Praise for *Love Teaching, Keep Teaching*

In *Love Teaching, Keep Teaching* Peter Radford offers an insightful pathway towards a school experience that is productive for youngsters as well as for those who teach them. The book is at times intensely personal, and it is well referenced and informed by a strong basis in psychology coupled with learning and leadership theory. The reflections at the end of each section encourage a positive questioning attitude to the way schools are at present and how they could be better.

A must-read for anyone who wants to delve into what makes teaching and learning tick.

Mick Waters, Professor of Education, University of Wolverhampton

Love Teaching, Keep Teaching is an important book. All too often, teachers enter the profession and are swallowed up by unrealistic expectations – whether this is to do with our own mindset, that of leadership, or the education system itself. This honest and heartfelt account seeks to challenge the relentless cult of 'outstanding' and rallies against an identikit model of teaching that seems to be increasingly prevalent in some of the darker corners of education. Celebrating the art of teaching and leadership, Peter Radford draws on research and his undoubted experience to give a clear insight into how to develop a school culture that values human flourishing. His book offers a timely reminder for us all of the need to refocus on the things that matter the most.

Jonathan Lear, teacher, speaker and author of *The Monkey-Proof Box: Curriculum Design for Building Knowledge, Developing Creative Thinking and Promoting Independence*

I think most of us in the teaching profession would be able to identify the myriad of problems present in the day-to-day realities of working in a school. What Peter Radford does in *Love Teaching, Keep Teaching* is provide excellent, well-researched and practical ways of dealing with them and in potentially transformative ways. He empowers the classroom teacher and reminds even the most experienced school leader how to make the most of their staff.

Peter believes that good schools start with the foundations of teamwork and valuing every individual, staff member and pupil – and he emphasises that good exam results are an indirect outcome of putting people first and valuing who they really are. He examines the power of 'starting with the end in mind' in our schools. If we want our pupils to go on to help the world to flourish then we'd better sit up and listen!

With the demands of teaching in schools seemingly going up and up, Peter Radford describes the difference that a genuine focus on staff wellbeing can have, and in terms that all teachers and line managers can understand. It is refreshing to read educational views and proposals for positive change from someone who has genuinely experienced life in the teaching profession first-hand. Peter carries us honestly through his own tough experiences of life in the school setting and offers convincing, empathetic and practical suggestions on how to move schools into the future.

I strongly recommend this book to any member of the teaching profession, whatever their role or level of experience. Honest, grounded and truly inspiring, it offers something for every teacher!

Martin Ashton, Deputy Head Teacher (Pastoral), Wells Cathedral School

This book beautifully refocuses your attention to what really matters in teaching and realigns our minds as to why we went into the profession. Amid the day-to-day running of schools and keeping our sights on the forever moving goalposts, it is so easy to forget what is most important and what our own values are. Peter's brave reflections on his own experiences have enabled him to understand what so many teachers and leaders are going through and to blend this experience with the works of renowned authors and academics into one easy-to-read book. *Love Teaching, Keep Teaching* combines research, strategies and excellent reflective questions to challenge your own thinking and the status quo. I wish I had this book years ago as it would have helped me to better understand why I do the things I do!

Krissi Carter, Principal, Burton Borough School

Love Teaching, Keep Teaching is the book I should have read 20 years ago! In many ways it is three books in one, covering the prevalent themes of the day: teacher wellbeing, school leadership and the future of the education system. It is philosophical and reflective but also eminently practical with plenty of prompts for further action and helpful diagrams to illustrate and summarise key ideas. The book stands upon an impressive evidence base, both educational and non-educational, and you will want a sharp pencil and a highlighter to hand in order to annotate and page-mark for future reference. However, the most powerful sections are the ones in which Peter refers to his own experiences with a fair degree of candour and courage.

Mike Foley, Head Teacher, The Thomas Hardye School

Love Teaching, Keep Teaching is both a moving personal story and an expert's user's manual on how to survive being a teacher. Peter tells his tale of the challenges faced by teachers every day, but never once falters from championing this great profession. He stresses the need for authenticity, being true to your values and having the courage to control your own destiny. This is a book about accepting your mistakes and yourself.

Reading *Love Teaching, Keep Teaching* will give you the confidence to either teach well where you are or to leave and find another profession – either way your own self-care is vital, and this book will help you reflect and act with integrity.

David Whitaker, Director of Learning, Wellspring Academy Trust

Peter Radford tells it as it is. With disarming honesty, he leads us into *Love Teaching, Keep Teaching* by informing the reader that he has quit the profession and by explaining exactly why. He does not spare himself and you soon realise that his own experiences have moulded the structure of the book. It starts with self-reflection and self-care, moves into a critical analysis of school leadership and finishes by taking a global perspective on what the education system needs to address in order to stay relevant.

This is a bold proposition – and it works. The blend of personal experiences, positive and negative, is narrated with skill. The book is brought alive by drawing on sources way beyond conventional teacher education books, ranging from *Zen and the Art of Motorcycle Maintenance* through to *That Will Never Work: The Birth of Netflix and the Amazing Life of an Idea.*

Love Teaching, Keep Teaching could not be more timely. The need for self-care is greater than ever as those in the classroom wrestle with adjusting to new ways of teaching that are counterintuitive and laden with uncertainty. This extends way beyond work into teachers' social and family lives, too – which also contributes to rising stress levels. All those working in schools right now are searching for professional and emotional lifelines, as they aren't being provided elsewhere.

The book has been written in an accessible style that will appeal to teachers and school leaders alike. It is invitational rather than didactic and lends itself to being read in an armchair because it is talking to you. Furthermore, the exercises – which serve as vital barometers to check our own wellbeing – can be undertaken privately and reflectively. Yet the learning takes us right back to what's happening in school and how positive cultures can be nurtured successfully.

This is a refreshing change from the canon of teaching manuals anchored in current English government policy with its reductionist focus on a knowledge-rich curriculum and behaviour regimes that render students as passive vessels to be filled. Here is a book that will take you above the fray and empower those working in schools.

Colin Diamond, CBE, Professor of Educational Leadership, University of Birmingham

This is an absolute must-read for anyone in teaching, or considering a teaching career. Peter Radford is an inspiring leader who practises what he preaches, and in *Love Teaching, Keep Teaching* he neatly distils how to deliver inspiration in the classroom and beyond. I cannot recommend it highly enough.

Will Collinson, Assistant Head Teacher (Pastoral), King Edward VI School

Peter Radford

Love Teaching

The Essential Guide to Improving Wellbeing at All Levels in Schools

Keep Teaching

Crown House Publishing Limited
www.crownhouse.co.uk

First published by

Crown House Publishing Limited
Crown Buildings, Bancyfelin, Carmarthen, Wales, SA33 5ND, UK
www.crownhouse.co.uk

and

Crown House Publishing Company LLC
PO Box 2223, Williston, VT 05495, USA
www.crownhousepublishing.com

First published 2020.

British Library Cataloguing-in-Publication Data

A catalogue entry for this book is available from the British Library.

Print ISBN 978-178583503-2
Mobi ISBN 978-178583527-8
ePub ISBN 978-178583528-5
ePDF ISBN 978-178583529-2

LCCN 2020946644

Printed and bound in the UK by
Gomer Press, Llandysul, Ceredigion

To all the great teachers I have known and worked with, and all those who have ever felt broken by the job: every day made a difference.

Contents

Introduction:

The Problem and How We Can Fix It

Teaching is the best job in the world. I have no doubt about it. To have the privilege of each day walking into a room and being able to shape and mould the minds and lives of young people is priceless. No matter the topic or the age group, no child leaves your classroom the same person as when they entered.

Philosophers have often posed the question, 'Is it possible to step into the same river twice?' since the water is continuously flowing onwards. Change is the only constant, and in much of life that change happens irrespective of our contribution. But in teaching the change *is* our contribution, and it is permanent. As Oliver Wendell Holmes Sr observed, 'When a man's mind is stretched by a new idea … [it] never shrinks back to its former dimensions.'[1] The transformation of the individual is irreversible. As teachers, we hold within our hands the future of the human race and the future of the planet. What job could possibly be more significant?

It is not only young people's minds that we shape through imparting knowledge and skills; we shape their personhood too. Our interactions with them, the teacher–learner relationship and the genuine friendship that develops in a positive classroom environment, have just as much, perhaps more, potency to impact the frame of mind, the outlook, the worldview and the attitude of an individual. We enable children to see the world differently.

A thank you card from one of my students said this:

> Every single lesson you taught was impressive: you made me think and I started to force the people around me to think as well … You made me realise the importance of changing the regular mindset people share … It took me some courage to

1 O. W. Holmes Sr, The Autocrat of the Breakfast-Table, *Atlantic Monthly*, Vol. 2 (1858): 502.

share my views on gender inequality with my parents. I hope you inspire and influence many others as well.

This is an amazing privilege. We are able to instil such intangibles as self-belief, confidence, openness, positivity, respect, wonder and insight. Young people can emerge from our classrooms and schools with the seeds of new possibilities firmly planted and nurtured. The imagination to do things differently, to mend that which is broken, to challenge the known boundaries of possibility.

Furthermore, teachers are the nurturers and overseers of a community. A school is an environment where children can feel like they belong. It is the first real place where they learn how to form and sustain meaningful relationships; how to navigate the minefield of people's differences and quirks; how to relate effectively so as to thrive socially and emotionally. Many of the children in our care will face their first friendship breakdowns at school, many will venture into the arena of love and suffer hurt and heartbreak, and many will experience bullying and be exposed to diversity and conflicting views. They will come face to face with difficulty, failure, competition and the consequences of inequality in our world.

All this they navigate while in our care. And as teachers we help them to navigate it, we are there for them when things get tough, we show them how to live. We get to shape the future. Now. In real time. Every single day we make an impact. A tangible, definite impact. Why would anyone want a different job?

Yet recent statistics tell us that teachers are leaving the profession in unprecedented numbers. Reportedly 20% plan to leave in the next two years and 40% in the next five.[2] Schools are haemorrhaging the lifeblood of education. And these figures are not simply descriptive of education-weary teachers entering the twilight of their careers. It was recently reported that in the London area, 43% of teachers leave the profession within five years of qualifying.[3] Something somewhere has gone very

2 S. Weale, Fifth of Teachers Plan to Leave Profession within Two Years, *The Guardian* (16 April 2019). Available at: https://www.theguardian.com/education/2019/apr/16/fifth-of-teachers-plan-to-leave-profession-within-two-years.

3 S. Weale, Teacher Crisis Hits London As Nearly Half Quit within Five Years, *The Guardian* (4 October 2018). Available at: https://www.theguardian.com/education/2018/oct/04/teacher-crisis-hits-london-as-nearly-half-quit-within-five-years.

wrong: in such an intrinsically motivating line of work, we somehow manage to murder a new teacher's passion and enthusiasm within five short years. With all that teaching has going for it, this indicates some major issues.

What has gone wrong and how to fix it is the subject of this book.

Why do I care? Because I am one of those statistics. I left, and I didn't leave because I don't enjoy teaching. I left because I had a breakdown. I came fully to the end of myself and knew that I had to get out to save my own sanity, my health and that of my family. Since then, I have reflected long and hard about what led me to that point. There were three main causal factors, which will shape the three parts of this book.

The first factor was me. I take full responsibility for my own degeneration. There is no point blaming others. It is futile and disempowering. You can't change others, you can only change yourself. If we are going to move forward, this has to be the starting point. I can change me. I fully believe in the ability of any human person to change. Responsibility means just that: I have the ability to choose my response. It was my mindset and the way I thought – my conditioning and my lack of awareness of just how negative these were in some respects – that played a big part in why I unravelled. In Part I, I will explore just that: our very common inability to effectively manage ourselves, whether due to a lack of self-awareness or of the positive coping and life skills that make for a balanced, healthy and fulfilled existence.

The second factor was the often dysfunctional and counterproductive leadership styles and structures to which I was exposed and of which I was a part. In my experience, leadership across the profession is shooting itself in the foot on a daily basis. Regrettably, little to no leadership training and development is given to leaders in the teaching profession. We promote someone to be head of maths because they are a good, competent and ambitious maths teacher, not because they are capable leaders and managers of people. We take individuals from the classroom where they are confident practitioners and place them in leadership and management positions, making them responsible for the wellbeing, progress and productivity of colleagues, and give them not one hour of training on how to do this.

The approach prevalent in many schools has somehow managed to eradicate the 'people element' from the role of a leader – for example, we refer to leadership positions as 'subject leader' or 'head of subject', as if leadership were essentially just an admin role. A head of English is not merely leading English as a subject; he or she is leading a team of English *teachers*. Here again we have the power to change things. The leaders in the profession are *us*, not just the senior leadership team (SLT). Looking back, I realise that I had a choice on a daily basis about what kind of leader I would be. I am ashamed to say that I was often the wrong kind. I put the task above the person over and over again. I communicated my agenda before listening to others, and I controlled and did myself what I should have been enabling and empowering others to do. I will address leadership, both in and out of the classroom, in Part II.

The third factor is the education system we have inherited but which we also perpetuate. This is the area in which we have a tendency to blame others the most. Education in Britain has become so politicised that changes are introduced at an astounding rate, which in itself generates anxiety. However, these changes are often counterproductive, short-sighted and motivated by short-term, synthetic improvements that will generate good headlines for re-election. They are not changes championed by the people on the ground who are doing the work. And rarely are they changes that are evidently in the best interests of all (or arguably even some) students.

We have a top-down education system: SLT receive their orders, who pass them down to middle leaders, who in turn pass them down to classroom teachers. I have often heard the following justification in a staff or department briefing, 'Sorry, but this is what we have to do now.' A resigned acceptance that unwelcome directives will keep on coming and our role is simply to shovel them. It is easy to shoot at whichever messenger delivers the news, but it is also futile. The profession has become utterly passive and reactive instead of proactive and innovative. Without realising it we find ourselves waiting for the next directive, ready to moan the hell out of it at the first opportunity. Then we retreat to our classrooms, our comfort zone, a little more anxious and troubled, and just teach the next lesson, hoping that at the first data collection point the student progress looks okay.

But this too is within our power to change, and that is regardless of which party is in government. Bad ideas coming from on high has always been the state of the world. To wish otherwise is to waste precious time and collude in your own demise, just as simply wishing that the ship you're on isn't sinking achieves nothing to prevent it from doing so. Our task is to find a way to grow something good out of it! Famously, Dale Carnegie wrote, 'If you have a lemon, make a lemonade.'[4] The systems, policies and procedures in our schools do not have to reflect the broken systems of government, or of the past, or of the school down the road. We do have at least *some* autonomy. There are a myriad of ways to go about doing education, which can tick the right boxes for inspection but are not limited by those boxes. Those boxes are not the aim or the purpose – they are just safeguards. Let's look at it differently: no architect considers the building regulations first and then aims to devise a structure which perfectly ticks each box. No, first she imagines and decides what it is she wants to create, then she finds a way to make it acceptable. The building regulations are not the point. We need to start dreaming all over again.

When it went wrong for me

In September 2016, I was sitting in my office staring at my inbox with my handwritten to-do list at my side, frantically trying to bash out replies to ten emails in the two minutes since the bell had gone for next lesson, which I was due to be teaching in a classroom on the other side of the school campus. As I typed, I crossed off those jobs on my to-do list while also adding new jobs which were emerging from the emails I was reading and responding to. I had just worked through my lunch break at a crazy pace to clear some of the backlog, so I was disheartened as I ran to my lesson that my list was now longer than it was at the start of lunchtime.

Back in my office later that day, I gazed at the computer screen and paused, just for a moment. I was overwhelmed by the feeling that no matter what I did to shift the work, it kept on growing. I felt as if I was

4 D. Carnegie, *How to Stop Worrying and Start Living* (New York: Simon & Schuster, 1948), p. 138.

drowning in quicksand: the more I thrashed and tried to help myself, the further in I sank. There were multiple plates spinning in my head, many starting to wobble, some already falling, but still more being added and spun. I remember foreseeing a moment of complete disablement and implosion, when this sense of being overwhelmed would be so great that I wouldn't be able to do anything at all. It scared me.

I had seen films and known former friends and colleagues who had suffered breakdowns, some to the extent of never being able to work again. Previously, I had never understood those stories or shown much empathy. The disability seemed so invisible as to be unreal to me. I didn't judge but I didn't relate. Until that day. On that day, I both saw it and felt it: a point not very far ahead when everything would come crashing down. That was the moment I sat up and took notice.

Around the same time I had two very vivid dreams. In one I was playing a classic game of musical chairs (always loved that game!). I was engaging with competitive zeal, as always. As the chairs were removed the organisers spaced out the remaining ones to make the challenge harder. In my dream, the game developed into a race. The pace was frantic. But each time I ran to circle a chair, it was moved. I would run to where the next chair was, but it too would be moved and obstacles placed in my way. I awoke panicking. I could not get to the chair.

My second dream was more sinister. A laughing face right in front of me – almost puppet-like but frightening, like a ventriloquist's dummy. I pushed it away but it wouldn't go. It was coming for me. It was hurting me. I couldn't get it away from me. And all the time it was laughing. In desperation, I took a knife and thrashed at the figure before me, plunging the blade violently into its chest. But it did no good: the face continued to laugh at me and my puny efforts to hit back. Needless to say I awoke in distress and thought, 'I need to do something about this.'

I don't claim to be a dream interpretation expert, but it seems obvious to me that there is at least some correlation between the themes of my dreams and my mental state at that time. I was an assistant head teacher in one of the largest secondary schools in the country, and I was suffering mild panic attacks on a daily basis. Although at first glance the problem might have seemed to be workload, in fact it was much more subtle than that. (Workload seems to be the default explanation for anything relating to teachers' wellbeing, which paradoxically sits alongside a common perception in wider society that teachers are work-shy: 'You already get 13 weeks' holiday a year – that not enough for you?')

My struggle with workload had at least as much to do with my own mindset and my approach to work as it did with my actual remit and day-to-day task list. However, I realised this only months and years later, after much counselling. It is for this reason that Part I of this book will address the way we think and the significance of developing positive habits that will foster greater productivity.

However, besides struggling with workload there was something potentially even more damaging going on. I was feeling increasingly disingenuous in my role. There was a huge amount of pressure to achieve better GCSE results and get a good rating from Ofsted. The approach largely being taken in my school, as in many others, was to heap ever greater pressure on teaching staff to up their game and extract more and better from their Year 11 students. Monitoring of teachers was constant. Monitoring of middle leaders monitoring teachers was constant. Procedures, internal reviews and audits and whole-school initiatives ostensibly aimed at 'using data more effectively' created unbearable pressure for middle leaders. The heads of department I line managed came to me in tears on a weekly basis. I empathised fully. However, I had been given a job and – this was the problem – my job was to enforce policy. Of course, that is not how I saw my role but, of course, that is what was expected of me. And the policies I was expected to enforce were policies I didn't believe in myself!

This is a ticket to hospital. When you find yourself doing something that is at odds with your core values it creates an inner tension, a stress that inevitably becomes internalised. In order to carry out the task you have to suppress the inner voice telling you that it's wrong. But that voice doesn't go away. Instead, it leads to living at a new level of disconnection with your true self. In short, you lose your authenticity. You become something you are not. You can't possibly believe in what you are doing, and therefore the whole workplace becomes a bitter place to be. The opposite is also true: Gandhi is reputed to have said, 'Happiness is when what you think, what you say and what you do are in harmony.' By implication, then, unhappiness is when your words, thoughts and deeds are in disharmony, when they are not aligned. This is unhappiness in the extreme and it causes stress, which has both a mental and physiological impact.

All of this relates to the crisis of leadership in teaching which I address in Part II – both the lack of any training and considered thought about effective leadership, as well as the typical bent towards top-down leadership models that consist either of shunting the problem ever downwards (let's find the scapegoat at all costs) or autocratic leadership styles that ultimately disempower, demotivate and ostracise staff.

The third factor which led to my breakdown, which correlates with Part III of this book, was the education system. What I experienced was, in some ways, tantamount to a crisis of faith. Not of the religious kind, but rather my faith in education. I had spent over 20 years of my career doing what I believed in. I am passionate about changing the world for the better and I am passionate about the power of education to accomplish just that. Intrinsic to my philosophy of education is my belief that our task as educators is not simply to produce good mathematicians or good geographers but good human beings. We are first and foremost not teaching history or science, we are teaching children.

I do not believe that education is a functional process whereby the teacher merely deposits his or her knowledge into the mind of the learner. Teaching is personal. Every child is different, unique, individual. It is the teacher's task to find 'the element'[5] in each child – the spark that switches them on – and develop that. It is the teacher's task to develop not just the academic ability of learners but also their social, emotional, moral, cultural and spiritual awareness. It is the teacher's task to guide and care for their students, to enthuse and inspire them, to help them enter the world as rights-respecting global citizens equipped to make a positive contribution to their families, communities and society – and, in turn, teach their own children how to be good, rights-respecting human beings.

This was my dream. This is what I had worked for and lobbied and argued for in every school in which I'd worked, and I felt that I had made some progress. And yet in that final year or so, I felt that my key achievements were being undone, one initiative at a time. All my sweat

5 See K. Robinson and L. Aronica, *The Element: How Finding Your Passion Changes Everything* (London: Penguin, 2010).

and toil to introduce changes at a systemic level – changes of which I was proud – were, in my perception, being rolled back and shelved in the name of better GCSE results.

I was devastated. Not just that my efforts were being undone but by the hopelessness I felt at the direction that education was taking. For the first time in my career I felt beaten. I felt (irrationally, of course) as if nothing made a difference. I'd been kicked one too many times and I had no strength left with which to fight. The system had won.

Or so I thought. On the other side of trauma, I have discovered new hope and optimism to build a better world, no matter what the context – particularly the potential for school leaders to be brave, authentic and innovative in building school communities that challenge the status quo and mould an education system fit for the 21st century. We certainly can't wait for politicians to do it for us. It's us or no one.

The low point

These three factors, taken together, represented a perfect storm for me. I went off sick, at first expecting to take just a few days to recuperate. But, as is the custom in schools, I continued to plan lessons, mark and keep on top of emails from home. Coupled with my own guilt at creating more work for others by being off work, my first week at home failed entirely to help me recover. During week two, I finally realised that I actually needed to stop and not just 'work from home'. So I allowed myself to pause. And a day later was when everything came tumbling down.

The tasks I had set for myself that day were to do a food shop and make a chilli. Two tasks that lie well within my capabilities and are both semi-regular occurrences. I decided not to rush (which is my default), but for some reason I didn't finish the shopping until after 2pm, despite having been focused solidly on doing that. I began to make the chilli, but when I looked at the recipe I suddenly felt totally overwhelmed. I didn't know where to start. I couldn't start. I was having a panic attack. I called my wife at work, who talked me down.

She said, 'You don't have to make a chilli. Just leave it … sit down.'

I said, 'Really, I don't?'

'No, it's okay. Just lie down.'

The next few months were hard. Small things overwhelmed me completely. I had gone from sustaining a massive remit in a big secondary school to managing to accomplish just a few, simple, mundane tasks per day – maybe. I'm grateful that over the following months the support of my wife, close friends and family, as well as counselling, enabled me to recover and change things. I started my own business shortly afterwards, although the road to full recovery took a full two and a half years. But I did come back!

I mentioned at the start that I left teaching, but I couldn't stay away because it is part of who I am and why I am. I still teach in schools every week. I am very much involved in education and speak to students and staff about the very issue that I think we all need to prioritise: *how to be better human beings*. I hope this book will help you not just to more fully embrace that goal yourself, but also to provide you with ideas and inspiration to shape our schools into places that make that goal their *raison d'être*.

This book is about three key aspects of improving wellbeing in schools:

1 Teachers and leaders improving their own wellbeing.

2 The role of teachers and leaders in improving wellbeing across schools.

3 The challenge to change the culture of our schools and education system.

I have also included an adaptable strategic plan template as an appendix. I am writing primarily as a teacher with some experiences and insights that have been invaluable to me and shaped my approach to life and education. I don't pretend to be a therapist or counsellor, and I wholeheartedly recommend, should you be feeling depressed or anxious, that you seek professional help.

Most importantly, I hope this book helps you *love teaching* again and reignites in you the passion for why you do it.

Part I

You – How to Live and Teach Well

Chapter 1

The Subtle Art of Achieving Balance

Mark Manson begins his excellent book *The Subtle Art of Not Giving a F*ck* by pointing out that we have a limited number of f*cks to give.[1] Though Manson uses the F-word quite a lot(!), in the interests of inclusivity I'm going to replace the F-word with the word 'stuff'. I realise it doesn't have quite the same kick about it, but you get the idea.

Every day we have the potential to get worked up about something – or wound up or hacked off or anxious or troubled or irritated or any number of other states of being – all of which Manson would sum up as 'giving a stuff'. His point, which I want to emphasise here, is that we have a choice about what to give a stuff about. He's not saying that we shouldn't give a stuff about anything. Quite the opposite. He's saying choose carefully what you decide to give a stuff about because what you choose to invest your emotional energy in will define your future.

If we choose to invest that energy in things that don't really matter, then some other aspect of our lives will suffer as a result. Because we only have a limited number of stuffs to give. We can't give a stuff about everything. Eeyore put it beautifully when he said, 'We can't all. And some of us don't. That's all there is to it.'[2] Love it. We can try, of course, but it's the beginning of our downfall if we do. The subtle art that Manson goes on to discuss is that of making sure we clearly identify what really matters to us and what doesn't. What is worth our time and energy and what isn't?

Life is short and precious, and personally I don't want to waste a second of it.

Case in point. This year I had a dispute with my neighbour. I've heard about people who have disputes with their neighbours, but I never thought I would be one of them. My neighbour, who enters his property

---

1 M. Manson, *The Subtle Art of Not Giving A F*ck: A Counterintuitive Approach to Living a Good Life* (New York: HarperCollins, 2016).

2 A. A. Milne, *Winnie-the-Pooh* (London: Methuen, 1926), p. 100.

by driving (legally) through my driveway, took issue with my adjustments to my own driveway – he now had to turn his steering wheel when previously he could drive straight. But it was his aggressive manner towards me that made my blood boil. Everything in me wanted to stubbornly refuse to acquiesce to his demands to readjust my drive. On a particularly confrontational encounter, I found myself physically shaking as I tried to remain calm regarding his request that I knock down a corner of my fence and move it by one metre.

My wife intervened: 'It's a fence, for goodness sake,' she said. 'It really doesn't matter, does it?' Well, clearly in that moment it mattered very much to me and my neighbour. But our mutually passionate care was making us both extremely agitated and unhappy. It took me a while to calm down, but I decided to choose to put the one square-metre-adjustment to my fence in the category of 'not worth giving a stuff about' and acquiesced to my neighbour's request. I think I have lengthened my lifespan as a result![3]

So, we can choose what to expend our time and energy on, but we frequently choose the wrong things. In large part, the shape and quality of our lives today is the product of our choices to date. Wherever you are right now, and however you are feeling about it, your choices have played a key role in leading you to this point.

In this chapter, I am going to suggest that there are three critical factors to achieving the balanced life you want to enjoy:

1 Fully accept responsibility.

2 Balance the ingredients.

3 Commit to do your best.

Let's look at them each in turn.

3 When you are agitated, your blood pressure reaches 150 in seconds, which, in turn, triggers the release of stress hormones. Over time these have a verifiable impact on life expectancy.

1. Accepting responsibility

Viktor Frankl was an Austrian Jewish psychologist who was imprisoned in a sub-camp of Dachau during the Second World War. He survived, but he lost his entire family during the Holocaust. He later wrote a brilliant book called *Man's Search for Meaning* in which he described how the Nazis took away every single freedom the prisoners had. He noted how some prisoners were broken very quickly – they despaired. A flicker had gone out and their demise was then only a matter of time. He also noted how in some inmates that flicker remained, and it often proved to be the difference between death and survival. He said: 'Everything can be taken from a man but one thing: the last of the human freedoms – to choose one's attitude in any given set of circumstances, to choose one's own way.'[4]

To choose one's attitude – this, Frankl claims, is a choice. It is at the heart of the notion of responsibility. What does responsibility mean? Response-ability. Flip it around: the ability to respond. In any given circumstance we have the ability to choose our response – which we do, every single day.

Every day in schools, in the words of Forrest Gump, 'shit happens'. Some of it predictable, some of it unpredictable. What is our default setting in situations of stress, when things are not going the way we would like? I suggest that our default setting is to blame.

I have sat in many staffrooms and faculty offices and the conversations don't vary all that much. In fact, they often fall into four distinct categories:

1 **'Little Johnny derailed my lesson again!' – aka: blame a student.**

We have all been there – great lesson, well prepped, a mix of activities, differentiated, good pace and challenge. But troublesome/troubled [insert name of choice] decided to be defiant/swear at me/kick another student. Such conversations are commonplace. Every school has a shortlist of 'known characters' who, come September, we hope aren't in our class and about whom we swap stories and commiserate together.

4 V. E. Frankl, *Man's Search for Meaning* (London: Random House, 2004 [1946]), p. 74.

2 **'Bloody SLT want us to do *what* now?' – aka: blame the SLT.**

Ah yes, the SLT. Those people who sit around creating new ways to hinder us from doing our jobs and who have forgotten what it's like to teach a 90% timetable. A new initiative or expected whole-school system that needs to be implemented across the board, or the dreaded data collection point and how it will be used creatively in new and unforeseen ways to catch us out and demonstrate that we're failing.

3 **'The government/Ofsted are changing it all again!' – aka: blame the government/Ofsted.**

Although some of us can remember a pre-austerity Labour government, the fact is that changes during the 2000s provided just as much fodder for complaint and discontent in staffrooms as the Conservative/Gove-era changes that continue to provide animated discussion today. We like to point out the short-sightedness of the government and laud our own on-the-ground, real-life educational wisdom whenever we can. It makes us feel better.

4 **'Can you believe what I had to deal with when I got home from school last night? And I still managed to mark a set of books!' – aka: blame life.**

Conversations quite rightly include what is going on in each of our lives, but like most people, we teachers will unwittingly find ourselves trying to score points by calling attention to and comparing our relative out-of-school hardships, because it helps us to justify why we may not be as 'on it' as we fear our colleagues may be. It can also serve to justify why the lesson we just taught was awful (even though we know it was down to the lack of prep we did).

All these conversations have one obvious common denominator: blame.

Here's the problem with blame: when we blame we adopt and fully accept a position of powerlessness. When we say: 'It's not my fault it went wrong,' we accept the conjoining assertion that 'There's nothing I can do to make it right.' The one statement is the same as the other. Someone else did it, which means I can do nothing about it, which means I am powerless.

It's the archetypal human coping mechanism as immortalised in the Christian creation story:

Adam: 'It wasn't me, it was that woman that you gave me – she made me do it.'

Eve: 'It wasn't me, it was that serpent that you made – he made me do it!'

When we participate in blame we give up. There is no hope for anything better, except perhaps winning the Lottery. The antithesis of blame is taking responsibility. Instead of blaming, ask questions of yourself:

- **When little Johnny disrupts my lesson:** Could I have handled that better? What could I do to prevent it happening again?
- **When bloody SLT have another initiative:** If I don't like/disagree with this, what am I going to do about it? I have a choice: (a) I can choose to get on board and make this work for me, (b) I can raise objections and negotiate changes or (c) if I truly can't stomach it, I can look for work elsewhere. I am in control.
- **When the government/Ofsted announces a change:** Instead of focusing on the things I can't change, what *can* I change? Could I still innovate within the confines of the current system and do something I believe in/adjust my approach?
- **When life is tough:** To what extent is my life the product of my choices to date? If I don't like aspects of my life, could I change them? I'm not merely a product or a pawn. I'm autonomous. I can take control of my life and refuse to be a passive recipient of what comes my way.

You can always choose your response. Equally, you can choose to live with the status quo and accept whatever hand is dealt to you, which is a perfectly valid choice and one which you are entitled to make. But then you must take responsibility for the consequences. You have chosen to do your job, in your department, in your school. You have given your consent. In which case it is bad form to complain when the choices others make which affect you are not to your liking.

You have the option to leave. No, really, you could leave. It is imperative that you realise this and accept it. Unless you do, you will remain a pawn in someone else's game – which is entirely your prerogative, but it does not have to be that way.

I am not suggesting for one moment that any of this is easy. I fully acknowledge that we face all sorts of circumstances in life which are entirely outside of our control, and sometimes those circumstances are traumatic and unjust. But unless we are willing to accept responsibility for our own lives, for our own responses to what happens to us, we won't achieve the balance we desire.

You are not a victim, even though you may have suffered unfair treatment or horrible situations. You are powerful.

However, we all have a tendency to make excuses at times. Here are three common ones:

- 'You don't understand. I'm trapped. I need this job – family and loved ones are depending on me.'
- 'You don't understand. I've tried before to change things and stick my neck out – those above me wouldn't listen.'
- 'You don't understand. I've tried every behaviour management trick in the book. I can't change Little Johnny – he's just feral.'

These may feel like very real obstacles to you at the time, but what such statements belie is the fact that actually, if you're honest, you've given up. When I say, 'you are responsible', I'm not being trite. I'm simply saying that if you are serious about wanting any or all aspects of your own life to change, it has to start with you. Because you are the only thing that you do have control over. Nothing else is truly within your domain. Today is the day that you can decide to take control. Once you accept responsibility, you have the power to change. Then you just need to decide what to do with it.

2. Balancing the ingredients

Life is complex, multifaceted and difficult. It is not one thing; it is lots of things. And keeping all those things balanced feels like a juggling act – but with far too many balls in play, especially if you are a teacher. In fact, the accepted wisdom in the profession is that teachers can't have a balanced life during term time, but the payoff is the long holidays when we get to even out the imbalance. I don't buy it: it's no way to live and it doesn't have to be this way.

The other juggling act we deal with is the job itself. The average classroom teacher is arguably employed to be all of the following, all at the same time:

- Life coach
- Trip coordinator
- Discovery guide
- Negotiator
- Academic
- Motivator
- Nose wiper
- IT specialist
- Fundraiser
- Counsellor
- Administrator
- Mediator
- Decorator
- Data analyst
- Behavioural expert
- Trainer
- Event planner

- Parent
- Entertainer

The job is, to say the least, diverse, and it requires us to know which role or responsibility to focus on when and for how long and with whom. The issue is this: you can't perform all of these tasks to an 'outstanding' level all of the time within the current system. No one can. The job is impossible.

This realisation can be a major discovery for many teachers, so skip over this part at your peril. I'll say it again: the job is impossible. You cannot do everything listed in your job description and included within the role for which you are employed and paid. It is only when you accept this fact that you will feel released to be a good teacher and empowered to be an agent of change. It is fundamental to the idea of balance.

Consider baking a cake. A good cake has the right balance of sugar and fat (generally speaking half and half – fat by itself is disgusting, the same goes for sugar, but in equal measure we love it – can't get enough). You increase the amount of fat and the sugar content is proportionately impoverished. And vice versa. It's not that you determined to reduce the sugar, you just majored on the fat, so the sugar, by remaining the same, became respectively less.

Grasp this principle and you will be a better teacher: with an imbalance of ingredients, the quality of the cake will be diminished. With an imbalance in life, the quality of life will be diminished. With an imbalance in your teaching practices, the quality of the teacher and their teaching will be diminished. *Balance the ingredients.*

The wheel of life – achieving balance

Life has often been likened to a wheel. It is fundamental to the Buddhist philosophy of balance: the idea of constant change and movement (impermanence) coupled with the acknowledgement that our existence is multifaceted (interdependence). The symbol is a popular coaching tool and the various spokes vary. Figure 1.1 is my version.

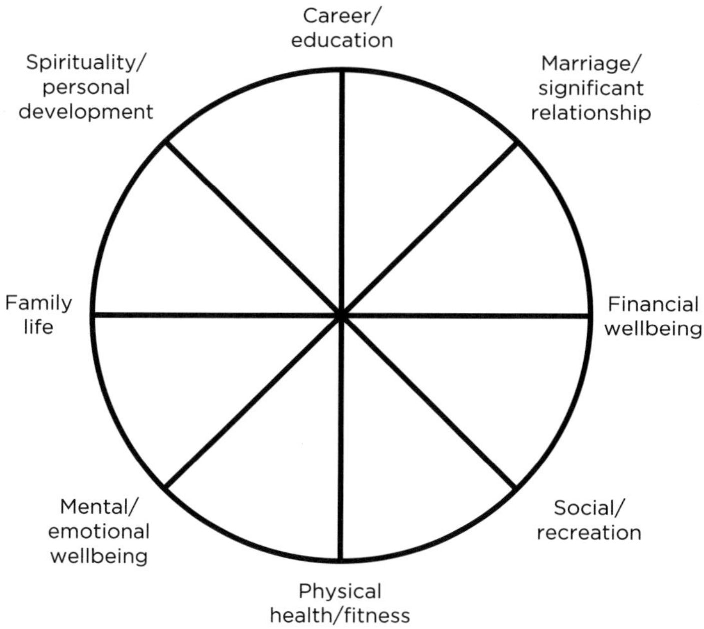

Figure 1.1. The wheel of life

Now have a go at scoring each aspect of your life, where the rim of the wheel represents 10 (the best it could possibly be) and the hub represents 0 (the worst it could possibly be). Pop an X on each spoke to illustrate where you are currently on the wheel. Then join up the X's so it might look something like Figure 1.2.

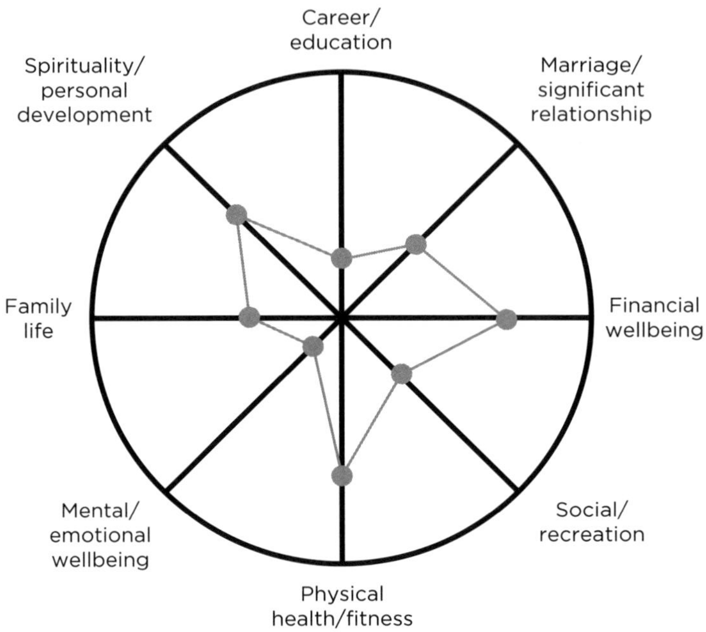

Figure 1.2. My wheel of life at the point of breakdown

Here's the point: life goes well when these things are in balance, not when they are all 10s. That is important to understand. Just as being a teacher is impossible if you take literally every line of the job description, so life is impossible if you buy into the notion that there is such a thing as a perfect life. There isn't. What there is are balanced and unbalanced people and balanced and unbalanced teachers. The former thrive, the latter survive ... maybe. But surviving is no way to live.

Look at your wheel and you will notice two things: (1) there are some aspects that are in a better state than others and (2) no aspect is a 10 (i.e. as perfect or good as it could conceivably be).

Here is my advice based on this exercise. First, make a decision to give serious attention to those aspects that are disproportionately low and to making them better. You can do this. You control which aspects of your life you give your attention to. Outline for each aspect how you would like it to be ideally. If you can see in your mind's eye where you want to get to, then you're already moving towards it. Your life will tend in the direction of your predominant thoughts. According to the Buddha, 'Our life is shaped by our mind; we become what we think. Joy follows a pure thought like a shadow that never leaves.'[5]

Second, be careful not to just cease giving attention to those aspects of your life that are high, although you may need to pull back and reduce your focus on some aspects. The aim is not for eight 10s; the aim is for balance. Eight 5s is better than two 9s, two 8s and four 2s. Remember the sugar: no action was taken to reduce it, yet it ended up disproportionately low because the other ingredients changed. Life is a constantly changing entity.

'For everything to stay the same, everything must change,' wrote Giuseppe di Lampedusa.[6] In other words, no aspect of your life will stay the same unless you give attention to making it so. There is no such thing as ticking over – the petrol gauge will run down to empty even if you go nowhere.

If your marriage is great now, if you just leave it alone it won't be great a year from now. If your physical fitness is great now, just leave it alone and a year from now you will be panting for breath at the top of the stairs. It takes constant input and effort just to maintain the status quo. However, if you want to make it better, that will take an extra special push.

So, do you want to make an extra special push? It's up to you. Which aspects of your life do you really care about? Are you giving way too many stuffs about one or two of them and insufficient to the rest? Or are you giving away your stuffs to things that don't even register on the wheel?

Now, what about teaching? Figure 1.3 represents my wheel of teaching – again, there are eight aspects which I think are essential to keep in balance if we are going to thrive.

5 E. Easwaran (tr. and intro.), *The Dhammapada* (Tomales: Nilgiri Press, 2009), verse 2.
6 G. di Lampedusa, *The Leopard*, tr. A. Colquhoun (New York: Pantheon, 2007 [1958]), p. 40. The original Italian reads: 'Se vogliamo che tutto rimanga com'è bisogna che tutto cambi.'

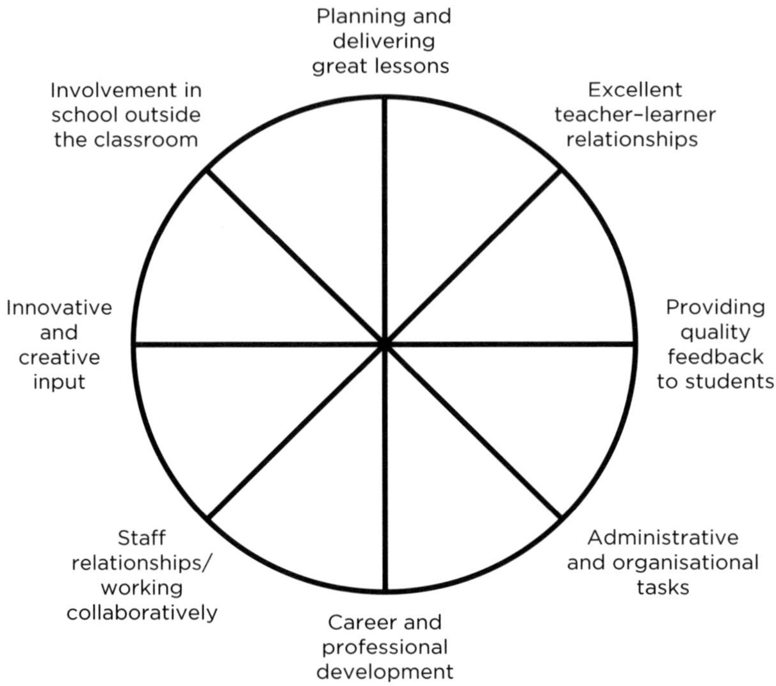

Figure 1.3. The wheel of teaching

First, without any further explanation, mark yourself on the spokes as you did before.

If you are in a leadership position, then the eight spokes of your wheel are slightly different, so mark them on the wheel of leadership (Figure 1.4) instead.

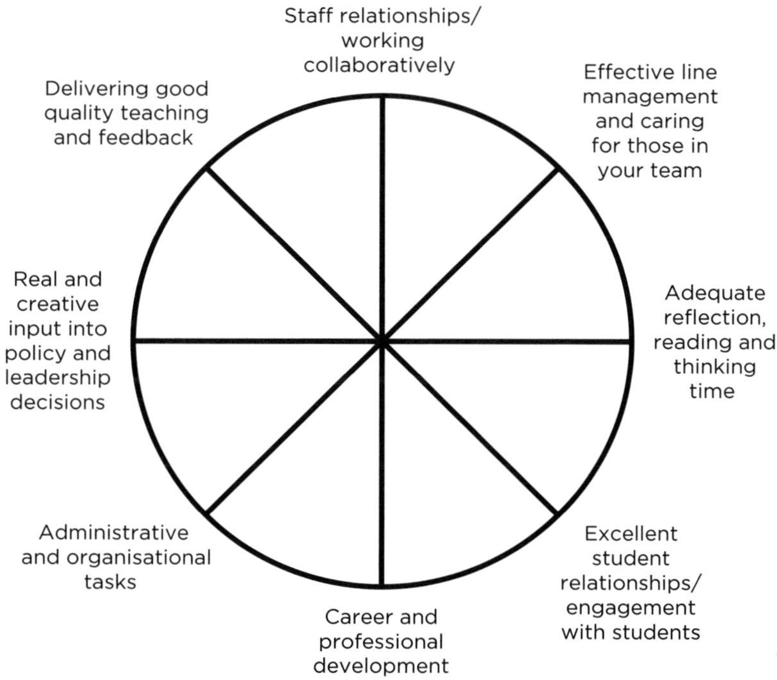

Figure 1.4. The wheel of leadership

In contrast to these components of being a balanced teacher/leader, I hear just three main messages being relentlessly pushed in most schools:

1 Pedagogy is everything: you are not teaching well enough.

2 Feedback is everything: you are not providing enough.

3 Progress is everything: you are not collecting and analysing enough progress data.

The truth is that, first, none of them is 'everything' and, second, there is so much more to providing quality education than pedagogy, feedback and progress. But there is no point in blaming; instead, we need to create more balance. Largely, this comes down to giving attention to the areas of lowest score and redressing the imbalance by reflecting on areas where we need to pull back.

We will explore the eight aspects of teaching in the next chapter, and consider the wheel of leadership in more detail in Part II.

The message from this chapter is that once you work out which areas of your personal and professional life are out of kilter or under addressed, then you can do something about them. You can re-evaluate what really matters: what to give a stuff about. The converse is that you begin to realise which things you have been giving too much time, attention and emotional energy to, and which ones, in the grander scheme of things, really don't matter so much.

3. Committing to your best (and the myth of perfect)

Nobody is perfect. This is a fairly universally held assertion. But I think it's wrong. Not because some people are in fact perfect, but because the statement implies an assumption: that there is such a thing as perfect, a standard to which we should aspire. I don't buy it. And not only that, I think the very idea is dangerous.

We have bought into this notion of perfection as a culture and as a profession. If we affirm the idea of perfect or outstanding, then we inevitably set ourselves up for repeated failure as we relentlessly try to achieve the unachievable. We need to bin the idea.

Carol Dweck's research on growth mindset illustrates this very well. In Dweck's studies, when students embrace the idea of 'clever', 'smart' or 'genius' as real things (known as entity theory) that we either do or don't have, they very quickly become demoralised and give up when they hit challenges or when their experiences provide evidence that they don't have what it takes. Conversely, students who adopt a mindset of continuous improvement (incremental theory), and abandon the notion of a preordained standard, tend to relish challenge and develop intrinsic motivation and engagement with the joy of the task itself.[7]

In other words, grading teachers or lessons on a four-point scale that effectively reinforces the notion of perfection has been an unmitigated

7 See Carol Dweck's studies in *Mindset: The New Psychology of Success* (New York: Ballantine Books, 2006) or *Mindset: How You Can Fulfil Your Potential* (New York: Constable & Robinson, 2012), or for a summary on praise watch 'The Effect of Praise on Mindsets' (2010) at https://www.youtube.com/watch?v=TTXrV0_3UjY&t=3s.

failure. The system explicitly asserts that 'requiring improvement' is a bad thing – as if no one in a higher category could ever require improvement! This is a system that labels teachers as 'inadequate' and hopes by doing so to inspire better things from them; a system that expects 'outstanding' all the time but actually obstructs teachers from giving the time and creativity necessary to teach great lessons with any consistency.

Hence, my third and final big point in this first chapter about balance is *there is no such thing as an outstanding teacher or an outstanding lesson*. There are teachers and there are lessons: your task is to be the best teacher you can be in helping your specific students to grow. Your only requirement is to be you. You are the best you there has ever been. I'm not being trite or facetious – I mean it. There has never been another you in the history of the universe and, after you die, there will never be another you again.

We don't look at the sun and ask, is it a perfect or an imperfect sun? It is the sun. It is perfectly what it is. We don't inspect a blade of grass or a leaf and ask, is it a perfect leaf or not? It is what it is. Perfectly. The notion that you are not a perfect human being is a nonsense. There is no such thing. You are a perfect you. And you are responsible for what kind of you you want to become and what kind of teacher you want to become. Your only responsibility is to do your best to become that.

This idea comes from Don Miguel Ruiz's fantastic little book *The Four Agreements*.[8] The fourth agreement is 'Always do your best,' with an emphasis on the word 'your'. No one else can say what *your* best is:

> All your life you tried to be good enough for somebody else ... you sacrificed your personal freedom to live according to someone else's point of view. You tried to be good enough for your mother, your father, your teachers, your beloved, your children, your religion, your society ... You can relearn how to love yourself by accepting yourself unconditionally.[9]

Your best is not a static thing. It changes every day. Your best first thing in the morning is different to your best last thing at night. Your best

8 D. M. Ruiz, *The Four Agreements: A Practical Guide to Personal Freedom* (San Rafael, CA: Amber-Allen Publishing, 1997).

9 D. M. Ruiz and D. J. Ruiz, *The Fifth Agreement: A Practical Guide to Self-Mastery* (San Rafael, CA: Amber-Allen Publishing, 2010), pp. 89–90.

at the beginning of term is different to your best at the end of term. Your best when your kids are ill or your husband has left you or your car has broken down is different to your best when everything is going beautifully. Your best is not the same as someone else's best. You are not supposed to be like them, you're supposed to be like you. You're supposed to be a you kind of teacher – and the best kind of you teacher you can be.

Seriously: don't give a stuff about outstanding if you want to be a genuinely good teacher, and certainly not if you're going to stay well. You are giving your stuffs about the wrong thing.

Now, some people reading this may realise that you, the authentic you, is not and never was a teacher. That's okay. That's a brilliant discovery. Find out what you are and do it. You went into the wrong profession – no worries, millions do. Be glad that you realised it now, but don't spend one further year trying to be something you are not. Your life is too precious for that. You have too much to offer the world.

Give yourself permission to be yourself and teach as yourself. Abandon perfect. Commit to do your best. But remember to balance being your best as a dad or mum, and as a teacher, and as a friend and as a partner, and as a caregiver, and so on. Don't rail against yourself for what you could have done differently. Tomorrow is another day, when you get to go at it again and be even better than today. Today you gave your best and you learned, so go to sleep with a clear conscience.

Chapter 2

The Eight Components of a Balanced Teacher

Although I've listed eight components on my wheel of teaching, it's difficult to say whether or not they all hold equal weight – in many ways they are interrelated and overlap considerably. However, I find it a useful exercise to examine each element as they all have a massive impact on our day-to-day work as teachers and whether or not we feel like we are doing a good job and maintaining balance.

It is my contention that these components must be in balance if we are going to thrive and progress, so let's unpack them one by one.

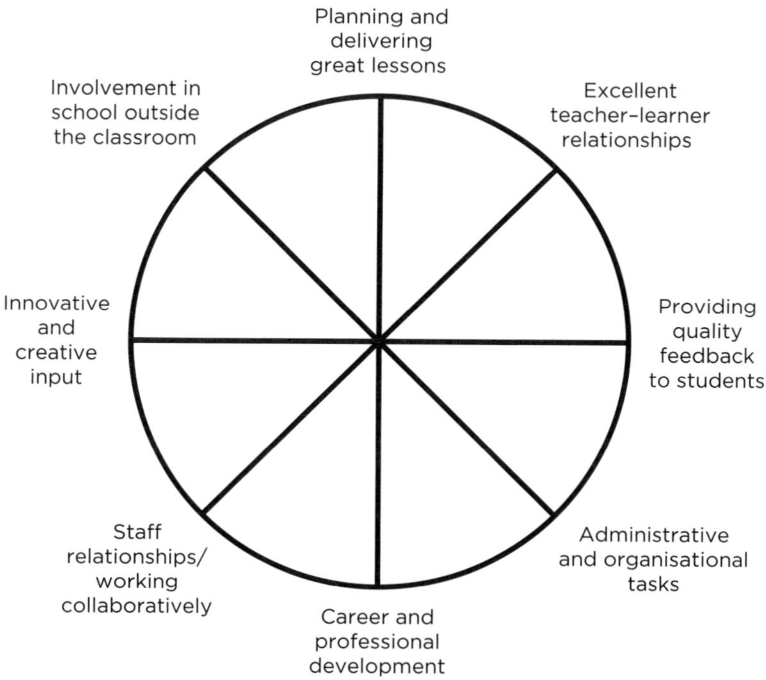

Figure 2.1. The wheel of teaching

Planning and delivering great lessons

In most people's minds planning and delivering lessons is what is meant by being a teacher. Of course, it's only a part of it, but it's a significant part. And if we don't feel like we are doing this well, then our self-confidence and sense of purpose is likely to plummet. Nobody wants to be rubbish at what they do. It is utterly demoralising and exhausting, not to mention personally diminishing, to go home at the end of a long day's work feeling like you haven't done a good job. And then to spend the evening planning for the following day with no sense that your hard work and time will yield any better results. Before too long you will give up – at least mentally.

We have all had teachers ourselves and we have all had both good ones and poor ones, so we know what it felt like to be in a poor teacher's class. And we never ever wanted to be that. But there's an assumption here that is wrong: I don't think there is any such thing as 'planning and delivering a great lesson'. Teaching isn't like delivering a speech or making a cake. It's not a one-way thing. It's not a functional task. This is educational philosophy from the 1950s: deliver your knowledge into the recipient's brain – job done. Like filling up a car with petrol. That's nonsense. Teaching is personal, interactive and transactional. The client is not a passive recipient, so the lesson cannot be a one-dimensional exercise. I realise I'm not saying anything new here. It's just that, unfortunately, the prevailing mechanisms and systems that have persisted for measuring good teaching don't adequately recognise the fluid nature of good teaching.

An English lesson for top-set Year 10s on Shakespeare is going to be a very different event to the same lesson with set 7. They cannot be judged in the same way and, here's what is important, you must not judge yourself in the same way. I don't mean that it's okay for one lesson to be good and the other substandard. I mean they should be totally different events with entirely different success criteria both for the students and for you. If you are going to achieve balance in this area, you must abandon the idea of 'well-behaved students working studiously' as any kind of measure of your success. Instead, I would suggest that you embrace a very simple question by which to self-evaluate after each and every lesson:

> Did I succeed in helping my students to grow today?

You should absolutely give a stuff about this, and if you don't you're in the wrong job. The various other measures will vary from day to day and class to class. You will have better days and worse days. You will have days when both you and your students are buzzing. But keep this as your baseline and you will have a better chance of maintaining balance. Absolutely aim to improve your pedagogy and share good practice, but there is no perfect lesson and there is no perfect teacher.

Reflection questions

- To what extent are you measuring yourself as a teacher by unreal perceptions and assumptions about other 'good' teachers rather than simply seeking to develop your own practice?
- Do you think you are helping your students to grow each day? If not, then who could support you or provide you with some objectivity to help you move towards this goal?

Excellent teacher–learner relationships

Excellent teacher–learner relationships go hand-in-hand with planning and delivering great lessons for the reason I've just outlined – that teaching is a personal relationship, not a functional one. If you don't have a great relationship with your students, then you are unlikely to teach great lessons. But, more importantly for you, you won't actually enjoy teaching. We can all probably think of a teacher or two about whom we have wondered why they ever entered the profession because they genuinely seem to dislike young people. However, much more common is the teacher who has a deep dislike for certain classes, and I can relate to that very well. My first real 'hated class' was 9R2 in my newly qualified teacher (NQT) year. I dreaded them, they dreaded me, and each lesson was a car crash. Until I made a decision to like them.

I genuinely did just that. I decided to smile and look pleased to see them, to joke with them and see the world from their point of view, rather than seeing them as the enemy: hostile, unpleasant and aggressive. From that day forward my relationship with them changed. They responded to my warmth, some more gradually than others, but essentially we were now working together rather than against each other.

That was one of the most important lessons I have ever learned about behaviour management. For students to like you, you have to like them. Building a relationship with young people takes time and effort, attention to detail, humanity, care and compassion. Although there will be students who never demonstrate any appreciation for the love and care you show, undoubtedly there will be those who do. And those occasional notes and cards make it all feel so worthwhile. Without doubt, the best teachers are the ones who care deeply about their students.

Reflection questions

- How do you make your students feel? Is your classroom a place of warmth and friendliness?
- How much on a scale of 1–10 do you care about your students? Where 1 is 'I don't really care about them as people – I just want them to hit their target grades so I don't get into trouble' and 10 is 'I care about each of them personally – their wellbeing and their reaching their potential is what gets me up in the morning'?

Providing quality feedback to students

We know what the research says: quality feedback is one of the top 10 influencers of student achievement.[1] The direct link between quality feedback and progress is undeniable. Yet 'marking', as it is still persistently termed, is most teachers' most hated activity. That is because it has been used to threaten and measure teacher performance and because we have misunderstood its purpose. Hence, many a teacher lives in fear of the dreaded book scrutiny. Lots has improved on this front, of course, but many teachers feel that the bar always seems to be too high in terms of what is expected of you and what you can reasonably do.

No one can flourish in any line of work if they are feeling guilty for not doing enough or fearful of being judged inadequate. Neither guilt nor fear is conducive to good, sustainable outcomes. In order to cope with the internal incongruency of these feelings, we reframe the task in our own minds to justify ourselves. One justification goes like this: 'The marking expectations are unreasonable and unfair. All my classes are big whereas my colleague has an A level class with four students in it. The system is unfair, so I'm not going to feel bad about not doing it.' Another goes like this: 'Students aren't going to read what I write in their books anyway, so it's a waste of my time. And if they want me to get through all this content, there's no way I can do that and spend time on feedback that isn't going to be used. I'll use just enough red pen to make the books look marked.' Either way we internalise 'feeling a bit bad' about it (which reinforces a negative view of ourselves as professionals), or else we kill ourselves following policy to the letter by marking well into the evenings.

If feedback truly impacts progress (which it does) then we should absolutely give a stuff about it. But something has to give to make it sustainable. Here is my working model as a secondary practitioner:

- **Feed back for redrafting only.** There is no point marking and providing feedback on anything unless you are going to insist on it being acted on and therefore ensure that it translates into progress.

1 J. Hattie, Feedback in Schools, *Visible Learning* (2013). Available at: https://visible-learning.org/2013/10/john-hattie-article-about-feedback-in-schools.

- **You decide.** You, the professional, decide how much individualised feedback is necessary and reasonable in order to achieve progress. Be bold about your decision. Don't apologise for it. If your students are making progress then you have evidence that your approach is working.
- **Feed back for progress only.** An assessed piece of work that is not fed back on and responded to by redrafting is a pointless exercise as far as teaching is concerned. The only appropriate place for summative assessment is the public examination. All other assessment should be formative.
- **Feed back in bulk.** Whole-class or group feedback is just as valid as individualised feedback in many circumstances. Writing the same piece of feedback 20 times is a waste of your time.
- **Communicate your policy.** Managing expectations is vital: students need to know not to expect red pen randomly in their books and only to expect feedback for the reason of redrafting/improving their work.
- **Set your own bar.** Don't set assignments that you know you can't adequately feed back on. If a student puts effort into an assignment and you don't provide quality feedback, it is a massive kick in the teeth to your student. It says: don't bother in future.

Much good stuff has been written about effective feedback in recent years, and regurgitating that is not my purpose here.[2] However, unless we nail what feedback is actually about and we are confident about the way we choose to approach it, it will continue to be the thorn in the side of many teachers.

Reflection questions

- Do you believe in the efficacy of the feedback you are giving? Which of your feedback activities make the most difference? Prioritise.

2 Claire Gadsby's *Perfect Assessment for Learning* (Carmarthen: Independent Thinking Press, 2012) is a good starting point.

- Are you blindly complying with a policy that you disagree with or has limited impact? Could you raise this with your line manager/SLT?

Administrative and organisational tasks

Emphatically, admin tasks are not why you became a teacher, but they are an unavoidable part of the job. The problems arise when they are not acknowledged as such – as if the administrative and organisational tasks involved in being an effective teacher are something you do on the side, at home or in-between the 'real' job of teaching. They are not an add-on; they are an integral part of the whole. The photocopying necessary for the great lesson you have planned is not incidental. The prep for the practical lesson you have planned is not an additional extra. The emails you need to send to check that risk assessments and arrangements are in place for the educational visit are not by the by. All of these things are essential.

Many teachers I know receive between 50 and 80 emails a day, and the average leader well over 100. It is quite possible for an email received during period 1 to have disappeared from the home page of your inbox by breaktime when you get to check your mail. There is a genuine problem with the email culture that has emerged which will not be solved by simply sending out some 'email etiquette' guidelines or having an email-free day every term. As a teacher, if you don't feel on top of the administrative element of the job, you can very quickly feel overwhelmed.

As we have seen, it is pointless to blame. You are responsible, and you must give a stuff about admin, or else you can't do the job.

- **Control your trigger finger.** Make up your mind that messages do not have to be responded to immediately. There was a time when we communicated by memos in pigeonholes and the school didn't fall down. We all need to slow down. However, the enemy of slowing down is the urge that says, 'But if I respond quickly now then it will be a quick job done and I won't have to add it to my to-do list for later.' I feel you, I really do. That is exactly how I think. But it's a false economy. It doesn't reduce your to-do list. Instead, you get an instant reply to your reply, which you then reply to again, which is followed by a further instant reply – or possibly more than one if you clicked 'reply all'. In other words, with each reply you add to your list of jobs or just don't ever get to your other jobs because you have become engaged in an ongoing conversation that is widening by the minute. Resist the temptation. Put it on your list and focus on your priority admin tasks.

- **Prioritise your admin tasks.** This is easier said than done, although there are plenty of time management books and techniques to provide advice on this. Try using the following method for prioritising your work.
  - *Now tasks*: tasks related to safeguarding and student wellbeing.
  - *Today tasks*: tasks related to effective teaching and learning and student progress. In here I would put admin for lesson prep, parental engagement and anything related to student experience at school that must be done urgently.
  - *This week tasks*: tasks related to school or department policy, educational visits, protocol and so on, or tasks that are not urgent.
  - *Periodical tasks*: these are tasks that fall at certain times in the school year, such as classroom displays, report writing or Christmas nativity rehearsals.

Whether via folders on Outlook or a good old-fashioned notebook, categorise the tasks that come in using these headings. Allocate a designated time slot once a week to address the 'week' tasks, and don't allow yourself to take action until then. Be strict with yourself. Only respond now to the 'now' tasks. Each day it's your 'now' and 'today' lists that matter – and, importantly, give yourself permission to chuck some of those 'today' things onto tomorrow's 'today' list. And plan ahead for the periodical tasks.

The key point is to stop having one list. It isn't a list, it's a noose. It will strangle you and starve you of the air you need to do your job. Some of the things on the 'week' list will have resolved themselves by the time you get to them. Some of them you will have sorted out in the staffroom through a chance face-to-face conversation. Don't go along with the view that everything needs to be done *now*. It doesn't. It is 100% acceptable to reply by saying, 'I'll get back to you on this on Thursday.'

You are in control. You decide what you give your attention to. You can slow down the pace. You don't find time, you make it. Take control of your time and you take control of your life.

Reflection questions

- Are you controlling your inbox or is it controlling you? Could you develop a better system or routine for keeping on top of admin?
- Are you giving too much of a stuff about certain admin/email related tasks? Look at your lists and rank them by importance: have you got your priorities right?

Career and professional development

Human beings are programmed for development. St Thomas Aquinas notably identified this as 'natural' and it became the third of his five primary precepts for what makes humans flourish – he calls it education. Aquinas drew on Aristotle's notion of *telos* or final cause. The idea is that all things have an ultimate purpose and each thing has potentiality. A thing's potential is to fulfil its nature. According to Aquinas, one of the marks of a human being is growth and development: knowledge and education.[3]

Aquinas was a scientist and an empiricist. He studied the natural world and drew conclusions based on observation. When we look at nature we see that all things tend towards growth and the fulfilling of potential – whether an acorn to become an oak tree, a rose bud to flower into a rose, a baby bird to fly or a baby human to walk, talk and reproduce. A flower

3 T. Aquinas, *Selected Writings*, ed. and tr. R. McInerny (London: Penguin, 1998), p. 270.

that never blooms is unfulfilled potential. A child that dies in infancy is tragically unfulfilled potential.

We often think of education as something that happens to us when we are young. School is associated with childhood. But this is a huge mistake. When we stop learning, growing and becoming, we run contrary to our nature as human beings. It also undermines our mental health and wellbeing. A commitment to lifelong learning is critical to maintaining a balanced life; the government regards it as one of the 'five ways to wellbeing'.[4]

In fact, when we cease growing and learning we begin to regress. Science tells us that all life is movement. Nothing is stagnant. Motion is the natural state of things. Newton's first law of motion is that an object in motion stays in motion with the same speed and in the same direction unless acted on by an unbalanced force. If everything is moving and you stop moving, then in relation to everything else you have regressed.

If you don't have clarity about where you are going, and you don't have a line manager who is talking to you about developing and growing, this will translate into frustration and dissatisfaction. You need a clear plan of continuing professional development (CPD). You need to feel like you have moved on this year; that you are a better teacher, manager, human being than you were last year. That doesn't need to mean promotion, a new job or extra responsibility, but it does need to mean that you are moving towards mastery in some way.

There is a problem here with the way the teacher pay scale works. A teacher can reach the top of the salary scale relatively quickly, and from there the only way to advance is by moving onto the leadership pay spine or taking on management responsibility. There is nothing to incentivise continuing mastery of the craft. We need to change this. Not necessarily by a never-ending pay spine but by establishing a culture of growth and development, mentoring and innovation.

If you don't have a plan for your professional development then discuss it with your line manager today. You are out of balance. And, what is worse, if you let yourself stagnate for even a few years, you will feel out

4 See Government Office for Science, *Five Ways to Mental Wellbeing* (22 October 2008). Available at: https://www.gov.uk/government/publications/five-ways-to-mental-wellbeing.

of touch and daunted by the very thought of learning a new skill or mastering an old one. Build continuous learning into your working life.

Reflection questions

- Do you feel you are still becoming a better teacher? How much effort and attention have you put into developing your craft in recent years?
- What is your vision for where you want to be in one year, three years and five years from now?

Staff relationships/working collaboratively

We are social animals. Our need for a sense of belonging has long been acknowledged as one of our core needs as human beings. This has nothing to do with whether we are introverts or extroverts. People need people. We thrive and flourish best when we work in harmony with others. A job we dislike can feel bearable if we get on well with our colleagues. The banter and social times grease the wheels of the working day. We commiserate and moan together and we celebrate Friday together. Good social connectivity in the workplace keeps many a person in a job they hate for far too long, such is its power to generate engagement.

However, the converse is also true. People can be miserable in a job they love and leave prematurely if they don't feel like they belong and don't connect and enjoy positive collaboration with colleagues. Businesses across the globe would enjoy greater productivity if they gave more attention to the social connectedness of their workforce and invested in building teams that work.

William Muir was an evolutionary biologist at Purdue University in the 1990s. Muir wanted to study productivity and for his case study he used chickens. It is easy to measure productivity in chickens – just count the eggs! He established two groups of chickens: group 1 comprised of average chickens which Muir left without intervention for six generations.

Group 2 comprised the most individually productive chickens and each year Muir selected the most productive and bred only from those chickens. Six generations later what do you suppose had happened? Group 1 was flourishing, but in group 2 all but three chickens were dead – the rest had been pecked to death. The individualistic one-upmanship culture of group 2 actually undermined productivity and progress. In contrast, a culture of collaboration and helpfulness generates growth and development, whether among chickens or humans.[5]

The faculty office and staffroom should be central to the design of any new school building because staff connection and communication are central factors to the organisation and smooth running of any given school day. School days have become shorter in recent years with lunch and breaktimes being squeezed. One in four secondary schools now allow only 35 minutes for lunch.[6] On one hand, this has reduced opportunities for behavioural incidents to arise during students' free time, but on the other, it has reduced opportunities for meaningful connection and support among staff. The pace of the day is relentless, and fewer teachers leave the isolation of their classrooms from dawn until dusk. This will never make for a happy staff or a culture of collaboration and helpfulness.

Reflection questions

- How often do you stay in your classroom rather than going to the staffroom/faculty space for coffee/lunch? Could you make greater effort to mix with others at these times, even if it means staying for half an hour longer at the end of the day?

5 See J. Amortegui, The Surprising Reason You Should Stop Trying to Be So Productive, *Forbes* (8 August 2016). Available at: https://www.forbes.com/sites/womensmedia/2016/08/08/the-surprising-reason-you-should-stop-trying-to-be-so-productive/#79cad5036e1a.

6 E. Busby, Children Miss Out on Making Friends amid Shorter School Break Times, Study Finds, *The Independent* (10 May 2019). Available at: https://www.independent.co.uk/news/education/education-news/school-breaks-lunchtime-friends-exercise-children-ucl-study-a8906756.html.

- Is your team collaborative and helpful or fragmented and dysfunctional? Could you do something to start bringing people together more?

Innovative and creative input

Your right brain – the creative, imaginative, intuitive part – is quite possibly starved of stimulation in many schools. That which makes us distinctively human is the very thing that we ignore the most. We will fail to flourish in any line of work that does not stretch us and does not utilise our skills and abilities. People the world over are employed to complete menial, repetitive tasks; we can do them but they don't make us jump out of bed in the morning.

Inevitably, we are increasingly finding ways to automate such tasks. Computers and artificial intelligence excel at performing high volume, repetitive tasks. According to Anthony Goldbloom, new technologies mean that computers can learn from vast quantities of data in order to, for example, grade an essay with accuracy and consistency. Recent trials have found them to be more accurate and consistent than teachers! A teacher might mark 10,000 essays over the course of her career, while a computer can mark 10,000 essays within minutes.[7]

Can humans compete with machines? Should we be worried? Goldbloom thinks not because humans can do what machines can't – namely, they can tackle novel situations. Humans can innovate. Machines can't. For example, Percy Spencer was a physicist working on radars during the Second World War. He noticed that his chocolate bar had melted from being in contact with a magnetron. He was able to synthesise his knowledge of physics with his knowledge of food and come up with an idea: the microwave.

This is what humans do best. When you feel like your job and worth is reduced to grunt work, you lose interest and motivation. When you are simply taking orders and routinely performing tasks that don't provide

7 A. Goldbloom, The Jobs We'll Lose to Machines – and the Ones We Won't [video], *TED.com* (February 2016). Available at: https://www.ted.com/talks/anthony_goldbloom_the_jobs_we_ll_lose_to_machines_and_the_ones_we_won_t.

stretch, you fall far short of your potential productivity. If you don't feel like you have any creative input in your team or workplace, then you will lose interest. If you aren't seeking to innovate within the classroom and are just regurgitating the same stuff year on year, you will find that your momentum slows and your enthusiasm wanes. To maintain balance and wellbeing you need to be creating.

Reflection questions

- When did you last do some blue-sky thinking about the way you deliver a certain topic in the classroom? Is there a novel and innovative way to deliver a topic you have taught in the same way for years?
- Do you feel you have a say within your team into how things are run and planned? The opportunity for creative input? If not, tell your line manager that you would welcome this.

Involvement in school outside the classroom

What, besides your subject area, are you passionate about? Find a way to invest yourself in this in your school community. When I look back at the highlights of my teaching career, most have been when I was involved in an activity that I was not expected or employed to do. I am passionate about human rights and seeing young people engage with important issues and resolve to do something to effect change, so I set up a 'Justice' group in my school. With those students we organised a charity day, parliament trips, an initiative to build a classroom for a school in Uganda, and a trip to Ghana. I love my subject, religious studies and philosophy, so trips to Rome and philosophy lectures and seeing students fired up about them fuelled my enthusiasm. I also love seeing students get excited about the arts, so along with a fantastic team of similarly passionate staff, I produced whole-school productions of *Bugsy Malone* and *We Will Rock You*. And, of course, there was my memorable and revolutionary interpretation of the Big Bad Wolf in the staff pantomime!

These highlights made school exciting. I was buzzing in the lead-up to and the aftermath of all these events for three major reasons:

1 I had the opportunity to give my time to something I love and am passionate about. Giving is one of the five essential keys to wellbeing.[8] The very fact that it is unpaid makes it much more rewarding and soul-enhancing than if it was remunerated. There is a fundamental psychological difference in your approach to activities that are freely given: you are there because you choose to be, not because you have to be. That means you are empowered.

2 Students see you in a different and more personable light, just as you see them in a more holistic way. This links back to the teacher–learner relationship discussed earlier. When students see you as a person with passions and interests, rather than an antagonist and source of 'suffering' in their lives, they respond to you entirely differently in the classroom. Equally, you will find that students you have found to be difficult or even unlikeable in the context of trying to teach them calculus, actually have plenty of positive qualities and some interests that coalesce with your own. You will find that you know how to engage them in the classroom more effectively because you know them better.

3 You get to work cross-departmentally with other staff and develop a sense of team and an appreciation of working towards a goal together that is enjoyable and fulfilling.

It is lamentable that in recent years the unrelenting focus on academic progress and the increase in associated workload has disincentivised many teachers from involving themselves in school life outside the classroom. Ironically, this in itself has contributed to a decline in teacher wellbeing. As staff are driven to achieve better results, so schools have cut out the very things that contribute to the enthusiasm and wellbeing of their teachers. Ideally, school leaders would rethink their approach to staff involvement in extracurricular activities because, in order for teachers to contribute in this way, other things may have to give.

8 Government Office for Science, *Five Ways to Mental Wellbeing*.

Could you take responsibility for choosing to prioritise some form of involvement in school life outside of your paid remit? Start planning something fun!

Reflection questions

- When were you last involved in an out-of-classroom activity, trip or group? How did you feel about your work at that time?
- What do you get excited about? Is there a way you could share this passion with students or staff at your school?

Now look back at your wheel of teaching: which spokes need some urgent attention and what are you going to do about them?

Chapter 3

Coping with Stress and Managing Your Mental Health

Ironically, as I sit down to write this chapter, I'm feeling quite stressed. I woke before my alarm this morning and immediately began running through all the things I had to do in my head. Not just today but over the next few weeks and months. A lot of them are new and big things, some require a big investment in time, some I've never done before and some have quite a lot riding on them. This is on top of all the niggly adminny bits and pieces that remain constant. Oh, and I've got to do my tax return too.

I can tell that my tether is shorter than normal. I can feel that I might snap at the kids or be impatient with anyone who takes up more of my time than I think appropriate. I can tell that I am likely to drive faster and get irritated with other road users. I can feel that very slight shortness-of-breath feeling that has in the past developed into a mild panic attack. Yesterday was Sunday and I didn't rest. I finished the day feeling knackered from doing lots of bitty jobs around the house. It's always bad to start Monday feeling tired.

I know all the theory, of course – the stuff I'm about to write about – and I'm doing it. I'm conscious of my mental health like never before. I can immediately recognise stress when I feel it. I have a number of strategies that help me to adjust my mindset and manage the symptoms. But it is worth noting at the outset that there is no stress-free life. There is no ultimate place of peace in which life doesn't challenge and occasionally trip us up. Recognising the signs of mental ill health is a constant. We all have emotions which change daily and hourly and even moment by moment. So, the need for self-awareness, positive coping mechanisms, and the ability to manage and regulate our emotional wellbeing is essential.

The two things I'm doing right now to manage my own emotions are:

1 Using positive coping mechanisms to pick myself up.

2 Recalibrating myself with reality:

- I'm reframing the stress-inducing situation in my mind.
- I'm adjusting my expectations of myself.
- I'm questioning my old assumptions which I know generate negative thoughts.
- I'm affirming the truths which I know generate positive thoughts.

I'll go through each of these in turn and explain how each one helps me to cope with stress and manage my mental health. However, please note I am not qualified to dispense therapeutic advice – I am simply passing on some of the principles that I have found to be most helpful as a teacher. I also recognise that everyone's context is very different and so you may choose to apply these principles in different ways depending on your own situation.

Positive (and negative) coping mechanisms

The starting point is that we all have mental health. To many this will be obvious, but to many it won't, so let's start there. Just as your physical health varies – you get a cold or twist your ankle and you get better – your mental health varies in the same way. Some days you wake up feeling good and some days you wake up feeling flat. On the days when you started out positively, 'shit happened' and a few hours later you were feeling low. Maybe you got to school and found yourself down for cover, or your partner was sharp with you, or your daughter was moody when you dropped her off for school, then your period 1 was disrupted, and by breaktime the day feels like it's already off track. Emotionally you are not feeling as well as you were first thing. Your emotional wellbeing has dipped. That's normal.

We must completely eradicate the thought that mental ill health is something scary or serious. Mental health and ill health is universal, which is distinct from mental illness or disorder. This is different. A mental illness or disorder is 'any condition characterized by cognitive and emotional disturbances, abnormal behaviors, impaired functioning, or any combination of these'.[1] The problem is that in many people's minds, mental ill health means mental illness. It doesn't.

I am not a doctor and in this chapter I will not be discussing the complexities of mental illness or disorders, or the complexities involved in managing or treating them. Suffice to say that one of the causes of a mental disorder or illness is sustained and untreated mental and emotional ill health. In other words, if we don't take our day-to-day mental health seriously and learn how to manage it, then we can find ourselves in a very dark place that will have far-reaching effects on our own and others' lives.

So, how to cope with the day-to-day ups and downs together with life's occasional (and sometimes frequent) storms?

We all cope every day (mostly very well) with the myriad challenges life throws at us. Humans are incredibly resilient creatures. Our instinct to survive serves us well and keeps us alive and kicking in the face of overwhelming difficulties. However, sometimes our survival instinct leads us to adopt coping strategies that don't do us any favours over the long term. Drinking alcohol is an obvious example. A beer or glass of wine when you get home is a nice treat at the end of a full-on day. It's not a problem. But over time, if we lean more and more heavily on it as a means to switch off and feel okay about life, it can become a problem. An alcoholic drink, like a bar of chocolate or a tub of ice cream, gives us a dopamine kick and therefore makes us feel better. Dopamine is the chemical released by our brain that gives us the feeling that we can cope. It's a natural chemical high.

Table 3.1 lists some very common coping mechanisms, all of which will generate a dopamine kick. Have a look and evaluate which mechanisms you commonly use.

---

1 See https://dictionary.apa.org/mental-disorder.

Table 3.1. Negative coping mechanisms

Negative coping mechanism	**Score each one on a scale of 1–5 (where 1 = I never do this, and 5 = I often do this)**				
Get angry/aggressive	1	2	3	4	5
Shout	1	2	3	4	5
Blame	1	2	3	4	5
Over-eat/eat junk food	1	2	3	4	5
Under-eat/excessive dieting	1	2	3	4	5
Drink more/smoke more/use drugs	1	2	3	4	5
Caffeine fix	1	2	3	4	5
Nail biting/fidgeting	1	2	3	4	5
Self-loathing/verbally beat yourself up	1	2	3	4	5
Spend more time alone	1	2	3	4	5
Become inactive/sleep or stay in bed more	1	2	3	4	5
Excessive use of social media/gaming	1	2	3	4	5
Self-harm	1	2	3	4	5

The problem with these negative coping mechanisms is that not only do they cause harm both to yourself and others over time, but neither do they actually fix the issue causing the stress or ill health. They may mask it, they may even make you feel better in the short-term, but they don't make the underlying source of distress go away.

We all have a 'stress bucket'. Each day some stress goes into the bucket. It may start with over-sleeping, which means you're running late, so some stress goes into the bucket. Then you can't find your keys and some more stress goes into the bucket. Then there are roadworks on the way to work and some more stress goes into the bucket. Then the photocopier jams so you have to make a last-minute change to your lesson plan and some more stress goes into the bucket. Then you have to arbitrate in a student bullying situation at breaktime so you miss break and some more stress goes into your bucket. And so on. Pretty quickly your bucket fills up. If your bucket gets full, eventually you will get to a point where you can't contain all that stress any longer, and you will flip out, or swear at someone, or 'lose it', or channel that energy in some other negative way. Your bucket spills over. We can all relate to this. We all have days like this.

Now, if this starts happening more regularly or you are living with a longer term stressful situation (like a difficult marriage, being a carer, a bullying boss or a bereavement) then you begin each day with your bucket already half full – or more. Your capacity for the small stuff is seriously reduced. You don't have the head space or the same level of emotional elasticity. You get to that tipping point far more quickly and you spill over far more regularly. And that's when your default coping mechanisms, if they are negative, can very quickly become significant. You become dependent on them and they begin to cause you harm.

Here's the trick: on the side of your stress bucket is a tap. If you can learn how to turn on the tap and release the stress, then you can essentially prevent it from ever getting to spilling-over point. There are various ways to turn on the tap, but the following four techniques are universally effective.

1 **Talk to someone.** This is number one for a reason. Studies have shown that self-disclosure 'produces the highest level of activation in neural regions associated with motivation and reward'.[2] When

2 A. F. Ward, The Neuroscience of Everybody's Favorite Topic, *Scientific American* (16 July 2013). Available at: https://www.scientificamerican.com/article/the-neuroscience-of-everybody-favorite-topic-themselves.

you feel like someone 'gets you', it elicits a chemical change in your brain.

However, people often say, 'What's the point in talking to someone? What can they do? They can't change the situation, they can't change my husband or bring my mum back …' That is not the point. You don't talk to someone so they can fix your problem for you. You talk to someone because the act of expressing your emotions verbally will help you to cope because you will feel that someone else understands what you are feeling.

This morning when I awoke feeling stressed I sat down to work, called my friend and colleague and said, 'I'm feeling a bit overwhelmed with everything.' This is often more difficult for males than most females because as men we have been taught since day nought to hide our emotions, 'man up' and be strong. As if strength and repressing emotion were somehow the same thing. Utterly ridiculous.

2 **Exercise.** A half-hour run, a walk or a swim will release a whole bundle of pleasure chemicals into your bloodstream which will give you a natural high that will last a good while. Studies suggest that team sports are best for good mental health but essentially any activity that raises your heartbeat will do it.[3]

   Sport is also stress-relieving because of its simplicity. There are fairly basic rules to most sports, and on the whole everyone agrees to them. Unlike with life, which is complex and people don't agree on much. Sport creates a safe zone in which we can operate without having to second guess every move and constantly adjust.

   The magic number that most scientists agree will elicit untold health and mental benefits is 30 minutes three times a week. But I admit that when I'm feeling at my lowest, my resolve to go out and run is also at its lowest. It is difficult to make myself do it when I'm not feeling perky. Try to make a fixed arrangement to meet up with a mate to go for a run or to a class. If they're expecting you, you'll go. Make it happen.

3 F. Bosely, What's the Ultimate Way to Defy Depression, Disease and Early Death? Exercise, *The Guardian* (3 October 2017). Available at: https://www.theguardian.com/lifeandstyle/2017/oct/03/exercise-depression-disease-death-sit-less-move-more.

3 **Get creative.** Sing, listen to music, dance, doodle, paint, play a musical instrument, write, design, build. Do something that allows you to express yourself. It is deeply therapeutic to create. And what you create is unique – it's you. Creating allows you to actualise the emotions that are locked inside. We all have a tendency to give our mental health less credence than our physical health. If you break a leg or injure an eye you go to hospital. Clearly it needs fixing. You don't struggle into work with a broken leg or a bleeding eye, telling your co-workers, 'Well, I can't possibly take the day off – Year 11 have got a mock next week!' Your injury is real and Year 11 will cope without you!

No one would judge you for going to hospital with a broken leg. However, we are still, on the whole, a long way off recognising the reality of our mental ill health. We somehow feel as if it is nobler to soldier on with a deeply debilitating emotional struggle. Whether it is due to a marriage breakdown, a bereavement or the cumulative effect of relentless pressure, the devastating effect of poor mental health is real. And we ignore it at our peril. Channelling that emotion into being creative can help psychologically to translate the invisible into the visible. It helps us to process the unseen by making it tangible.

4 **Be kind.** When I am low, I am usually low about what is happening to me. I will usually be fully engaged with my problems, my worries, the pressure I feel, the struggles I am experiencing. Even though some of those concerns are to do with others – like bringing in enough money to support my family or not wanting to let my students down – the bottom line is that *I* feel stressed about what *I* need to do. I am thinking of myself.

Studies show that dopamine and oxytocin are released when you do something kind for someone else – when you make someone smile.[4] This is different from doing the normal stuff you do for others (which you may well feel is underappreciated and a cause of your emotional low). This is about going out of your way to do something unexpected, helpful or kind for someone who crosses

4 J. Baraz and S. Alexander, The Helper's High, *Greater Good Magazine* (1 February 2010). Available at: https://greatergood.berkeley.edu/article/item/the_helpers_high.

your path, who may well be a stranger. When you focus on making someone else happy, you feel happier too. You are empowered. Recognising that you have the ability to help or lift or energise another person is empowering. Furthermore, your kindness will usually (although not always) elicit a positive response – a smile, a thank you, a word of appreciation. It's called the 'helper's high'. Try it and see!

Each of these will turn on the tap of your stress bucket. Work to make them your default settings and you will learn to manage stress more effectively.

Recalibrating Yourself

The following steps, which I now take when responding to stressful situations or taking care of my mental health, derive from a cognitive-behavioural therapy (CBT) technique known as the ABC Model of stress.[5] Understand and apply this model and it will change your approach to stress forever:

A = the adverse or activating event

B = your beliefs

C = the consequential emotion

The critical question here is: does A cause C or does B cause C?

Here is an example: I leave for work 20 minutes before I need to arrive. A few miles along, a tractor pulls out in front of me on a single-lane country road. I slow to 15 mph. I'm annoyed. I'm driving right up the tractor's backside looking for any possible passing opportunity. Eventually the tractor turns into a field and I seek to make up for the fact that I'm now running late by driving faster. I'm closer to the rear of every car I now encounter. I overtake more aggressively than usual. I get to a junction and find myself in a queue behind about ten cars – far more than

5 J. Selva, Albert Ellis' ABC Model in the Cognitive Behavioral Therapy Spotlight, *Positive Psychology* (29 April 2020). Available at: https://positivepsychology.com/albert-ellis-abc-model-rebt-cbt.

usual. What am I feeling? Stress, frustration, anger, irritation – that is, C, the consequential emotions.

If you ask me in the moment what is causing my stress and frustration I will tell you with absolute clarity, 'That bloody tractor!' But it's not true. The tractor was the activating event or the adverse situation. My stress is actually caused by B – my beliefs. Here's how ...

Two beliefs have generated the stress I am feeling in this situation: (1) that there should be no other road users, obstacles or roadworks that will impede my desired driving speed, and (2) that being a few minutes late for work is a really bad thing.

Is belief number 1 rational? Of course not, it's ridiculous. Rationally, I know there could be any number of obstacles on the road. If I change my belief to accommodate this reality, then I will leave home a little earlier and consequently the slow-moving tractor may even prove to be a mildly interesting distraction rather than a trigger for my frustration.

Is belief number 2 rational? No. This is trickier because there may be a knock-on effect from being late – like inconveniencing someone else or having to teach my lesson minus the photocopies – all of which are surmountable. Actually, I'm more concerned about the fact that turning up late to a briefing will make me look bad in front of my head; in spite of the fact that I'm usually punctual and she will probably think nothing of it. This probably indicates that what I'm battling with is more a core belief drilled into me from way back that being late is a moral evil(!) and I'm a bad person if I keep somebody waiting. I stumble into the meeting and mutter my excuses ('Bloody tractors – I'm so sorry ...'), only to find that everyone else is much less bothered by my tardiness than I am. Fundamentally, I was worried about failing to meet my own self-imposed standards of perfection.

CBT asserts that C always derives from B, not A. This is empowering because it means that if you change your beliefs, you can change the consequential emotion. Of course, this is easier said than done, but it's a brilliant starting point to begin to move forward.

There are three very common beliefs to be aware of, and which one you default to may well be causing you substantial distress:

1 **Optimism:** the belief that everything should always go well all the time. This is like me believing that I should make my best time ever every time I drive to work because nothing will ever go wrong. Is it rational? No. And when life doesn't conform to my beliefs I get upset.

2 **Pessimism:** the belief that everything will always go wrong all of the time. 'Bad stuff always happens to me. Oh, here we go – just my luck – of course there's a tractor in the way! There would be, wouldn't there?' Is this rational? No. When life happens to go well, pessimists may unconsciously seek to self-sabotage their success because it undermines their core belief that life is unfair and the self-worth they derive from feeling like they have it harder than everyone else.

3 **Realism:** this is the mean between these two extremes. The belief that 'shit happens' or, as the old saying goes, 'Some days you're the pigeon, and some days you're the statue!' Some days will be great and some won't, and that's okay. You can try to maximise the positives and mitigate the negatives, but certain things are outside your control, so just roll with those days and chalk them up to 'good learning experiences'. Rational? Yep. Less likely to result in extremes of emotion? Definitely. Your beliefs determine your emotions.

The message here is that you can choose your emotions. As we saw in Chapter 1, even when he experienced the depths of human suffering, Victor Frankl understood that you can choose your response: whether to believe that a better day is coming or whether to despair. You choose your beliefs.

I don't wish for a minute to make this sound easy, but I do think it's simple. Our beliefs are usually deeply entrenched and intertwined with a whole host of powerful memories and experiences which we cannot simply erase. But we can gradually reprogramme ourselves as we become aware of the negative or destructive beliefs or agreements we have internalised over the years and seek to replace them with positive, liberating beliefs and agreements.[6]

Let's apply this thinking to a typical stressful teaching day:

> I arrive at school having dropped off my own kids at school. I have some copying to do for lesson 1. I am teaching four out of five lessons today. There is a staff briefing before registration. In my free period I am hoping to get some marking done as well as prep for tomorrow, but I know that I may have to cover someone or deal with something unexpected and it may not happen. I collect in work in two lessons and set homework in two. I now have two extra class sets of work to mark. I have a departmental meeting after school followed by a brief catch-up about the Christmas play. I need to keep on top of my emails throughout the day. After the meetings I try to finish the marking and prep I need to do. I then go home in time to cook dinner for the kids and get them to their early evening clubs. I do some marking while watching the netball, swimming and so on. When I get home I work for an hour from 9 to 10pm and scoop up the emails I haven't got to yet. My desk at school is a mess. I would like to go in earlier tomorrow to get a head start, but that will mean changing my childcare arrangements ...

Consequential emotion: stress. I have too much to do today and I already feel behind. I'm getting further behind by the hour.

What is causing the emotion? The instinctive answer is: school, my job, school policy.

No, that's A – the adverse activating event. What beliefs are at play here? What are the beliefs that are causing me to feel stressed? There is not a set answer to this question. The narrative will be different for different people. There are a multitude of different beliefs in play which collectively can cause a perfect storm of negative emotion if they all coincide.

Here is one possible set of beliefs that may be triggering a negative emotional response:

- I should be able to **handle** this.

6 For more on this see Ruiz's *The Four Agreements* and what he calls the 'domestication' of the planet.

- My desk should be **tidy**, like [insert colleague's name] always is.
- I'm a **bad** teacher if I don't have students' work marked and back to them by the next lesson.
- Every lesson must be **outstanding**.
- It's never **okay** to be late.
- I must look like I'm **coping** – showing weakness is **bad**.
- I must be a **perfect** mum/dad/wife/husband, which means being as present as possible at home but also bringing in a **decent** income.

I could go on ... But you may notice a common theme here: the belief that I should be meeting a certain standard and I should meet it all the time. The standard is evident by the subjective terms in **bold** which indicate an internalised bar and a varying position in relation to that bar. None of these terms – like **decent**, **bad** or **handle** – are absolutes. They will all mean different things to different people. You have a bar in your own mind that you expect yourself to live up to. It is the culmination of all your core beliefs. You hold yourself accountable to it. And when you don't live up to it, in your own judgement, you feel stress. The thoughts give rise to feelings, which in turn trigger behaviours (like working later and faster or speaking more sharply or curtly), which in turn feed back into your thoughts, as Figure 3.1 illustrates.

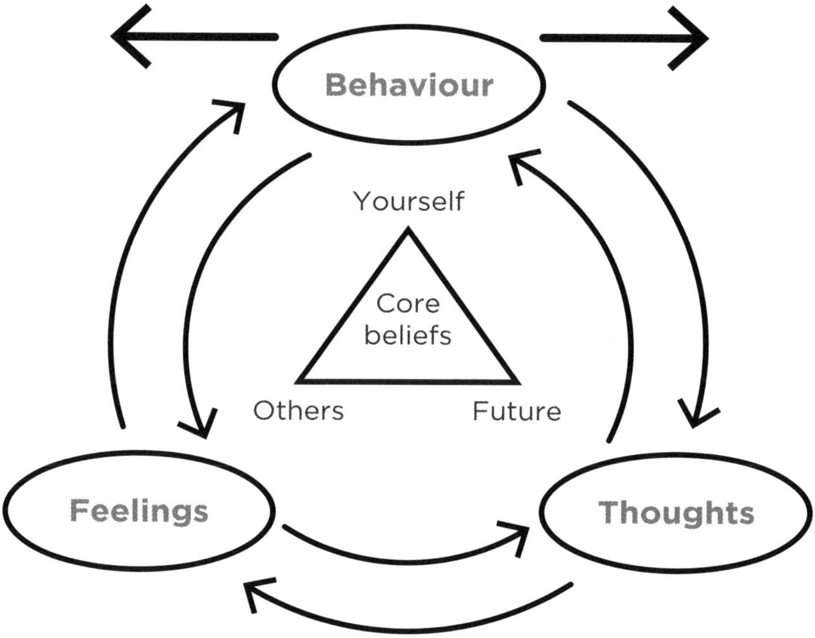

Figure 3.1. How feelings, thoughts and behaviours influence each other

Is your bar right? No, it isn't – principally because there is no bar. As we saw in Chapter 1, there is no perfect teacher and no perfect human being. There is you. And your capacity today is different to your capacity tomorrow or next year or after a sleepless night.

Of course, minimum standards are expected of us in all lines of work. What I'm referring to is our internalised reinterpretation of those standards and the way we add to them with our own pre-programming to expect far more of ourselves than the Teachers' Standards ever did.

So, given that our internalised bar is of our own making – a belief – we can change it or at least re-examine it and check whether it's true. This is the process I went through this morning:

1 **Reframe the situation**

- Does everything you think you have to do actually have to be done?
- Does it have to be done today?

- Do you personally have to do all these things?

I look at my list and I think no, no and no. I reframe the reality I'm facing. The truth is that there are some things I need to do today, but some things can wait until tomorrow and next week, and some I personally don't need to do at all. I'm feeling better already!

2 **Adjust your expectations**

- Is the time frame you have imposed fixed or have you made it up?
- Is the expectation on performance or outcome fixed or self-imposed?

I look at my list. Some of the deadlines I have no control over. Some I've just made up – so I can change those deadlines. Some I can liaise with whomever I need to and look to move the deadline. The second point is trickier. I want to do every job well. I want it to be excellent. But who says what is excellent? Who says that what I'm currently doing is not excellent? The fact is that the main judge I'm trying to please is the relentless slave-driver in my own head. I don't know how he got there, but he's pretty loud and annoying! But I'm getting better at answering back. Something like this: 'What I do doesn't have to be perfect. I don't have to reach somebody else's standard. I'm just going to be me. I'll do my best given the time I've got. I'll focus on the moment, on getting started, and I'll put my best into it. I don't need to worry about the finished product.'

3 **Question your assumptions**

- What underlying core beliefs are generating the negative feelings you are having?
- Are these beliefs rational?

Identifying these core beliefs is not easy and usually requires some help. Through the course of a good number of counselling sessions, I managed to put my finger on some of my core beliefs. Here are three of my own big ones – either they will resonate with you or you will think they are crackers:

- Suffering is virtuous: the more I suffer by working extremely hard, the more valid I am.

- Busyness is admirable: the busier I am, the more impressive I am.
- Perfection is expected: falling short is unacceptable.

There is a minefield of issues with any one of these core beliefs, and unpacking them has been quite a journey. The fact is that although I have tried to reprogramme myself, to a significant extent they are still a default setting that I revert to when I'm under pressure. Are they rational? Definitely not.

4 **Affirm the truth**

- What can you change/control?
- What can't you change/control?

In conjunction with questioning the assumptions that I used to think were truth comes the affirmation of their antithesis, which I now believe to be truer. Working out what these are for you will not be an overnight process, but it is necessary if you are going to live a richer, freer life. Here is what I'm affirming right now:

- Suffering is not virtuous, and neither is busyness. I am valid and valuable because I am a unique human being. I am not a victim. I can choose what I give my time and attention to. I can choose what to prioritise. I can adjust my workload in any number of ways. I am responsible.
- There is no such thing as perfect; there is only growth. I will do my best today and seek to improve on that tomorrow. I am a work in progress. There is no finished product. I will do my best to adapt to the things that come my way that I can't control. I am not expected or obliged to be anything other than myself.

I don't know about you, but I'm definitely feeling better! I would recommend wholeheartedly that if you think you might be struggling because of some entrenched core beliefs that are negatively shaping your approach to life and work, then try working through them with a friend, coach or counsellor. Taking control of your thoughts and choosing to change your mind is the beginning of a healthier mental existence. As the philosopher William James reputedly said, 'The greatest weapon against stress is our ability to choose one thought over another.'

Figure 4.1. Plato's Cave

Chapter 4

Changing Your Mindset: Getting Out of the Cave

Plato suggested that people everywhere live their entire lives like prisoners trapped in a cave (Figure 4.1).[1]

In the darkest part of the cave the prisoners are chained up, their viewpoint confined and they can only see the inner wall of the cave on which they observe shadows. They believe these shadows to be real. They are the only reality they have ever known. They discuss these shadows and come up with names for them and theories to explain their movements and appearances.

Unknown to the prisoners, behind them in the outer part of the cave are puppeteers holding aloft different objects which deflect the light coming from a fire at the cave entrance. It is the puppeteers who, by deflecting the light, create the shadows the prisoners see.

One day a prisoner escapes. She makes her way to the outer part of the cave and discovers the source of the shadows. She begins to realise that what she thought was reality is artificial. It is a reality that has been handed to her. She then goes further, past the puppeteers, past the fire and makes her way out of the cave. There she discovers true reality. The world unfiltered, the truth as it actually is, undistorted by the versions presented to her. Plato calls this truth the world of Forms. He suggests that our entire existence is a dance of shadows, and that we discover our true purpose in life when we commit to finding the truth and questioning the untruths we have been fed throughout our life. This, Plato says, is the philosopher's challenge. All those who embark on this journey are philosophers.

Plato was a student of Socrates. He furthered the Socratic method for which Socrates was arrested and executed by the Greek authorities of his day – that is, the crime of questioning everything. Or what the

1 This is my paraphrased version based on Plato's allegory of the cave from *The Republic*, tr. H. D. P. Lee (London: Penguin, 2007), 514a–520a.

Greek authorities called 'corrupting the youth'. It was on this principle that the first Western university was founded: Plato's Academy in Athens. It is the basis of the educational project: we discover truth by asking questions. There is nothing that should be exempt from questioning – no question which should not be asked – which is why the Athenians found Socrates' teaching such a threat. Those in power would always much prefer to have a passive, accepting population to oversee. Perish the thought that the people start thinking for themselves! Today, just as then, the teacher's primary task is to pique the curiosity of students, to generate and develop their questioning nature, and enable them to progress in their journeys of discovery. Yet I fear we have ourselves become the antithesis of what we are actually employed to do. We are prisoners in a cave, having fully accepted the norms, the system, the expectations and the untruths under which we have been reared. We don't buck the system. We don't challenge the status quo. We don't question authority. We don't expect different. In fact, we often become the enemy of change ourselves. We are so wedded to how things are that we fear anything that could possibly set us free and make things better. We are safe in our moaning. We are secure in our discontent.

In Plato's analogy, the philosopher, having discovered truth and reality beyond the cave, resolves to go back. She cannot keep this knowledge to herself. She feels compelled to tell her fellow prisoners of the wonders that lie beyond the shadows. But when she returns they won't listen. They scoff and are disbelieving. They have no appetite for change. They have become complacent in their imprisonment. Still, she pleads with them and relays stories and possibilities about the world beyond. In the end, the prisoners become angry, rise up and kill her. They silence the voice that challenges their view of reality. This, Plato says, is what humanity has routinely done to those visionaries and leaders who have sought to challenge the accepted norms. We don't need to look very far for other examples: Jesus, Mahatma Gandhi, Martin Luther King Jr, Oscar Romero.

People are always resistant to change. We find security in whatever meta-narrative we use to decipher and make sense of the world. This is why religion in all its forms continues to be such a powerful and enduring phenomenon: religious systems provide people with a lens or narrative with which to make sense of the world and their place within it.

But freedom lies in the uncomfortable journey of questioning accepted wisdoms and seeking truth. I worry that our classrooms have become places where we seek to reinforce conformity and passivity rather than places that call on our young people to challenge, question and venture to create a better world. And this is set to continue as long as we ourselves passively accept the cave into which we were born and do not honestly evaluate our own assumptions and mindset.

Are you in the cave?

I would argue that we are all, at least to some extent and in some areas of our lives, in the cave. You may have ventured out in some respects. You may have sought to forge your own route in some ways, but there is no arrival point in life – there is only continuance. As soon as you stop growing you start regressing. There is no such thing as a stagnant human being. You are regressing as soon as you stop progressing.

Our schools are also in the cave, and this can make it exceptionally difficult to find freedom and authenticity as teachers. I am acutely aware of just how powerful the threat of Ofsted and inspection is in the minds of most teachers and leaders: it looms large and can thwart and stifle original thinking and innovation. 'We have to do this for Ofsted,' is a commonly heard mantra in many school faculties. We have to be willing to question directives, including those from Ofsted or the Independent Schools Inspectorate (ISI), if we are going to build authentic schools that serve the best interests of our children. And that means all of us, from the NQT to the head teacher to the governors. Because the standards set by Ofsted/ISI, as with all standards, are made up. They have changed and they will change again. They are not truth; they are a shadow.

I wrote in Chapter 2 of the need for continuous professional development, of the need to keep learning. What I am referring to here goes a step deeper – of continuous personal development, of mindset change, of identifying some of the assumptions (the shadows) that you have come to accept as real but which may be keeping you from enjoying your life and teaching and which are keeping you trapped in the cave.

Recognising that you are not happy with the status quo is the start of your journey out of the cave.

The shadows

The shadows represent the assumptions we all make. The things we think are true but actually aren't. There are three big ones:

1 Assumptions about what is possible.

2 Assumptions about purpose.

3 Assumptions about identity.

Assumptions about what is possible

'You can't do that!' We all heard those words very early on in our lives. Our instinctive reaction when we were young was to say, 'Why not?' But very quickly we accepted the limitations we were given and internalised them. We learned to see obstacles as boundaries to confine us rather than as opportunities to be overcome. At the age of 8, I started having trumpet lessons. It was my granny's idea but I was keen. I had about 10 lessons, but in that short amount of time I couldn't reach the high notes. So I quit. I concluded that I couldn't play the trumpet. It didn't occur to me that with practice I could develop that ability.

We all have stories like this one. We gradually and unconsciously drew the confines of our own existence and potential as we met with impediments and interpreted them as objectively binding parameters for our lives. Sometimes they were reinforced by others: 'You'll never be as artistic as your sister – she's the arty one.' Much of the time they were just assumed: 'We're not rich – that's how the other half live.' Our mindset was shaped.

As we saw in Chapter 1, Carol Dweck calls this entity theory – the view that intelligence or ability or talent is a fixed entity that you either have or don't have in a certain discipline. She contrasts it with incremental theory – the view that we can all make incremental progress in all activities; what matters is effort and purposeful practice. Dweck coined the terms fixed mindset and growth mindset to describe the mode of thinking that evidence shows determines our level of development and growth: 'Students who believed their intelligence could be developed (a growth mindset) outperformed those who believed their intelligence was fixed (a fixed mindset). And when students learned through a structured program that they could "grow their brains" and increase their intellectual abilities, they did better.'[2]

Obviously, this has huge implications for the way we go about education, but my purpose here is to ask you personally to what extent might you have limited yourself and believed the shadows because you, like me, accepted entity theory? More importantly, what are you still believing and accepting now that keeps you from exploring new and exciting possibilities in life and work?

Henry Ford said it brilliantly like this: 'Whether you believe you can do a thing or not, you are right.'[3] We stay in the cave every time we consciously or unconsciously accept the thought that 'I can't do that.' Henry Ford is also reputed to have said, 'I cannot discover that anyone knows enough to say definitely what is and what is not possible.' This is the kind of brave thinking that gets you out of the cave!

If your default assumption is to think 'I can't', then question that thought. Question the directive, question Ofsted, question the government, question the head, question your line manager. It is the beginning of your journey out. Do you feel trapped? You're not. Do you feel that no one's listening? They are. Do you feel like there is no point in trying? There is. Do you feel like you've tried everything? You haven't. Do you feel like you're failing? You're not. Question what you think you know. A different reality is possible.

Assumptions about purpose

What is it all for? Why do you exist? There are plenty of philosophies on this and I'm not about to attempt tell you which one is true, if any. But I

2 Dweck, *Mindset: The New Psychology of Success*, p. 116.
3 H. Ford. quoted in *Reader's Digest* (filler item), vol. 51, September 1947, p. 64.

am going to question the assumptions we have been fed by our culture, some of which may or may not be pertinent to you.

- **The point is to get more stuff.** The classic consumerist tale: your value is defined by your net worth. I am successful if I own my own home. I am successful if I drive a nice car. I am valuable if I earn a good wage. The more stuff I own, the more significant I am. Of course, it doesn't take a genius to point out just how flawed this theory is and yet it is astonishing how placidly we subscribe to it.

  This pursuit of stuff is an unrelenting and unfulfilling pursuit. J. D. Rockefeller was once asked, 'How much money is enough money?' His answer: 'Just a little bit more.'[4] If we buy into this assumption we can find ourselves on a treadmill that only gets faster. With each pay rise we adjust our lifestyle to absorb our new income level, so we still feel like we haven't got enough. We are endlessly looking at what we haven't got or can't afford which perpetuates a dissatisfaction that is unending.

  The shadow isn't real. Stop chasing it.

- **The point is to get security.** I heard a teacher say just recently (having been told that his school was opting out of the teacher pension scheme) that the only reason he became a teacher was 'for the pension'. I was honestly shocked, although on reflection perhaps I shouldn't have been. What he was articulating was that innate need for security that we all desire. Maybe you wouldn't put it quite like that but there are plenty of people who ended up in teaching because it was a 'safe' career or because they didn't know what else to do. I remember my own dad sitting at the dinner table and warning me and my siblings that self-employment was risky – not to be toyed with. He said: 'You need to have a job that's secure, with a pension. Like being a teacher. At least then you'll always have something to fall back on.'

  I don't doubt his good intentions. It's perfectly understandable. But in my view it leads down a path that keeps you in the cave. Risk-averse. Accepting the system. Keeping your head down. Missing out on the fullness that life has to offer. And it's flawed too, of

4 See https://www.newworldencyclopedia.org/entry/John_D._Rockefeller.

course, just as that teacher discovered. Certainty in an uncertain world is impossible, a shadow. The truth is that nothing is secure – even the teachers' pension scheme. Even the Great British pound. Even democracy itself – as the past few years have shown.

The shadow isn't real. Stop chasing it.

- **The point is to get position.** I am valuable if I have seniority, if there is someone beneath me who has to do what I say. Or perhaps it is less egotistical than that: I am valuable if I have been given responsibility, if I have climbed the slippery pole and can say that I am the head of something. Oh, how we love to have important-sounding job titles, when in reality it's just a rearranging of the chairs. We are still taking orders from someone. We probably have more things to worry about, more stress, less time to enjoy our increased income and less time with those we love. It's a false economy, a shadow. The thing we thought would make life better has actually made it worse.

  It's not that there is anything wrong with wanting responsibility or to be in a position of leadership, the question is *why* we want it? Who is it for? Who are we trying to impress? Have we just bought into the system because we assumed that is what you are supposed to do? Or because we felt flattered to be offered the role? In fact, position by itself means nothing, only what we do with it. Question the system.

  The shadow isn't real. Stop chasing it.

Assumptions about identity

We have been conditioned since the day we were born with expectations about how we are supposed to be. Based on boys' and girls' gift cards alone, girls have been conditioned to think they are supposed to like ponies, fairies, cupcakes and pink, and boys are supposed to like dinosaurs, trucks, football and blue. We never had a choice in this. It was forced on us. And in a myriad of other ways we have been repeatedly told how we *should* be, which has constrained us from simply being ourselves.

Social media, and the media in general, has exacerbated this identity crisis. We are exposed daily to the intricacies of other people's lives and activities, but not the whole of their lives – just the best bits. We instinctively compare ourselves to others, even though we know they only post the most flattering selfie, the happiest family picture and share the job promotion but not the action plan or capability procedures they have been put on. All of it together paints a vivid picture in our minds: this is how I'm supposed to be in order to be happy, valued and accepted.

In teaching, we are presented with examples of what an outstanding teacher should be like. We are shown videos or observations of outstanding teachers. We are given the Teachers' Standards and the Ofsted framework which set out how we should perform in the classroom. All of this is well intended and supposedly designed to raise standards, except that is an attempt to make teaching an exact science when it isn't. Arguably, it is more of an art than a science. Some academy trusts have taken a rigorously prescriptive approach to marking, lesson starters, assessment for learning, lining up, dress code, behaviour policy and so on, all seemingly based on the notion that good teaching must look a certain way. And that good progress must look a certain way. And that good behaviour means silence. And good students will have their top buttons done up and their skirts below the knee.

None of these assumptions are true. They are shadows.

All of these expectations get projected onto the average teacher, and it leads to a relentless feeling of failure that no one can live with for any period of time without serious consequences for their mental and physical health. The truth is that every student is different. Every lesson is different. Every class is different. Every teacher is different. We will grow truly brilliant schools when we embrace this rather than fight against it. You don't need to be or teach like anyone else. As my good friend Emily often tells me, 'You do you!'

Getting out of the cave

Behind the prisoners in Plato's Cave there is a partition from where the puppeteers deflect the light and shape the prisoners' version of reality. As we have seen, these shadows (assumptions) aren't real. The prisoner escaping the cave, then, must now deal with the deflectors responsible for shaping those assumptions.

The deflectors in our own lives and careers are the expectations of others: our parents, our teachers our mentors, the media, Ofsted, our culture or religion, our peers and so on. They have shaped our mindset in the past and have the power to continue to control our lives, but only to the extent that we let them. We are all a product of our pasts to some degree. For example, I am one of five children. My mum was a teacher and my dad was a banker. What did we five children become? Four teachers and a banker! And I thought I became a teacher of my own free choice. We know this about society. We largely stay within the confines established by the norms and expectations of the people around us. Mechanics give birth to mechanics, musicians give birth to musicians, university graduates give birth to university graduates. In fact, social mobility in the UK has been stagnant for a number of years.[5] For better or worse, humans the world over are shaped by the mindset and frame of reference of their parents and early influences.

Sometimes life pushes us out of our comfort zone and we are exposed to forces which make us question the version of reality we have been handed. However, we would all do well to consciously challenge our deflectors and question why they continue to hold sway over our lives. Breaking free is hard to do, but it is absolutely necessary in order to escape from the cave.

Why do these forces hold so much power over us? Ruth Berenda conducted a famous experiment on peer pressure in the 1950s and found that 75% of the time people of all ages will go along with what they know to be wrong because that is what the majority are doing.[6] Why is this

5 R. Adams, Social Mobility in UK 'Virtually Stagnant' Since 2014, *The Guardian* (30 April 2019). Available at: https://www.theguardian.com/society/2019/apr/30/social-mobility-in-uk-virtually-stagnant-since-2014.

6 R. W. Berenda, *The Influence of the Group on the Judgments of Children* (New York: King's Crown Press, 1950).

the case? A significant part of the answer lies in our quest for validation: the deflectors have power over us to the extent that we seek validation from them.

Where does your validity come from? Are you valid because your dad is proud of you? Are you valid because your boss recognises you? Or because you have 1,000 followers on Instagram? Or because Ofsted said you were outstanding? Or because your social class thinks you do a 'respectable' job? I think not. Every one of us is valid and has infinite value simply because we are human beings, each with the potential to make an invaluable and unique contribution to the world. And yet we constantly make choices – many of them contrary to our best interests – in order to achieve this elusive validation.

Does our validity as teachers or as schools come from a judgement by Ofsted or ISI? I recall the announcement by the head teacher in one of the schools where I taught that the outcome of the Ofsted inspection was requires improvement rather than the good we had all been hoping for. Of course, there were tears and an overwhelming sense of demoralisation. But I also remember thinking: 'We are the same school today as we were yesterday.' Yesterday we were confidently providing an education that we believed in; today that education had been invalidated. Except, of course, in reality nothing had changed. How we *felt* about ourselves and what we did had shifted because we placed great import on this judgement. But that is on us.

I was struck by a head teacher I met recently who placed great import on a different measure. She leads one of five secondary schools in her town, and inevitably there is rivalry between them. She said:

> We didn't get the 'best' results in the town, but I know for a fact that every one of our Year 11s got what they needed to access their post-16 choice, and we were the only school in the town to have no students hospitalised during exam season due to stress and mental ill health. Personally, that matters more to me than the percentage 9–4 statistic or an Ofsted judgement.

As it happens, Ofsted rates the school as good, but arguably that is by the by. The point is that their number one aim is the wellbeing of their students rather than validation by Ofsted, and that results in an entirely different mindset.

I heard a fascinating Buddhist tale about a particular method some villagers had for catching monkeys. They would attach a narrow-necked jar to a tree containing some nuts. During the night a monkey would come out of the forest, smell the nuts, put its hand into the jar and grab a handful. But then, with its hand now balled into a fistful of nuts, it couldn't get it out of the jar. So it sat there all night, and in the morning the villagers would knock it on the head with a stick. All the monkey had to do to go free was to let go of the nuts.[7]

Are you doing the same thing? Clinging on to the very thing that is keeping you a prisoner? How much are you limiting your own freedom, as well as your progression as a teacher, because you won't let go of your need for validation from the deflectors? Are you reluctant to pursue your true dreams and be your authentic self because you fear the opinions of others? If you want to be free, you have to let go!

Of course, this isn't easy and it's an ongoing process for all of us, but it cannot be bypassed if you want to live life authentically outside the cave. When I am feeling stressed, I have found it helpful to attempt to identify who it is I am seeking validation from. Often, the answer is that I am trying to live up to a standard that is in my own head. But that raises the further question: why is that standard or expectation in my head in the first place? How did it get there? And the answer, for me, was that I had adopted it in early childhood. I had internalised a belief in a standard of perfection that I felt I must meet based on my conservative Christian upbringing which categorised anything short of perfection as sin.

I still battle with this idea every day, although now I am aware of it, I can notice it, question it and challenge it. Even as I write this chapter, the nagging thought persists that what I am writing is not good enough and could be better. But then I take control and affirm, 'No, it is me, today, doing my best.' There is no standard that I have to live up to; there is just my best today. Some people will find this helpful, some won't, and that's okay. I don't need the validation of everyone. I don't need everyone to like my book.

---

7 This story also appears in Robert Pirsig's *Zen and the Art of Motorcycle Maintenance* (New York: William Morrow, 1974) as the South Indian Monkey Trap, consisting of a hollowed-out coconut, chained to a stake and containing rice. The principle is the same: the monkey is trapped by an idea which has become deadly.

Validity is not derived from others. It is intrinsic. An artistic masterpiece that is only appreciated after the artist's death is the same masterpiece it was before the artist's death. The artist didn't become more talented posthumously. Their validity didn't change and nor did the validity of their work. They were authentic, not a copy. They didn't live by someone else's standards.

If you are going to succeed and flourish as a teacher, then you need to get out of the cave. No one should spend 40 years of their life trying to be anything but themselves. You will be miserable. Either be an authentic teacher or don't be a teacher. Question everything. Be yourself in the classroom. Do what you believe in the way you believe it should be done. Be open. Keep learning. Do your best. Believe in possibilities. Believe in what you do. Teach because you believe in teaching and not for any other reason. And gradually try to let go of your need for validation.

You are valid. You do you.

Chapter 5

The Six Psychological Needs of Human Beings

Let's talk about addiction. It is a commonly held belief that drugs are dangerous. And that experimentation with drugs over even a short amount of time leads to addiction. And therefore we should steer clear of using drugs. Better still, we should criminalise drugs, thereby keeping people away from these dangerous substances. This basic belief informed the decision of many countries to criminalise drug use towards the end of the 19th and beginning of the 20th centuries.

There is some evidence to back up this thinking. In the 1960s, experiments were conducted with rats using 'Skinner boxes' to test various theories of animal learning. The rats, who were kept in solitary confinement, were able to self-administer drugs by pressing a lever, which they did, consuming large amounts of heroin, morphine, amphetamines, cocaine and other drugs. There was clear evidence: drugs are dangerous. Keep people away from drugs.

In the 1970s, Dr Bruce Alexander revisited the research and wondered whether it was flawed. He devised a different experiment in which a rat was placed in a cage with the same accessibility to drugs but some other things too: other rats as well as balls, slides, treadmills and climbing apparatus. He made a 'Rat Park'. He discovered that drug consumption was hugely reduced. The drug hadn't changed. The rat hadn't changed. What had changed was the cage.[1]

Around the same time, a human experiment was underway. It was called the Vietnam War. The United States was shipping out vast quantities of heroin to its troops in Vietnam and it is commonly reported that approximately 20% of all American troops were using heroin on a regular basis towards the end of the war.[2] This posed a concern as the war

1 B. Alexander, Addiction: The View from Rat Park (2010). Available at: https://www.brucekalexander.com/articles-speeches/rat-park/148-addiction-the-view-from-rat-park.

2 A. M. Shuster, G.I. Heroin Addiction Epidemic in Vietnam, *New York Times* (16 May 1971). Available at: https://www.nytimes.com/1971/05/16/archives/gi-heroin-addiction-epidemic-in-vietnam-gi-heroin-addiction-is.html.

wound to an end: what are we going to do with all these drug addicts when they return to civilian life? Well, as it happens, they needn't have worried because, on return, 95% of those who had been using heroin stopped.[3] Just like that. No withdrawal. No cold turkey. Just stopped. What had changed? Answer: the cage.

This challenges many of our long-held assumptions about drugs. You see, it's not the drug itself that is dangerous, so much as the combination of the drug together with the reason for its use. When the soldiers returned from Vietnam they were reunited with their families and loved ones. They again found purpose, a community and a sense of belonging. Their psychological needs were now being met through positive healthy mechanisms, and their interest in the synthetic high generated by heroin was no longer necessary or even appealing. (I am not suggesting the soldiers were just fine – many suffered from post-traumatic stress disorder – but that some of their psychological needs were being much more adequately met at home than they were while on duty, and this was a major factor in their rapid rehabilitation from drug use.)

All social animals have basic psychological needs. For human beings, a number have been suggested over the years. Self-determination theory cites just three: autonomy, competence and relatedness.[4] Consistency theory suggests four: attachment, control, pleasure and self-enhancement.[5] Abraham Maslow famously spoke of five: physiological, safety, love, esteem, and self-actualisation.[6] I don't think there is any real contradiction between these theories, just different levels of detail and terminology. I have amalgamated some of these theories to arrive at six basic needs which I have found to be a useful framework for assessing the suitability of our cage (which we will consider in more detail shortly):

1 Being understood

2 Belonging

3 Achievement

3 J. Clear, How Vietnam War Veterans Broke Their Heroin Addictions (excerpt from *Atomic Habits: An Easy & Proven Way to Build Good Habits & Break Bad Ones* (New York: Penguin Random House, 2018)). Available at: https://jamesclear.com/heroin-habits.

4 See https://selfdeterminationtheory.org/theory.

5 M. Dahlitz, Basic Psychological Needs, *Science of Psychotherapy* (23 November 2016). Available at: https://www.thescienceofpsychotherapy.com/basic-psychological-needs.

6 A. H. Maslow, A Theory of Human Motivation, *Psychological Review*, 50(4) (1943): 370–396.

4 Purpose

5 Autonomy

6 Love

When these needs are being met, we are more likely to be emotionally healthy and feel happy. When any of these needs are lacking, we instinctively look for other ways to get the feeling that, ideally, is generated by their fulfilment. One way or another we self-medicate – sometimes with drugs and alcohol, sometimes with shopping, sometimes with sex, sometimes with social media, sometimes with gambling or whatever. None of these pastimes may be bad in themselves, in moderation, but – and this is the critical point – when used to fulfil a psychological need they quickly become dangerous or at least problematic.

Understanding the ways you fulfil your own needs is essential to managing your own mental health. When you are feeling low there is a reason for it, and chances are that one or more of these needs is not being met. There is a deficiency. Now, with the possible exception of love, all the other needs are significantly affected by your work. If you are part of a team or school culture that does not adequately address these needs, then the team will be dysfunctional, job satisfaction will be low, your engagement with teaching will diminish and you will find yourself hating going to school. The Sunday night sick-feeling starts becoming something you just live with and accept. And the job is reduced to a counting activity: number of days until the weekend, number of weeks until half term. That is no way to live and it is seriously damaging over time – not to mention the fact that it directly undermines your ability to teach great lessons and to love doing so.

Here is another example of what I mean: depression is an increasing concern in most Western countries. Despite ever rising living standards, more and more people are experiencing depression and anxiety and turning to chemical antidepressants. At one time, depression was primarily explained as being due to a chemical imbalance in the brain which can be adjusted with medication. However, Johann Hari, author of *Lost Connections*,[7] points out that over time medical professionals

7 J. Hari, *Lost Connections: Uncovering the Real Causes of Depression – and the Unexpected Solutions* (New York: Bloomsbury, 2018).

have found that the dosage needs to be continually increased to produce the same effect, which suggests that the underlying cause of depression is not biological.

Hari tells the story of a psychiatrist named Derek Summerfield who travelled to Cambodia when antidepressants were just being introduced there. He began to inform fellow professionals about these new wonder drugs, but they explained that they already had antidepressants. He didn't understand. They told him about a rice farmer they had treated. He had worked in the paddy fields until he stood on a hidden landmine and lost a leg. He recovered and used a prosthetic, but it caused him extreme pain. The situation deteriorated until the farmer couldn't get out of bed, cried most of the day and was suffering from acute depression. The doctors went to him, listened to his pain and sought to understand how he felt. Then they had an idea: rather than working in the paddy fields, what if they could get him a cow? Then he could become a dairy farmer instead. This is what they did. Within a month all the symptoms of depression had gone. 'You see, doctor,' the local doctors said, 'the cow was an antidepressant.'[8]

They were right. By prescribing a cow they were solving the problem that had caused the depression in the first place. And the cause was arguably not dissimilar to that of US soldiers in Vietnam: lack of purpose, low achievement, disconnection from the community, not being understood, no autonomy. Current psychological and medical research verifies this: only in a minute number of cases does it appear that there is a purely genetic or biological explanation for depression.[9] Overwhelmingly, the problem is environmental: your cage. And your psychological pain is a signal to you that something is wrong.

Here, then, are the six basic psychological needs that shape the cage we each live within. When any of these are in deficit we are likely to find ourselves reaching for an artificial stimulus in order to compensate. Consider whether they are being met in your own workplace as well as in your broader life.

8 J. Hari, Is Everything You Think You Know About Depression Wrong?, *The Guardian* (7 January 2018). Available at: https://www.theguardian.com/society/2018/jan/07/is-everything-you-think-you-know-about-depression-wrong-johann-hari-lost-connections.

9 Hari, Is Everything You Think You Know About Depression Wrong?

Being understood

I am putting this need first because it cannot be overstated. It should also be acknowledged that some of these needs interrelate. Along with belonging and love, being understood is a subset of our relatedness or attachment needs – for example, you are much more likely to feel understood if you feel like you belong. But not necessarily, and the thriving existence of the counselling profession demonstrates just that. We often find it helpful to talk to someone entirely unconnected to our usual circle of contacts, even (or perhaps especially) a complete stranger. This is because we feel we can be honest and open with someone who is bound by the strictures of confidentiality in a way that we cannot with friends and family. We may also value the insight of a professional who understands the complexity of the human brain and some of the deeper reasons behind our feelings and behaviours, who can therefore offer analysis without judgement.

Whatever the reason, as I mentioned in Chapter 3, scientists tell us that the critical chemical that provides us with the feeling that we can cope is dopamine. When dopamine levels are high we have what we might call bounce-back-ability or resilience: we can roll with the knocks, we can handle being sworn at by a student, we can chalk up a bad lesson to a bad day and not let it bother us. When dopamine is low we struggle to do that. A poor observation, a negative remark by a colleague or an incident with a student knocks us and leaves us feeling low for the rest of the day, the evening or even the whole week. Then we begin approaching other things negatively, which in turn generates more bad feelings, and a difficult start to the week turns into the week from hell.

Dopamine is secreted by the brain at optimal levels when we talk about ourselves and thereby feel understood.[10] When someone gets us. When someone listens to our feelings and affirms them. Not necessarily agreeing with our perspective but agreeing that the feelings we are expressing are real feelings, whether or not they have arisen for legitimate reasons.

I have learned this the hard way, and slowly, from my wife. Many times she has, understandably, felt like having a rant, as we all do – whether about me or the kids or the in-laws or anything else. And I have

10 Ward, The Neuroscience of Everybody's Favorite Topic.

admirably (in my mind) attempted to help her be rational (yes, patronising git) and to lay out for her the reasons why she should not, or need not, feel the way she does. My arguments are robust. My logic difficult to refute. But utterly futile and entirely missing the point. Because by arguing against her emotional state, I am in fact negating it. 'I know I'm not being rational,' she would say. 'Just let me rant!'

And that is what we all need: to rant and to have a safe space in which to do it and persons to do it with. This is why our staffrooms and faculty offices are so important. There has to be a space where we can let off steam. It's not that staffrooms should degenerate into places of moaning. That is nearly (but not quite) as bad as not having them at all. Our presence affects the temperature in the staffroom. We can be an empathetic listening ear and we can also offer hope and perspective. So, when you're having a bad day and you're tempted to remain in your classroom at break and lunchtime – don't! Get out there and get it off your chest.

Of course, there will be times when the staffroom isn't the right place to sound off (or certain colleagues aren't the right people to sound off to), or it would be unprofessional, inappropriate or indiscreet to vent. In which case, go and see your line manager, the head, your SLT link, a governor or a trusted colleague and let them know how you are feeling. Nothing will change by keeping things to yourself. You won't be doing yourself any favours by going home and having an extra drink or taking it out on the kids. Lead by example and demonstrate that it is okay to talk about your feelings.

Reflection questions

- Who can you go to at school with whom you can be honest about your feelings?
- How often do you share how you're doing with your line manager or someone in a senior position?
- If you don't share how you feel in the staffroom, faculty office or similar, why not?
- When you don't share your feelings in these contexts, what do you do with those emotions? How do you manage or not manage them?

Belonging

Do you feel part of a team? What is the atmosphere in your team? Is there an inner circle and an outer circle? Are there favourites in the team? Who are the newbies? How do they feel about the team? Are there in-jokes that you don't get? Is the team inclusive? How long did it take for you to feel part of the team? Is there a pecking order? Are you accepted in the team? Do you feel valued? Do you think you would be missed if you left? Do you know how you contribute to the team? Do you know your role within the team?

What about outside of work? Are you the black sheep of the family? Are you accepted? Do you feel like there is a group that you could call your own? Is there a friendship or social group, a sports or religious group that feels safe for you?

We all need to feel that we belong. If your answers to the questions above reveal a lack of a sense of belonging then this will be getting you down and you will find a way to self-medicate. If your social, family and outside-school sense of belonging is strong, then you will be more able to cope (at least for a while) with not feeling that sense of belonging in school. It can carry us. We have all been the new person at some point. We don't implode. We know it takes time. But if after a short time we feel like we still don't belong in our team at school, then we will fail to flourish.

Again, we all have a part to play in this – to be the welcoming person who makes a new staff member feel at home quickly, to bring cakes on our birthday, to show an interest in others, to bring some humour and banter to the table, to smile, to make an effort to find out how our colleagues are and know what is going on with them, to communicate and share information.

The single most effective way to establish a sense of team quickly is to help someone out. Do something for a colleague that is appreciated. Offer a lift home when they are stuck. Offer to cover a lesson so they can leave early to pick up their sick child. Share your lesson plans and resources. Say thank you. Remember birthdays. Go out for the staff meal, even if you feel a bit tired and it's a longer drive home for you. Share your coffee. And do it all expecting nothing in return, not counting the favours that other people owe you and not keeping score. Just being inclusive and friendly for the sake of it – because it's kind. Don't wait for someone else to change the atmosphere in the team. As Gandhi said, 'As a man changes his own nature, so does the attitude of the world change towards him.'[11]

The magic of kindness is that it inspires kindness from others. Not always, and not always immediately. But generally, and generally you will find that your sense of belonging improves too.

Reflection questions

- Reread the questions at the start of this section.
- If you don't feel like you belong, have you shared this with your line manager? Could you?
- What have you brought to the team recently? Are you outgoing? Are you giving?
- How often are you staying in your classroom by yourself because you feel safer there?

Achievement

In my experience, achievement comes up over and over again for teachers because of the nature of the business we are in. Our 'product' is not a straightforward one. I'm unable to count the number of sales I've made in a day, a week or a year. Or the number of customer complaints I've handled. Success, and therefore achievement, in teaching is far more nuanced because our product is people.

This is a problem for statisticians and analysts who understandably want to reduce everything to numbers in order to measure impact and identify reasons for underperformance. Achievement is a relative concept:

11 M. K. Gandhi, *The Collected Works of Mahatma Gandhi*, vol. 12 (April 1913 – December 1914) (Delhi: Publications Division, Ministry of Information and Broadcasting, Government of India, 1964), p. 158.

whenever we quantify achievement we do so in relation to something else, a measure of some kind. But which measures are the appropriate ones to use? Evaluate against the wrong thing and you will feel like you are constantly failing; evaluate against nothing and you can't identify whether you have achieved anything at all. We very easily fall into the McNamara fallacy: we measure what is easy to measure and we ignore what is difficult to measure.[12] The conclusion: what is difficult to measure is not important or, worse still, doesn't exist.

What is easy to measure in education? Public exam results. What is difficult to measure? Everything else. I will discuss this in more detail in Part III, but for now I just want to note that, unfortunately for teachers, all of our effort, planning, nurturing and extracurricular activity, all of our marking, admin and emails get reduced to a single figure per child, on which we are judged as either failing or succeeding: a grade in an examination. The only other explicit, recorded numerical judgement will be a formal lesson observation or two – a snapshot of between 20 and 60 minutes in an entire year.

We all know that there are a multitude of factors that contribute to the academic success of a student. Great teaching is, of course, one of them. But the Year 11 teacher has no control over the students they inherit at the end of Year 10 or the quality of the teaching they experienced over the 11 years leading up to that time. Not to mention the fact that the grade boundaries change every year and Ofsted keeps moving the goalposts in terms of what is expected or required to be good or outstanding. When you take into account changing exam specifications, the impact of social and economic deprivation, special educational needs and disability (SEND), English as an additional language, looked-after children and the massive impact of parental engagement (or lack thereof), measuring the impact of one teacher becomes almost impossible.

There is a very real sense among most teaching staff that no matter what we do, we will fail. And even if we get our best results ever, the bar will be raised again next year in the flawed pursuit of ever-increasing progress scores. Not only is the job, as it is described in most job descriptions, impossible, but objective numerical success is also impossible given the prevailing system of measurement. We are set up to fail before we even

12 See https://expertprogrammanagement.com/2017/07/the-mcnamara-fallacy.

start, which is why thousands of demoralised teachers are leaving the profession.

Teachers are daily performing a job which, by all the mechanisms generally utilised, can't help but leave you feeling as if you are underachieving. And acknowledging this fact is the beginning of coping with it more effectively. We looked at the ABC Model of stress in Chapter 3 which shows that if you change your beliefs, you can change your consequential emotions. Teachers who continue to enjoy teaching do so, in part, because they have managed to recalibrate their own expectations to align more fully with reality, rather than the relentlessly optimistic unreality of the educational system. Every school has them – those calm and unruffle-able teachers who, no matter what new initiative or specification comes along, they just keep on doing their thing. They have seen it all before: 'Oh, I remember this – it came round in the 1990s! We're doing it again, are we?'

They know there's nothing new under the sun, often just the repackaging of an old idea. They know that it won't last and that things will change again. It's not that they aren't open to learning or changing or growing (well, some of them aren't), it's that over time they have developed a better grasp on reality and an understanding of what is necessary to sustain a balanced lifestyle. Namely, rejecting a literal interpretation of the job description and accepting the reality of the complexity of student progress and development.

In other words, it's not all on you if your students don't hit their target grade. All you can do is your best. As we saw in Chapter 2, the fundamental, bottom-line question is: did I help my students to grow today? The problem is that we don't tell young and trainee teachers this at the start. We set the bar as high as we possibly can and peddle the impression that everyone is doing it like this all the time. And we put would-be teachers through a training experience so gruelling that many quit before finishing or leave within five years of starting. No one can live with a permanent sense of underachievement.

Reflection questions

- How much are you expecting of yourself, and is it reasonable or even possible?
- How do you view your impact in the classroom, and do you need to take the pressure off yourself where progress data is concerned?
- Could it be that less is more: that when you focus less on the data and your 'performance', you enjoy teaching more, which will inevitably result in better student progress?
- Have you discussed your sense of underachievement and impossible expectations with your line manager, or are you trying to present the appearance that you are coping just fine?

Purpose

Why do you do the job you do? Having clarity on this will help you to feel motivated and engaged; not having clarity will impact significantly on your engagement and sense of worth.

Everyone needs a purpose that is 'other-people centred'. All human beings have an innate desire to contribute to the wellbeing of others. We feel good when we help someone else. This is a biological as well as a psychological fact. Interestingly, some years ago an experiment was done to assess the impact of financially incentivising people to give blood. People who were considering being a donor were offered US$7 each time they donated blood. The result? Blood donation decreased! People were less likely to give blood when the sense of altruism, of doing something selflessly for others, was removed.[13] There are many similar experiments which affirm this finding. However, the most obvious proof is the selfless devotion and expenditure we invest in our children, with little thanks or appreciation for most of their upbringing. We do it because we love them and find genuine delight and happiness in providing for them.

13 H. Abolghasemi, N. S. Hosseini-Divkalayi and F. Seighali, Blood Donor Incentives: A Step Forward or Backward, *Asian Journal of Transfusion Science*, 4(1) (2010): 9–13. Available at: https://www.ncbi.nlm.nih.gov/pmc/articles/PMC2847338.

A profession like teaching also generates an obvious sense of purpose. To many outside of education, teachers have an enviable job because each day we have the opportunity to make a real and tangible difference to the lives of young people. Theoretically, this psychological need should not be in deficit for teachers, and yet it is. This is because we have replaced the true purpose of our profession with a synthetic and altogether inferior one. Take your pick from the purposes below:

- To be graded outstanding by Ofsted/ISI.
- To get out of special measures.
- To get from requires improvement to good.
- To get our best results ever.
- To improve our percentage of A–A*.
- To improve our percentage grades 9–4, including English and maths.
- To reduce the number of exclusions.

I could go on. What do all of these objectives have in common? They include no reference to a person, student or society. It is not that schools formally adopt these statements as their vision statement and stick them on the ethos page of their website or prospectus. It is that in the day-to-day communication and business of our schools they have become the primary starting point. They are what is talked about. Data, percentages and inspection judgements are what you would think it was all about if you walked into most schools in the UK or sat in most SLT meetings. It happened accidentally. We didn't deliberately lose sight of why we run or work for these institutions, but gradually teaching has become depersonalised. If challenged we might acknowledge that 'Yes, of course, it's all about the children.' But that's not good enough.

Children can't be the afterthought – they have to be centre stage – because the knock-on effect of removing explicit, personalised language of care and development from our schools is that we lose that innate motivation to contribute to the wellbeing of others. The thing that inspires us most and generates all that goodwill and enthusiasm is lost.

There is something deeply uninspiring and demotivating about doing a job in order to tick a box for Ofsted or notch up our percentage average. That is not our purpose as teachers. Don't ever buy into it. Our purpose is to change lives. To help young people grow and develop; to inspire a generation of compassionate and resourceful global citizens who will make the world a better place; to shape the future of humanity; to grow human minds and make them sparkle with hope and fresh ideas; to help our students discover and appreciate more of the wonder of the universe and the boundless possibilities that lie ahead. That's our purpose.

Reflection questions

- Has teaching for you become less about the students and more about the numbers?
- Do you remember why you became a teacher? How did you articulate it then? How would you articulate it now?
- Is the true purpose of teaching front and centre in your mind?
- How could your classroom/faculty area effectively communicate this purpose visually as a reminder for you, your colleagues and your students?

Autonomy

Our freedom is important to us: the sense that we have some control over what we are doing and how we do it. This desire has driven the human race ever forward – to shake off the shackles of autocracy and dictatorship. Trace it back through human history and the quest for freedom has toppled empires, fuelled revolutions, motivated exploration and discovery, and formed the founding of a New World and a new form of government, as it then was, in the United States of America. Globally, legal slavery and child labour are today at an all-time low, while the number of countries where men and women have an equal right to vote, as well as the proportion of girls in primary school, are at an all-time high.[14]

Any and all efforts to subjugate and repress the human will are bound to failure. And yet despite the inestimable liberating effect that education has had on humankind, in general, many of our schools are the most autocratic, prescriptive and regimented institutions in modern society – possibly second only to prisons or the armed forces. We tell people how to dress, when to eat, when to go to the toilet. The day is governed by bells and timetables. We have policies prescribing procedures for how students line up, how to start lessons, what those lessons should include, how students' books should look, how feedback must be given, how progress should be recorded, what you can and can't say to a student, how to seat your students, how to run your classroom, what sanctions are permitted. There are rules concerning language, phones, piercings, nail polish, hairstyles, shoes.

I won't get into the whys and wherefores here, but suffice to say that many schools treat their staff only marginally better than their students. Our schools are remarkably autocratic, hierarchical institutions and many teachers feel like they don't have control over how they do what they do. The micromanaging of teachers is demeaning and can become debilitating over time. If you are unable to go off-piste, to put yourself into your lessons, then you begin to feel like a cog in a wheel, rather than a person in a team. You feel devalued, replaceable, unimportant.

We each need to believe that we are bringing something of value to the table and that what we are bringing is appreciated. We need the freedom to use our creativity and to feel like we are trusted. When we are overly controlled or micromanaged it can feel as if we are not trusted and are expected to just follow orders. This approach negates our sense of self – it is a rejection of our individuality and uniqueness – and it results in a lowering of standards. A box-ticking, bare minimum mentality develops which is focused on covering our backs rather than giving of ourselves freely and having the opportunity to innovate.

---

14 H. Rosling, *Factfulness: Ten Reasons We're Wrong About the World – And Why Things Are Better Than You Think* (London: Hodder & Stoughton, 2019), pp. 60–64. Out of 195 countries, only three still have legalised slavery compared to 193 in the year 1800. Conversely, 193 countries have equal voting rights compared to just one in 1900.

Reflection questions

- How free are you to be yourself in your teaching role?
- To what extent is your opinion sought and valued?
- Do you feel like your ideas are listened to and make an impact?
- Have you accepted too readily the constraints and demands that have been placed on you by leadership? Could you have spoken up or resisted sooner?

Love

I come to love last not because it is less important but because it is likely to be a psychological need that is met beyond the context of your school or work (notwithstanding the many successful relationships that have begun there). Even so, it matters greatly to our mental health and our ability to flourish as teachers or in any other line of work. It links closely to purpose, since for most of us those we love are the primary purpose of all we do in life.

The evidence is resounding that the quality of our happiness and fulfilment in life is directly proportional to the quality of our close relationships. We are relational beings. We function at our best when those relationships are strong and healthy. Our capacity for love appears to be a uniquely human phenomenon and lies at the core of our psychological make-up. We neglect our love relationships at our peril. When we peel away all the other aspects of life, it is our love relationships that matter most. On your deathbed you will not be asking to be brought evidence of your outstanding lesson observation, your framed degree certificate or your vast collection of designer shoes. You will be asking for the people you love. They are all that matters. The Beatles were right: all you need is love. Or, as Nat King Cole sang: 'The greatest thing you'll ever learn is just to love and be loved in return.'

Poets and philosophers have written endlessly about love. We need love just as we need oxygen. How ironic then that our closest relationships are the first things we sacrifice for the sake of success, money, achievement, notoriety and validation. How many kids have lost their parents not to war or disease but to teaching? How many wives and husbands have lost their spouse in the same way? It is deeply upsetting. As I write this, my eldest daughter is just eight months away from leaving home for university, and I have recognised – perhaps a little too late – that many of the lessons, thinking, inspiration and time I have poured into other people's children, I have neglected to pour into my own.

Balance. The wheel of life. Yes, I can tell myself that I did it to put a roof over their heads, to provide for them and ensure they had as many opportunities as possible, and that is valid. But there were definitely times when they were deprived of me: my attention, my time, my focus, my interest, my wisdom, my enthusiasm, my mind.

It's not good enough to put family on hold until the holidays. Your spouse, your partner, your children, your siblings – they need you in term time too. You will be a better teacher when you get your priorities right and get your life in balance. You can't neglect your love relationships and get away with it for long. It will take its toll.

Reflection questions

- How much time do you invest in your love relationships during term time?
- To what extent are you being neglectful of those you love most?
- Are you lonely? Do you feel alone? To what extent is this because you are not prioritising this aspect of life sufficiently?
- What could you do today to let your loved ones know what they mean to you?

Having self-assessed how well your psychological needs are being met, consider – if they are not in a healthy state – how well you are coping. How are you self-medicating? You will be doing so somehow. What are you doing to numb the pain or fill the void or distract you? Is it becoming a problem? Your pain is a signal – it's telling you that something needs to change. Endeavour to treat the cause, not the symptom.

Chapter 6

Recalibrating: Resisting Busyness and Embracing Your Why

Busy is the new normal. It used to be the case that when you asked someone, 'How are you?' the standard answer was, 'Fine, and you?' Now there is a deep sigh followed by, 'Busy!' And what is crazy is that we like it that way. We wear our busyness like a badge of honour. We brag about it. We attempt to out-do each other in busyness competitions:

> I was marking until 11pm last night!
>
> Well, I was marking until midnight!
>
> That's nothing. I had an afterschool club, a meeting with a parent, a safeguarding issue to deal with, then went home and cooked dinner, took the kids to swimming club, helped my daughter with her homework, put them to bed, then marked until 1am and got up at 5.30am to finish off – and I'm teaching a five-period day today too!

I've heard one-upmanship conversations like this on countless occasions. And I've kept quiet. Many years ago I resolved, as a general rule, not to work in the evenings. I would stay late at school and go in super early if necessary, but I needed to keep work and home separate. I'm not saying that it is the best method, and possibly it contributed to my breakdown, given the speed and focus I had to give to work during the school day. I certainly didn't eat lunch for five years.

But I remained silent in such conversations because I felt that to admit that I didn't work late into the evening would not have gone down well. Within the value economy of the staffroom I would have scored low. It would have been unacceptable and I would have felt embarrassed. How absurd that we should be competing with one another over who is the busiest, whether explicitly or implicitly. How is it that we have come to measure our worth and validity by how busy we are? Surely, it is obvious to all that we cannot simply keep getting more and more busy.

Tony Crabbe points out:

> Today you will consume the equivalent of 174 newspapers' worth of content (five times as much as you would have in 1986) … And as our tools for productivity improve, we communicate more. For example, in 1986 the average worker produced the equivalent of two and a half newspaper pages of content per day. In 2011 it was estimated this amount had risen to six complete newspapers each and every day. That's a two-hundredfold increase in output! Every action we take, every email we send, has a consequence for someone else.[1]

The irony is that the technology which was designed and sold to us to 'make our lives easier', by enabling us to do more in less time, has actually led us to speed up. We have adjusted our expectations in sync with our new capacities. I now expect to get an answer to an email by breaktime, action it by lunchtime and evaluate the impact by the end of the day. The same process used to take a week. We have become calibrated to a new normal. One that is faster.

Before email we couldn't send a message to a colleague at 2am. Now we can. Of course, we still don't *need* to, so why are we? Recent research by psychologist Stephanie Brown suggests that we are actually addicted to busyness.[2] It makes us feel important and gives us the sense that we are needed. But frenzied activity is also very effective at distracting us from the pain or void we feel when our core psychological needs are not being met. In the teaching profession, we have almost an entire workforce self-medicating their psychological ailments by doing more and more stuff faster and faster.

This is why I think it is misguided to ascribe the exodus of teachers from the profession simply to workload. There is a very real sense in which we are our own worst enemies. We are creating the workload that we then blame for our stress. We have acquiesced to this new reality, become complicit in its proliferation, and now we are hooked.

In the same way that many of us are addicted to social media (each new alert you get on your phone elicits a dopamine spike in your brain, a

1 T. Crabbe, *Busy: How to Thrive In a World of Too Much* (London: Piatkus, 2015), pp. xix–xx.
2 S. Brown, *Speed: Facing Our Addiction to Fast and Faster – and Overcoming Our Fear of Slowing Down* (New York: Berkley Publishing, 2014).

literal mini high[3]), we are also addicted to email. I recall once 'bragging' to my family about the 90 emails a day I received (a number that will seem pathetically small to some, but for me represented a tangible way that I could communicate to my brothers and kids how important I was). Of course, we all exaggerate somewhat too – for example, we know that many of those emails are unimportant, lots of them are junk and some we don't even open, but we quote the number at its max because we have bought into the idea that our value is derived from how busy we are and how many people want to contact us.

The truth is, of course, that the number of emails you send or receive, or the number of meetings you have – far from demonstrating your importance and efficiency – may actually be evidence of quite the opposite. A sign that you are not doing your job well because you are simply reacting and using that as an excuse (or avoidance tactic) to justify why you are not giving concentrated time and effort to longer, more impactful work that requires quiet, thinking time, creativity and meaningful dialogue. Or perhaps your busyness is self-imposed to enable you to 'legitimately' avoid aspects of your job that you don't like. Busyness is often a mask – a justification for teaching poor lessons or not giving quality feedback – or, worse, camouflage for a failing marriage or home situation that you don't want to address.

Psychologist Stephanie Brown suggests that our society is dominated by impulse.[4] We have started to instinctively and automatically open our inbox and check for messages, or log in to our Twitter account or Instagram feed. We feel dismay if there are no new messages, so we take action to generate more messages. A teenager may post a new selfie and immediately receive 100 likes from her followers. The responses and resultant dopamine spike are instantaneous, which feeds the desire to do it again. We may not be craving more emails consciously – we may actually assert that we want less, but unconsciously we participate in the same basic addictive cycle.

Some have even suggested that we need the equivalent of Alcoholics Anonymous for busyness addiction. The only problem is that we would

---

3 T. Haynes, Dopamine, Smartphones & You: A Battle for Your Time, *Science in the News* (1 May 2018). Available at: http://sitn.hms.harvard.edu/flash/2018/dopamine-smartphones-battle-time.

4 Brown, *Speed.*

need entire stadiums in order to accommodate all the sufferers who would sign up! The fact is that if we are going to love teaching, and keep teaching, then we have got to address the busyness epidemic.

But there is a deeper, underlying cultural problem. Dan Ariely, professor of psychology at Duke University, tells the story of how he was once locked out of his house. He called a locksmith who got him into the house within two minutes and charged him US$120. This led to a conversation about his pricing strategy. The locksmith explained that years ago he was a very poor locksmith. He would arrive at a client's house, spend half an hour fiddling with the lock and usually end up breaking it. He would go off and get a new one, fit it and then charge the customer US$120 plus US$25 for the new lock. No one ever complained about the price – the customer was very appreciative and he was often given a tip. 'Now,' he says, 'I'm very good at my job, I charge the same amount yet people complain about the price and never tip!'[5]

The customer is now getting a much better service and avoiding the inconvenience and extra expense of waiting on the kerbside and paying for a new lock, so why are they disgruntled? Arguably, somewhere in our collective subconscious, we have bought into an idea that effort and time should be rewarded rather than impact and results. We are actually (and rather bizarrely) happier to pay for incompetence rather than competence, and by participating in this false economy we, in turn, feel the need to present an impression of busyness to those around us. We instinctively tell ourselves that in order to feel satisfied after a day's work, we need to have been furiously active. It doesn't matter whether we have achieved much, just so long as we expended an excess of energy.

This has got to stop because it is a recipe for burnout and breakdown. This was a key realisation for me personally after my breakdown. I identified in myself a core belief that suffering is virtuous, which on reflection is rather questionable. However, the idea that suffering is good for you and is a measure of your worth is not uncommon, and is certainly prevalent in many religions.

Undoubtedly, I didn't feel that I was sufficiently acceptable to God, my boss, the world or myself unless I could, in good conscience, breathe a

5 See O. Burkeman, Fetishing Busyness, *Oliver Burkeman Is Busy* [audio], *BBC Radio 4* (13 September 2016) at 03.57. Available at: https://www.bbc.co.uk/sounds/play/b07v07pb.

huge sigh of relief at the end of the day and believe that I had suffered: 'Phew, made it through another day! Still standing.' It is how I valued myself. It is how I legitimised my existence, my share of oxygen.

There is a close correlation between the furious activity we generate in our busyness and the sense that suffering for a cause is virtuous. In the case of your own teaching career, could it be that your survival depends on a radical recalibration that explicitly rejects this belief? Personally, I have managed to let go of this idea (although it still rears its head quite often) and now live a more healthy and balanced life.

Recalibrating

Ironically, technology – much as it has been a factor in our ever-increasing busyness – may actually end up being our saviour. The world of education is lagging behind many other sectors in finding new and innovative ways to do things. Technology has opened up opportunities for remote and international working, so for many jobs it makes no difference whether we are in an office in London, a call centre in India or on holiday in a ski chalet in the Alps. So long as the job gets done, where we do it doesn't matter. Indeed, in many cases it may lead to greater productivity and profit for work to be done from home, as it cuts out the wasted commute time, the cost of office space and the distractions of other workers.

Of course, undertaking education remotely is not so straightforward (as we have found during the coronavirus lockdown), and I am not suggesting that it is necessarily desirable. My point is that a more flexible approach to work in many sectors has forced a shift in the focus of management attention away from hours worked or physical presence in front of a computer and more towards outcomes and productivity. This is a critical shift.

In business sectors that have experimented with this home working, at first management was twitchy: 'How can we be sure that people are doing their jobs if we can't monitor their physical presence and check up on them in an office?' Well, as it happens, quite easily. It just means monitoring their impact rather than their timesheet. It means valuing competence and results rather than activity and effort. It means rejecting the myth of redemptive suffering and embracing a belief in human potential. I will explore this more in Part II and its implications for leadership. Here, I would like to focus on how you as an individual think about what it is that makes you valuable, valid and legitimate. It is not about how busy you are or how much you suffer. It is about your unique and creative impact on others.

Jeff Gunther, CEO of a US-based medical technology company, experimented with flexible working some years ago. He decided to switch his company to what is now called a ROWE: a Results Only Work Environment,[6] a concept conceived by former human resources officials Cali Ressler and Jody Thompson of Best Buy.[7] He told his staff that their job description was just the same, but from now on the only thing they would be judged on was their results; how they worked, where they worked, when they worked was entirely up to them. At first, not much changed. As creatures of habit most people still turned up at 9am and knocked off at 5pm. But gradually they became more comfortable with working more autonomously. After the trial period was over, Gunther decided to switch to ROWE permanently: productivity was up, stress was down, employee retention had improved and almost all staff reported feeling more engaged and happy in their jobs.[8]

What about you? If you assess your approach to the different activities in your day, are you results focused or process focused? Arguably, it's not the activity that matters but the outcome. It's not how many books have been marked according to department policy, it's whether your feedback made any difference to student progress. It's not whether the lesson started and finished on time, it's whether the students learned. It's not whether there was silence or disruption during the lesson, it's whether students engaged with the topic. It's not whether the data analysis is handed in on time, it's whether it will inform planning and help students to progress regardless of prior attainment. It's not whether every tutor session is spent doing an activity, it's whether students are happy and

6 See https://www.gorowe.com.

7 C. Ressler and J. Thompson, *Why Work Sucks and How to Fix It: The Results-Only Revolution* (New York: Portfolio, 2011).

8 D. McNair, Getting Results: Local CEO Tosses the Time Clock, *The Hook* (14 May 2010). Available at: http://www.readthehook.com/67646/getting-results-local-ceo-tosses-time-clock.

supported. It's not whether homework was set by all staff in accordance with the homework timetable, it's whether homework actually helps students to learn and grow. I could go on …

We must start asking fundamental questions about why we are doing what we are doing, assessing the impact of all our activity and then radically adjusting what we do so that it aligns with our purpose. Which brings me neatly to the final aspect of Part I: finding your why.

Finding your why

If you haven't already, watch Simon Sinek's TEDx Talk 'Start with Why'. Seriously, watch it now before you read the rest of this chapter – it's only 20 minutes long.[9]

Sinek makes a brilliant point: our brains work from the inside out, and so does any successful institution. His Golden Circle – which asks what, how and why – is a great illustration of the importance of recalibrating. What's important here is your why at the centre: when you start with this, the how and the what have meaning, integrity and coherence.

We know *what* we do: I teach religious studies and philosophy according to the AQA specification.

We know *how* we do it: I use a three-part lesson plan that includes some assessment for learning, some teacher input, some independent learning, success criteria and a plenary with appropriate pace and challenge.

Want to be in my class? Hmmm …

Let's start with *why* instead.

Why do you do what you do? I inspire and equip students to think differently about the world, value diversity and build a fairer future.

How do you do it? I teach varied and exciting lessons using a variety of methods that are tailored to the students I teach and which challenge them to grow their brains every day.

9 S. Sinek, Start with Why – How Great Leaders Inspire Action [video], *TEDx Talks* (28 September 2009). Available at: https://www.youtube.com/watch?v=u4ZoJKF_VuA.

What do you do? I teach the best subject in the world: religious studies and philosophy (oh, and I make sure I cover the spec along the way).

Want to be in my class?

Damn right you do! Can you see the difference?

I know why I became a teacher. I know why I still teach. Do you?

Now have a go at doing what I've just done in your own words and for your own subject or key stage. How does it feel? Read it out loud. Do you believe it? Do you believe *in* it? Do you believe in what you do? Because if you don't, your customers will know it and they won't buy. It's exactly the same in the business world. What Sinek is saying is that people buy with their emotions. They buy an idea, an ethos, a mission.

Sinek uses the example of Apple because the company has clarity about why it does what it does: 'We believe in challenging the status quo. We believe in thinking differently.'[10] People who buy Apple products do so with the same sense of belief. They are like disciples. They won't touch anything else. They will go with Apple to the edge of the world. Microsoft doesn't have disciples, at least not in the same way. There is no global loyalty to brands like HP or Asus. We will buy them if they suit, if they are at the right price, but we aren't loyal to them. There is no clear message, no passion, no vision. The same goes for you and your lessons. The students will come – they have to – so you will have customers. Some of them will like what you do, some of them won't. There will be a general mix of passivity, disruption, apathy and a bit of progress. But no one is writing home about it, and neither are you. And that is the problem.

You don't believe. And if you don't believe, neither will they. Having clarity about your why will keep you fresh because there are no end of ways to achieve your why. Each year, instead of just churning out the same old stuff like Groundhog Day, counting the weeks until mocks, then reports, then exams, then the summer (over and over again for 40 years), you will be thinking, 'What can we do this year to blow our students' minds and help them to get passionate about changing the world?'

10 S. Sinek, *Start with Why: How Great Leaders Inspire Everyone to Take Action* (London: Penguin Random House, 2009), pp. 40–44.

Apple made computers until they made the iPod and revolutionised the music industry. Until they made the iPhone and revolutionised the phone market. Until they made the Apple Watch. What will they do next? You know it will be something innovative and disruptive because innovative and disruptive is in their DNA – it's their why. What will *you* do next?

If you've lost your sense of why or struggled to articulate it, then try this to help you rediscover your why.

Step 1: Make a list of all the most memorable, significant stories from your life so far – be specific

- Events that have hurt you the most/events that have helped you the most.
- Things that have shaped you/times when something significant happened.
- Times when you felt happiest/times you felt most unhappy.

Step 2: Identify any themes in these stories or events

- Do you always end up feeling the same way?
- Does a similar thing seem to keep happening?
- Do the stories have anything in common?

Step 3: Identify what you love doing and what you care deeply about

- My contribution: what I love doing/what gets me motivated.

- My impact: what I care about/feel strongly about.

Step 4: Draft your why statement[11]

A why statement takes the following format:

- To _________ [write the thing you can do or the contribution you make], so that _________ [write the impact or effect you want to have].

This is my own why statement:

- To challenge unfairness and get people to think for themselves, so that people can live life better and build a fairer future.

Have you ever stepped on some bathroom scales – the old kind with the spin dial – and had a bit of a shock? Perhaps your heart sank when you saw that you had gained a stone, or you had a sudden moment of elation when you saw you were a stone lighter than you thought. Then you stepped off to double check and saw that the scales had not been set to zero at the start! Either you breathed a huge sigh of relief or you felt deflated for the rest of the day. Very quickly, with the turn of a lever, you recalibrated the scales – that is, you aligned the scales with reality rather than leaving them aligned with an illusion.

Over the course of many years as teachers and leaders, we have established a way of living and working that is out of kilter with reality. We have grown accustomed to it and accepted it as non-negotiable. My purpose in Part I has been to question some of the factors that have resulted in this 'normal', which I believe is unhealthy, unbalanced and unsustainable. Recalibrating means resetting your mindset, your expectations and your motives to align with the truth. You have to do this for yourself.

What is the truth? I think I'll leave that question for another book! More appropriate is to ask the question, what is *your truth*? What do you want your life to look like? How do you want to feel at the end of a working week? Are you living and teaching according to your core values? Are

11 This exercise is adapted and abridged from S. Sinek, D. Mead and P. Docker, *Find Your Why: A Practical Guide for Discovering Purpose for You and Your Team* (New York: Penguin Random House, 2017), ch. 2.

your thoughts, words and actions in harmony? This is what is meant by authenticity: being true to your truth.

History has taught us that societal change rarely comes about due to a groundbreaking edict from a powerful government or leader. In the main, governments are always playing catch-up, adjusting and responding to the movement of the people. Movements are what change the world. The current green revolution (admittedly still in its infancy) demonstrates this. Governments have quite definitely not led the way on climate change: they have been lobbied, cajoled and pressured by activist groups and coerced by industry and consumer demands. So it will be with teaching. If we each take responsibility for reflecting on and changing our own lives and teaching habits, and choose to live and teach with balance, integrity and authenticity, then we will slowly but surely change education for the better.

Part II

Leadership – How to Lead People, Not Schools

We are all leaders. This is important to state at the outset of Part II. Whether in your friendship group or with your own kids as a parent or in a sporting context, we all utilise leadership skills all the time. Leadership is not something relevant only to a few people who fulfil formal management roles in hierarchical organisations.

This is even more true in schools. Every teacher is a leader in their classroom of the students they teach. Every member of support staff is a leader of the students they care for. Beyond this, a huge proportion of teaching staff also hold a teaching and learning responsibility of some kind. In many schools and organisations, there is a tendency to associate leadership with those at the very top – those in *senior* leadership. Not only is this inaccurate, but it can also reinforce the problem we explored in Chapter 1 of passing the buck and claiming powerlessness with regard to institutional change. And that just leads us back to perpetuating the status quo.

I believe in the power of every one of us to effect change. Furthermore, I believe that we each have more power and influence to effect change than we think, so Part II is certainly not only for senior or aspiring senior leaders. It is for all of us.

If our schools are going to change and become thriving centres of innovation and discovery, venturing forth with a workforce of enthused, healthy and balanced teachers, then how we view leadership needs to change radically. The challenge to lead bravely and authentically needs to be taken up by all of us – because the tendency to blame the SLT is the same tendency as that of the SLT to blame Ofsted. There is much about the world, and education, that we cannot control, but there is much that we can. The challenge for brave leaders (all of us) in education today is to major on the things we can control and change them. If we each focus on our own domain, where we do have influence, we can each determine to run that part of the world honestly, authentically, compassionately and sustainably.

The content of Part II has significance for every aspect of school life: from how you run your classroom and get the best from your students, to how you run a two-person team meeting with your teaching assistant, to how you go about implementing a new school policy change or recruiting new staff. Schools are communities of people; secondary schools, in particular, are conglomerations of lots of micro communities: the maths department, the PE department, the admin staff and so on. We each have sway within these micro communities. It is all too easy to say, 'If I were the head teacher I'd do this or that ...' The corollary question is, are you? Are you doing this or that within your sphere of influence? Because, chances are, if you are not doing it now, then you won't when you are in a position of greater responsibility.

No matter what your current job title or department, if you try to understand people a bit better and find out what makes them tick, you will be more effective in leading and influencing others – and, in turn, be a more effective team player yourself.

Chapter 7

The Truth About Staff Engagement

A recent survey conducted by the polling organisation Gallup, which has surveyed millions of employees around the world, found that in the UK:

- 11% of staff are engaged.
- 68% of staff are disengaged.
- 21% of staff are actively disengaged.[1]

The same survey found that employee engagement in the United States is considerably higher at 33%. However, neither statistic is a recipe for a productive working environment or for an outstanding school. As Michael Barber and Mona Mourshed observe, 'The quality of an education system cannot exceed the quality of its teachers.'[2]

There is no way that any school can sustainably provide an excellent education if between 68% and 89% of its staff are not engaged in what they are doing. Yet, at times, that is what senior leaders seem to be attempting to do: to somehow bypass the teachers and get to outstanding by setting higher targets, giving more directives, being more prescriptive and focusing on attempting to drag underperforming staff up to satisfactory levels using methods that often prove counterproductive. Not only will this not work, it will also make things worse.

As long as the majority of your team are disengaged, you are going nowhere fast. And more directives are only going to hack people off even more. They may jump through your hoops and do what you say, because most people are relatively compliant or scared of the consequences. But

1 G. Gyton, Just One in 10 Brits Feel Engaged at Work, Says Gallup, *People Management* (18 October 2017). Available at: https://www.peoplemanagement.co.uk/news/articles/one-in-10-brits-engaged-work.

2 M. Barber and M. Mourshed, *How the World's Best Performing School Systems Came Out on Top* (London: McKinsey & Co., 2007), p. 19. Available at: https://www.mckinsey.com/industries/public-and-social-sector/our-insights/how-the-worlds-best-performing-school-systems-come-out-on-top.

any progress made will be undermined because they have lost the passion and the love for what they do.

Let's assume that we do want to improve staff engagement – where do we start? Most leadership teams race straight for the bottom – the 21% who are actively disengaged, the persistent underperformers. We need to get their standards up and deal with underperformance. Right? Wrong.

I've been in many an SLT meeting where we traffic-lighted the teachers in the school. Then we poured our time, effort and resources into those few 'red' teachers who we deemed were letting the side down. Not only did our attempt to drag them into the 'amber' zone consume a huge amount of leadership time, energy and expense, but it also generated further disengagement because they shared their disgruntlement about being targeted in this way with others or they struggled to cope with the extra intensity and pressure of being monitored more closely. Other staff empathised with them and, in turn, felt greater anxiety too. Realistically, however, some of the 'red' teachers are unlikely to change very much. Some of them are in the wrong job, pure and simple. Some of them are going through broader issues in life which mean, rightly or wrongly, that their focus is not on their teaching. They are not your priority.

Instead, what if you could shift 30% of those disengaged teachers (the middle category) into the engaged category? What would that do for your productivity? What would that do for the feel of your school? The atmosphere in staffrooms and faculty offices? It would make for a totally different culture.

Transforming outcomes is about transforming the culture of school: how we, as leaders, can transform the environment, the feel and the way we go about things in our school communities and classrooms. The teachers and students didn't start off disengaged – almost all of them started out quite keen. Something happened to wear them down. And it's no good blaming – that will get you nowhere. Change has to start with you.

Employee engagement: key statistics

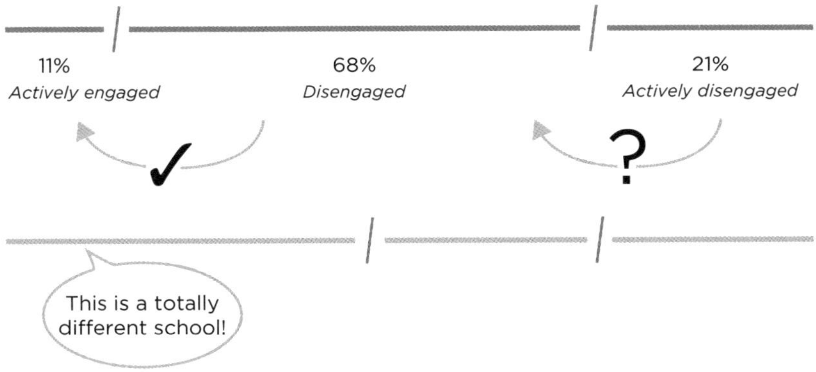

Figure 7.1. Employee engagement – key statistics

Another statistic from Gallup suggests an answer: 75% of people leave their job because of their direct line manager.[3] People don't leave jobs, they leave bosses. That's the issue. As leaders, we have failed. There is nowhere else for the buck to stop. We missed the point when we got promoted. We thought we were leading departments, projects and schools, but in fact we were leading people. It's just that no one ever told us how to do it.

It is one of the peculiarities of the way the education system works that the only way in is at the bottom: we do degrees in a subject specialism, then we teach that subject, then we get promoted because we are good at teaching our subject, then we find ourselves in a totally different job – now leading fellow teachers, but with no associated training or development. No guidance on people management, team dynamics or leadership models. Nothing on time management or motivation. Just placed in a role and expected to get on with it.

In most of my teaching life, line management has been fairly non-existent. It's just not a thing. It's not that I had bad line managers as such, it's just that there was no expectation on either side that this would mean anything more than an annual performance review. And this is

3 J. Robison, Turning Around Employee Turnover, *Gallup Business Journal* (8 May 2008). Available at: https://news.gallup.com/businessjournal/106912/turning-around-your-turnover-problem.aspx.

the problem. The profession as a whole has not grasped the invaluable significance of effective line management and leadership training. We have not appreciated the significance of all of our leaders, and indeed the leadership role that every individual staff member plays, in leading the students they teach. We have simply not invested in helping our people to develop their leadership and people management skills.

Furthermore, in most schools I have encountered, there is a significant gulf between senior leadership and the rest of the staff. Here is a question: if you were to ask your middle leaders how they see themselves – whether as part of the school leadership team or the teaching staff – what would they say? My guess is that most would align themselves with the teaching staff rather than the SLT. And that is a problem. Your middle leaders don't see themselves as leaders. They are largely disenfranchised, they don't feel part of the decision-making team, they receive orders and directives like the rest, they are often not included in key consultations, and they don't have the time or energy to engage further because, out of all the teaching staff, they are the ones being squeezed most (from above and below) and are seldom given adequate time to do their jobs properly.

Your middle leaders are the key to your school's transformation. If you can shift your middle leaders into the engaged category and enable them to become brilliant leaders of people, then nothing can stop your school. They are the engine of your school. They can inspire, enthuse and re-engage the teachers they line manage, but not if they are the ones who are most stressed out.

Think back to your own school days for a moment: who was your favourite teacher? Probably a name or a face comes to mind. Mine was Mr Miller in Year 5. Absolute legend! Now consider why they were your favourite. Try to come up with a couple of reasons.

I've asked this question to many people, many times, and they tell me things like:

- He made me feel like I could achieve.
- She always smiled at me.
- I loved her enthusiasm.

- She took an interest – I felt valued by her.
- He was great fun – I loved his lessons.
- He loved his subject – he gave me a love for it.
- I never felt judged by her – she was always approachable.

Rarely does anyone say anything about what that teacher taught them. How come? As the old saying goes, people will forget what you said and forget what you did, but they will never forget how you made them feel. I would argue that your favourite teacher was your favourite teacher because of how he or she made you feel. Equally, you may well remember the teacher you hated most for the same reason: how he or she made you feel.

This demonstrates a critical fact about leadership. For most of us, that favourite teacher was the first great leader we encountered (besides our parents – who may or may not have been great). If you fast forward and think of your favourite leader or boss – who it would be and why – we would find a similar list of qualities emerge. Because great leadership is first and foremost about our ability to infuse self-belief and enthusiasm in those we lead, so they cannot help but want to follow.

Every day you have an impact on those around you. If you are in a leadership role, then that impact is multiplied. Every day you have the capacity to make those around you feel valued or devalued, acknowledged or overlooked, enthused or dejected, listened to or ignored, accepted or judged, important or invisible.

If only we recognised more acutely just how significant each of our transactions are with our colleagues. If only we realised the power of our words and actions and their potential to uplift or undermine. If only we had seen great leadership modelled within schools so that we had a blueprint to follow. This starts at the top. Middle leaders will only develop brilliant leadership skills if they are brilliantly line managed themselves. The significance of a senior leader's line management meeting with a middle leader cannot be overstated. The multiplied effect of how that person feels when they leave your office and go back to their faculty area is massive. They will pass along that same feeling to their own team, for better or for worse.

Transactional analysis has some useful insight on this. Eric Berne talks of 'stroking'. A stroke, he says, is a 'unit of social interaction'.[4] A stroke can be either positive or negative, big or small. For example, when a person walks past you in the corridor, catches your eye and raises their eyebrows, that is a positive stroke. Your presence was acknowledged in the interaction. Psychologically that matters because your subconscious keeps score. If, on the other hand, you passed your line manager, or any other colleague, in the corridor and they walked straight past you without any acknowledgement whatsoever, that would be a negative stroke. You might not think anything of it consciously – you know that school corridors are busy and that everyone is in a rush – but your subconscious is keeping count.

Contrast these minor strokes with the impact of walking into the faculty office at breaktime and your line manager looking at you directly, greeting you, asking how you are and whether she can get you a cup of tea. Massive positive stroke. Further still, she passes on to you some feedback from a student who told her that she loves your lessons. Huge stroke. How you respond to either of these interactions will, of course, generate a positive or negative stroke for your line manager.

Conversely, if you pop by your line manager's office to ask them a question and they don't so much as look up from their laptop and give you a blunt response in an irritable tone, then this is a pretty big negative stroke. It will leave you feeling like you're an imposition, that you're disliked and that your questions are stupid. Chances are none of these assumptions is true, but your line manager was insufficiently aware of the significance of her interaction with you and let her own stress levels negatively impact on the way she communicated.

Over the course of any given day, then, we accumulate a catalogue of strokes. And if, on balance, the negative strokes outweigh the positive ones then we are likely to feel depleted, devalued, insignificant, demoralised. Over time a norm is established. A culture is reinforced which either feels positive, affirming and uplifting or drains, negates and diminishes us. We each have the power to influence the atmosphere and mood of our social spaces and interactions. But it is the responsibility of

---

4 See http://www.ericberne.com/transactional-analysis.

leaders to set the bar – to lead by example and create the conditions in which people can do their best work.

Therefore, line meetings (or your informal interactions with those you line manage) are the single most important meetings in the school week. More important than lessons. Their multiplied significance can so transform the level of engagement, and thereby the quality of teaching, that you owe it to your students and to their education to look after your people. Nothing you do this week is as important as the time you give to those you line manage. Nothing. Those meetings should be protected above everything else. They should be timetabled and regarded as contact time. They are not additional extras *if* you have time. They are the core activity of leadership. The first job of leadership is not the students or the school; it is the development of those you lead. If your team is enthused, engaged, aligned and on point then the student experience will be brilliant. You won't need to worry about it because that is what your fabulous staff are doing. Your job is to lead your team.

Do you know how engaged your staff team is?

Gallup have been surveying employees for many years and have, over time, come up with 12 questions that most succinctly measure the level of employee engagement in the workplace: the Gallup Q12.[5] The following are my own version for teachers along with a thirteenth question which I think is important. I call them the teachers' dozen.[6]

1 Are you clear about what is expected of you as a teacher?

2 Do you have the necessary resources, facilities and environment in order to teach consistently well?

---

5 See R. Nishioka, Use the Gallup Q12 Questions to Manage Your Manager, *Business 2 Community* (5 October 2017). Available at: https://www.business2community.com/human-resources/use-gallup-q12-questions-manage-manager-01926550.

6 Duncan, Gallup's 12 Employee Engagement Questions + 1 It Forgot!, *Vetter* (n.d.). Available at: https://www.getvetter.com/posts/174-gallup-s-12-employee-engagement-questions-1-it-forgot.

3 At your school, do you have the opportunity and freedom to teach in the way you teach best every day?

4 During the past week, have you been acknowledged or affirmed by a colleague or leader for teaching well or doing good work?

5 Does your line manager, or another colleague, seem to care about you personally?

6 Do those you work with encourage your development as a practitioner and a professional?

7 In your school, do your opinions, ideas and suggestions seem to make any difference?

8 Does the focus and mission of your school make you feel that your work as a teacher is important?

9 Are your colleagues committed to delivering a brilliant education and not settling for 'good enough'?

10 Do you have a good friend at your school?

11 In the last six months, has your line manager discussed your progress with you and offered constructive feedback?

12 In the last year, have you been given opportunities to learn new things and develop as a professional and as a person?

13 If you have a new idea or suggestion that can help your school, is there a regular means or opportunity for you to communicate it to senior leadership?

These questions provide an accurate account of the key factors that make people tick. Understanding what makes people feel motivated and engaged goes hand in hand with what I have already discussed about how you make people feel. What is interesting is that these questions correspond with the six psychological needs explored in Chapter 5. If you have skipped straight to this section of the book, then please go back and read that chapter first.

As I observed in Chapter 5, with the exception of love, each of the other five psychological needs are significantly influenced by your work and your work environment. As a leader then, it is your responsibility to have your finger on the pulse of how each of your teammates are doing in these areas, because it is your job to do your best to address those needs in the workplace. Table 7.1 shows how the five psychological needs match up with the teachers' dozen.

Table 7.1. How the five psychological needs correspond with the teachers' dozen

Psychological need	The teachers' dozen (reordered to align with the five psychological needs)
Being understood	5. Does your line manager, or another colleague, seem to care about you personally? 7. In your school, do your opinions, ideas and suggestions seem to make any difference?
Belonging	9. Are your colleagues committed to delivering a brilliant education and not settling for 'good enough'? 6. Do those you work with encourage your development as a practitioner and a professional? 10. Do you have a good friend at your school?
Achievement	1. Are you clear about what is expected of you as a teacher? 2. Do you have the necessary resources, facilities and environment in order to teach consistently well? 4. During the past week, have you been acknowledged or affirmed by a colleague or leader for teaching well or doing good work?

Psychological need	The teachers' dozen (reordered to align with the five psychological needs)
Purpose	8. Does the focus and mission of your school make you feel that your work as a teacher is important? 11. In the last six months, has your line manager discussed your progress with you and offered constructive feedback? 12. In the last year, have you been given opportunities to learn new things and develop as a professional and as a person?
Autonomy	3. At your school, do you have the opportunity and freedom to teach in the way you teach best every day? 13. If you have a new idea or suggestion that can help your school, is there a regular means or opportunity for you to communicate it to senior leadership?

Use these questions with your team, but also use them to self-evaluate your role as a leader. The research is clear: the more attention you give to ensuring that these questions can be answered affirmatively by those you lead, the greater their engagement will be. It is also worth giving some thought to the same questions with regard to your students. The level of student engagement in your classes is affected by exactly the same factors. We are each leaders in our classrooms. And yet I have never, in any behaviour management handbook or training I have come across, encountered the Gallup Q12. Your students will be engaged to the extent that their psychological needs are met.

What are you building?

In their book *Built to Last*, James Collins and Jerry Porras examine the practices of a number of visionary companies.[7] The companies they analyse are those which have stood the test of time and proven their success and longevity far beyond the life of one dynamic leader or product, like Disney, Procter & Gamble and 3M. The authors set out to discover what it is about these companies that has set them apart from the competition, and they discovered they all have one key trait in common. Each company places the company itself, the core team – literally the 'company of people' – at the centre of everything they do. They believe that the people don't exist for the product, rather the product exists for the people.

Collins and Porras use an example. Imagine you needed to tell the people of London the time – before the age of pocket watches. You could go about it in two ways. Firstly, you could employ a time teller – someone with a really loud voice who will yell out the time every hour on the hour. Of course, sometimes the time teller may be sick or hoarse, and eventually they will get old and want to retire. The second option is to build a clock that will work every minute of every day. A mechanism that will communicate the time itself without the need for constant interference or assistance; a mechanism that will stand for years and even centuries, 24 hours a day, rain or shine, and ring out the time for all to see and hear.[8]

It is fairly obvious which option is better. But here is the point: the clock is the team. The clock is the system, the means of delivery, and in all these visionary companies this awareness was central. The principal focus and priority was on investing in and developing the 'clock': a clock that is so good, so tight, so robust and so effective that the time takes care of itself. For example, Disney has kept growing long beyond the life of Walt Disney because he invested in the team: 'Above all, there was the ability to build and build and build – never stopping, never looking

---

7 J. Collins and J. Porras, *Built to Last: Successful Habits of Visionary Companies* (London: Random House, 1994).

8 Collins and Porras, *Built to Last*, p. 22.

back, never finishing – the institution … In the last analysis, Walt Disney's greatest creation was Walt Disney [the company].'[9]

It is our role as leaders to focus firmly on our teachers, on creating a team that works and knows where it is going. When we do that, and do it properly, they will be the individuals who find new, innovative and exciting ways to make the vision a reality. Or as Richard Branson put it, 'Train people well enough so they can leave, treat them well enough so they don't want to.'[10]

Invest in your team.

9 R. Schickel, *The Disney Version: The Life, Times, Art and Commerce of Walt Disney* (New York: Simon & Schuster, 1968), p. 44, quoted in Collins and Porras, *Built to Last*, p. 22.
10 See R. Branson, Twitter post (27 March 2014). Available at: https://twitter.com/richardbranson/status/449220072176107520.

Chapter 8

The Art of Motivation

There are four key takeaways for school leaders from the previous chapter:

1 Your middle leaders are the most important asset in your school.

2 Line meetings between staff and managers/leaders are the most important meetings in the school day and need to be timetabled and protected.

3 Middle leaders require training and development in people skills, management skills and effective leadership.

4 Middle leaders need to be involved in the decision-making process and consulted on all major policy decisions.

These four priorities will transform your school. The culture of your organisation will coalesce around the ethos, enthusiasm and engagement of your middle leaders and their proficiency (or otherwise) in effectively managing and motivating their teams. However, to take the education we provide to the next level, we also need to rethink our assumptions about motivation and how they inform the way we go about engaging our teachers.

In Chapter 2, I described William Muir's experiment with super-chickens and his conclusion that overall productivity suffers when individual success is achieved at the expense of suppressing the productivity of others. This speaks to the kind of culture we are establishing in our schools: either one of collaboration and helpfulness or individualism and one-upmanship. In the short term, a superhead or new departmental head can appear to be shaking things up and improving standards. Sometimes this is done by actively culling staff and sometimes by establishing a fairly ruthless culture of fear. Over the long term, however, this approach is likely to lead to unsustainable work patterns, which in turn will lead to high staff turnover and a miserable working environment.

If we want to achieve lasting success then we must take seriously the fact that humans (like chickens) flourish in an environment where they feel safe. The 'stick' approach to motivating staff has been proven to be counterproductive (as I will show later in this chapter). Performance-related pay, far from incentivising higher standards, tends to feel more like a threat, which induces fear and performance anxiety. I have already referred to the problems and complexities associated with measuring only the data generated by public exam results. To use this as a justification for withholding a pay rise or progression on the pay scale undermines all of the hard work and effort that goes into fulfilling the incredibly broad remit of the average teacher. It generates resentment and leads to a box-ticking culture in which staff work strictly to the minimum standards: 'Right – if that's how they're going to be, I'm not going to give extra time to run clubs or invite students back after school for additional support.'

This is dangerous for a school, but it is a sentiment I have often heard from teaching staff. The whole school system depends on the goodwill of its staff. The system banks on it. In any people-centred profession, goodwill, trust and social capital are the currency of progress. If you take that generous spirit for granted, don't acknowledge it or, worse, insult it, then you have got nowhere to go and nothing to build with. Remember: the team is the engine.

A culture that undermines this social capital is dangerous for a further reason. I am aware of occasions when safeguarding concerns were ignored by staff because addressing them would generate so much extra paperwork that they just couldn't afford to go there. Any extra time or work will not be acknowledged or even considered when it comes to the narrow data collection exercise that is used to measure teacher performance. This cannot be right. When our measuring system actually undermines our duty of care to the children we are there to protect, something is seriously wrong.

The fact is that, over the course of a day, an average teacher in a secondary school will have direct contact with around 150–180 students, including interactions at break, lunch, on duty and in corridors. Every day, there will be students in the classroom who are noticeably withdrawn, struggling socially, academically or mentally. The teacher faces a choice: do I address this by asking the student how they are and/or getting them to stay behind at the end of the lesson to check in on them?

Or do I just leave it and tell myself that their tutor or head of year will pick up on it?

If I take the first option, I know that I am creating work for myself that I don't have time for and for which I will receive little credit or thanks. If I take the second option, I can stay on track and cope with my workload. However, to take the second option and keep a clear conscience, I have to do one of two things:

1 Tell myself that it's not my job: I'm not a social worker, I'm a maths teacher. That's what pastoral staff are employed for.

2 Over time I become better at not 'seeing' in the first place. If I don't look for problems, I won't spot them so often and then I won't feel like I have to act on them.

The only other thing I can do to appease my conscience is to fire off an email to the head of year: 'Noticed Shannon was not herself today. Thought I should let you know …' I dump it onto someone else who is already overwhelmed by how many students they need to look out for.

All of these responses are hugely problematic for student wellbeing, and potentially have very serious repercussions for students, some of whom may slip through the net altogether and become another statistic, another suicide, another abuse case because we missed the early signs.

If you are a teacher then, yes, you are a social worker. Obviously not in the same sense as a trained, professional social worker, but in the sense that your duty of care is to the whole child, not just the maths part or the history part of their brain. You are, first and foremost, a teacher of children, not a teacher of a subject. But I understand why you feel the way you do. We are expected as teachers to provide all-round care and support for students, but the significant role we play is ignored by the mechanisms used to measure our performance. Ironically, it is entirely feasible for one teacher to be denied a pay progression for providing a better standard of care to students, while another is rewarded with higher pay for ignoring the more complex needs of students! This is wrong.

Stick-based motivation does not work in most cases. When a high quota or target is set, it tends to create performance anxiety, which not only inhibits creativity and positive thinking but also leads to lower standards, corner-cutting and even unethical behaviour. The Volkswagen emissions scandal in 2015 is just one example of unethical data reporting motivated by the expectation to meet a target and the threat within the company of falling short.[1] Mis-selling in many industries (think of payment protection insurance by banks) demonstrates the negative impact of placing pressure on the fulfilment of arbitrary goals within arbitrary timescales. The danger is increased in people-centred professions: a number of hospital scandals within the NHS over the past decade have been linked to pressure on staff to meet government targets.[2]

Dan Pink explores the stick approach in *Drive*. When we utilise the stick as a way to motivate our staff, especially in people-focused jobs, it has the effect of undermining the much stronger intrinsic motivator of altruism. We have already seen in Chapter 5 how offering a financial incentive for blood donation led to a reduction in willing donors. The powerful altruistic motivator was undermined by the offer of a reward. The same is true of threat. Pink describes an experiment to incentivise parents to bring their children to a private day care centre more punctually by introducing the threat of a fine for lateness. However, it actually led to an increase in the number of parents arriving late. Previously, the motivation for punctuality was the relationship with the teachers who cared for their children and the parents' sense of moral obligation not to inconvenience them. By imposing a fine, that motivator was replaced by a transactional mentality: 'I can just buy more time if I'm running late.' According to Pink, 'The punishment didn't promote good behaviour; it crowded it out.'[3]

Back in the 1960s, social psychologist Douglas McGregor distinguished between Theory X and Theory Y approaches to human motivation and its implications for effective leadership.[4] According to his research, extrinsic motivators of threat or reward assume that humans are essentially lazy, avoid responsibility, dislike work and need to be controlled. This is Theory X. Theory Y, on the other hand, suggests a more

1 R. Hotten, Volkswagen: The Scandal Explained, *BBC News* (10 December 2015). Available at: https://www.bbc.co.uk/news/business-34324772.

2 At Stafford Hospital, for example,: BBC News, Stafford Hospital Scandal: The Real Story Behind Channel 4's *The Cure* (19 December 2019). Available at: https://www.bbc.co.uk/news/uk-england-stoke-staffordshire-50836324.

3 D. Pink, *Drive* (New York: Riverhead Books, 2009), pp. 52–53.

4 D. McGregor, *The Human Side of Enterprise* (New York: McGraw Hill, 1985), pp. 33–34.

optimistic view of human nature: that people seek responsibility and are happy to work on their own initiative. If this is the case, then extrinsic motivators of reward or threat will have little effect. In fact, they can be counterproductive, even hindering progress and impact.

By way of example, author and entrepreneur Tim Ferris gives some advice to writers in avoiding writer's block: 'My quota is two crappy pages per day. I keep it really low so I'm not so intimidated that I never get started.'[5] Writers, and anyone for that matter, can struggle to get started and excel when they feel that the product has to be perfect, when they are anxious that their work is not good enough and will be judged negatively. If you are told you have to write 20 pages today or make 20 sales today, otherwise you will be deemed to have failed, then you may struggle to get into a flow. Also, once you meet that target you are more likely to stop. Conversely, when the bar is set low it is much easier to get started. If you start with a much lower target, which you very quickly meet, you are then intrinsically motivated to keep going and see how far you can go. There's no pressure. The working environment is much more conducive to progress and productivity. But here's the uncomfortable truth: higher targets lead to lower performance. What are the implications of this for the way we use targets in school?

This brings us back to the environment of the super-chickens versus the collaborative chickens. When teachers feel safe, invested in and valued, when their psychological needs are met and they have the freedom to be themselves, they flourish, innovate and give far beyond the call of duty. A culture like this is either established or undermined by the team leader.

Another study of relevance was conducted by Sam Glucksberg of Princeton University, which is referred to as 'the candle problem'.[6] Groups are provided with the following items: a candle, three matches and a matchbox filled with thumbtacks. The task is to pin the candle to the wall in such a way that when the candle is lit no wax drips onto the floor. Groups approach this in different ways, none of which will work except for the solution – which is to pin the box itself to the wall as a platform

5 G. Roy, 5 Writing Lessons from Tim Ferriss, *Medium.com* (27 January 2015). Available at: https://medium.com/@eBooksIndiaMag/5-writing-lessons-from-tim-ferriss-2c11b39f6584.
6 S. Glucksberg, The Influence of Strength of Drive on Functional Fixedness and Perceptual Recognition, *Journal of Experimental Psychology*, 63(1) (1962): 36–41.

for the candle. Invariably groups arrive at this solution after a few minutes – it just requires a little lateral thinking. Here's what is interesting though: when groups were timed and financially incentivised to solve this problem as quickly as possible, in test after test they completed the challenge *three minutes slower* than groups who were not incentivised. The incentive made people less, not more, effective. It challenges what we thought we knew about motivation.

In an alternative version of the candle problem, the groups were provided with the same challenge and the same equipment; however, this time the equipment was laid out like this: a candle, some thumb tacks, the empty box which the thumbtacks came in and three matches. This time the incentivised groups won every time. This conclusion has been verified and reinforced by many studies since, and it tells us something essential about human motivation and productivity. Namely that for straightforward, left-brain, mechanistic tasks, carrot and stick can lead to improved performance. However, in tasks that require right-brain, creative thinking, innovation and imagination, traditional incentives make people less effective. The way the candle problem was presented the second time around made it a much more clear-cut task.

Teaching is a task that requires considerable right-brain, innovative, imaginative as well as emotional engagement, so carrots and sticks are counterproductive in generating greater productivity or improved outcomes. It is the intrinsic motivation of the joy of the task itself that is a far more powerful motivator, especially in teaching. If the culture of our schools and departments leans towards extrinsic motivations and short-term success assessed by narrow data measures, the effectiveness of our teachers will be stunted. If instead we cultivate freedom, innovation and major on the joy of teaching and of shaping young lives, then effectiveness will go through the roof.

Who sets the temperature gauge that determines the culture of your teams? The team leaders. Invest in your middle leaders and transform the culture of your school.

Intrinsic motivation

Imagine it's 1995 and you are presented with two contrasting business plans for a new encyclopaedia. One is backed by Microsoft, with all its market dominance, and involves employing hundreds of specialists to write thousands of articles which will be sold on CD-ROMs or downloaded from the internet. The second proposes to ask thousands of writers to write and edit millions of articles for fun. No remuneration will be offered. No incentive given.

Which would you have predicted would be most successful? Daniel Pink suggests that back then you wouldn't have found a single sane economist who would have backed the success of the second venture. Yet, by 2009, Microsoft had pulled the plug on their online encyclopaedia, Encarta, whereas Wikipedia now has some 52 million articles translated into 309 different languages and continues to flourish.[7] Wikipedia tapped into what Pink calls Motivation 3.0 – intrinsic motivation. Doing something for the love and joy of the task itself rather than for extrinsic reward.[8]

This concurs with Abraham Maslow's work on motivation: that the basic motivators of safety and material gain are much less powerful than the drive generated by belonging and self-esteem. But most powerful of all is what he calls 'self-actualisation' – the sense that I am doing what I am supposed to do. I am being and becoming a fuller and more developed version of myself.[9]

If you are going to draw the best out of your staff and enable them to do what they do best more effectively, then leaders at all levels need to fully grasp the import of harnessing and optimising intrinsic motivation. Jeff Gunther states: 'Management isn't about walking around and making sure people are in their offices, it's about creating conditions for people to do their best work.'[10] What kind of culture, what kind of conditions have we created in our schools? To what extent have they become places which actually stifle innovation, cripple ingenuity, suffocate free thinking and penalise creativity? Pink advises: 'Think of the great artists of the last hundred years and how they worked – people like Pablo Picasso,

7 See https://en.wikipedia.org/wiki/Wikipedia:Size_comparisons.
8 Pink, *Drive*, p. 70.
9 A. Maslow, *A Theory of Human Motivation* (St Paul, MN: Wilder Publications, 2013 [1943]).
10 Quoted in McNair, Getting Results.

Georgia O'Keefe, Jackson Pollock … Nobody told them, "You must paint this sort of picture. You must begin painting precisely at 8.30am. You must paint with the people we select to work with you. And you must paint this way." The very idea is ludicrous.'[11] Great work is accomplished when there is room to breathe. And importantly, when there is personal, emotional buy-in to the outcome or mission of the project.

Here's a question: how do you get a whole army of people to do a job that involves regularly wiping up human excrement and vomit, working irregular hours, including being on call every night, without paying them a penny but rather requiring an investment of thousands of pounds of their own money for the privilege of doing it? Answer? You give them the chance to give birth to their own baby.

Every parent knows the massive investment of money, time, energy and hard work involved in raising kids, yet we do it willingly and even take delight in it. Yes, even in the ostensibly nastier, more menial and thankless aspects of it. We do it year in, year out. We do it because it's our baby. I can deal with my own kid's sick and nappies and crying and interruptions, and I have discovered far deeper reserves of patience and resilience than I ever thought possible. But hand me someone else's child and I am physically repulsed by their vomit, I have no patience for their crying and I cannot abide their noise. It's not my baby.

Clearly, we value what we love and believe in, what we grow and nurture, what we give birth to, far more than something that is shoved into our arms or imposed on us, something in which we had no creative part or say. We don't care in the same way if we have had no investment or involvement in its conception.

I'm still talking about leadership. Any management-driven target, project or initiative that is rolled out from the top down without consultation, communication and the involvement of the team is destined for mediocre success at best and abject failure at worst. You can come up with the finest school improvement plan in the world, but if your people aren't on board with it, it will fail. If they don't buy in, if they don't believe in it, if it doesn't feel like theirs, there won't be the emotional and personal investment to make it a success. In short, they just won't care enough.

---

11 Pink, *Drive*, p. 106.

Performance goals versus learning goals

Carol Dweck highlights the difference between performance goals and learning goals – for example, getting an A in French (performance goal) versus being able to speak French (learning goal). Even though both can fuel achievement, only one leads to mastery. Dweck found that giving students a performance goal (e.g. getting a high mark in a test) was effective for straightforward problems but it inhibited their ability to apply concepts to new situations. By contrast, students given learning goals scored significantly higher on these novel challenges. They also worked longer and tried more solutions.[12]

Learning goals also have far greater potential to generate emotional buy-in over the long term. It is difficult to get excited about meeting a number or a standard. A short-lived high is generated by getting an A grade or being judged outstanding, but it doesn't last. It doesn't have the depth of feeling to drive us forward day after day. It isn't an intrinsic goal. Furthermore, such gradings are arbitrary. Grade boundaries change every year. Ofsted criteria shift every few years. The standards are someone else's, not yours. Anyone who has endured an inspection that was disappointing, even though you know and have the evidence to prove that your school and teaching is far improved on what it was, will know the utter debilitation this generates. We know that there is more to it than a simplistic, performance goal might indicate on first glance.

A learning goal, on the other hand, can last a lifetime and lead to real, sustained and tangible progress, rather than the synthetic, manipulated and short-term progress often generated by the data collection that is designed to evidence performance goals. Compare these two contrasting performance management targets, for example:

> Target 1: Ensure that 75% of your students meet or exceed their target grade.

12 C. S. Dweck, *Self-Theories: Their Role in Motivation, Personality and Development* (Philadelphia, PA: Psychology Press, 1999), p. 17.

> Target 2: Find new ways to inspire each of your students to love learning, achieve their goals and become even more exceptional human beings.

Which one is most motivational? Which one resonates most with your inner desire and intrinsic motivation as a teacher? Which one aligns with your why – the reason you became a teacher?

The first is a performance goal and acts as an extrinsic motivator, especially when used in a performance management context. The second is a learning goal which harnesses intrinsic motivation and allows you to invest yourself in your students. Some will argue that target 2 is no good because it cannot be measured. I would challenge this. It can be measured; it's just harder to do. Target 1 may be easy to measure, but what is easy to measure is not necessarily the most important thing, as Robert McNamara discovered during the Vietnam War. He was secretary of state for defence and insisted on judging the success of the US war effort by simplistically counting the number of casualties on each side. On that basis the United States were winning. Only they weren't because war is far more complex than that.[13] Just as education is far more complex than counting the grades 9–4.

In order to measure target 2 we have got to get smarter at measuring more effectively and more broadly. We have been lazy. But even if there are some things we can't count, or can't count now, that doesn't mean we shouldn't value them and make them a priority. It may be impossible to measure the impact of my care of a student on the way she treats her workers when she takes on her first management role, or the impact of the help I put in place for a neglected student on the way he cares for his own children when he becomes a father, but that doesn't mean these things don't matter. As William Bruce Cameron said, 'Not everything that can be counted counts, and not everything that counts can be counted.'[14]

---

13 See https://expertprogrammanagement.com/2017/07/the-mcnamara-fallacy.

14 W. B. Cameron, *Informal Sociology: A Casual Introduction to Sociological Thinking* (New York: Random House, 1963), p. 13.

Autonomy, mastery and purpose

There are three factors which research shows are critical to increasing and harnessing intrinsic motivation: autonomy, mastery and purpose. I have touched on all three already at different points, but it is worth tying them together and prompting some reflection on each one in terms of how we can change the way we lead schools in order to create healthy, flourishing teaching environments.

Autonomy

Edward Deci and Richard Ryan are proponents of self-determination theory, which focuses on the extent to which human behaviour is self-determined and self-motivated. They argue that we have three innate needs: competence, autonomy and relatedness.[15] (Again, consider how these correspond with the six psychological needs discussed in Chapter 5.) Their research has found that job satisfaction, and therefore performance, was higher in contexts where employees were offered 'autonomy support' – the opportunity to take on new projects, provide creative input and exercise some degree of choice over what to do and how to do it.[16]

The key principle here is to see your employees as partners, not as resources. The leader's role is to create the environment that enables them to do their best work with as few constraints and restrictions as is possible. Pink cites the example of the Australian company Atlassian, which experimented with what they called 'FedEx days': employees were told they could work on whatever they liked for a day. The only condition was to produce something and present it the next day. That is why they were called FedEx days – you had to deliver by the next day. They found that staff voluntarily worked longer because they were working on something that mattered to them – their 'baby'. The experiment also generated some of their most lucrative ideas and future products, which

15 R. M. Ryan and E. L. Deci, Self-Determination Theory and the Facilitation of Intrinsic Motivation, Social Development and Wellbeing, *American Psychologist*, 55(1) (2000): 68–78.

16 P. P. Baard, E. L. Deci and R. M. Ryan, Intrinsic Need Satisfaction: A Motivational Basis of Performance and Wellbeing in Two Work Settings, *Journal of Applied Social Psychology*, 34(10) (2004): 2045–2068.

prompted them to turn FedEx days into 20% time: everyone is free to devote their time to whatever they want for 20% of the working week. 3M's Post-it notes emerged from the same concept, as did Google's Gmail, Google Translate and Google News.[17]

When you give people greater autonomy they draw on their intrinsic motivation and access their right-brain creativity – and as a result, they can take your school far further and far faster than all your top-down new initiatives put together. Your people are the engine.

Pink's 4 T's are worth pondering as you do an 'autonomy audit' on your school:[18]

1 Task – how could you give teachers greater freedom over what they do day-to-day?

2 Time – how could you give greater flexibility over when they work and where their time is spent?

3 Technique – how could you give greater autonomy over how teachers teach?

4 Team – how could you involve staff in decisions about who they work with and how they will work best with those people?

Of course, in a profession like teaching there are greater restrictions than in some other industries, but there are undoubtedly many as yet unexplored ways that we can make teaching much more flexible. Devote a team meeting to brainstorming this!

Mastery

This is where performance management and appropriate goal-setting can either genuinely help your staff to develop, or stifle and depress them. Aim to set learning goals, not performance goals, and place meaningful CPD at the core regardless of where teachers are on the pay scale.

17 Pink, *Drive*, p. 93.
18 See https://www.danpink.com/audit.

Embed a growth mindset in your school community. Many teaching staff have a fixed mindset about their own capacity to improve, as well as that of their students. Challenge entity theory and look to develop a culture in which incremental growth is the norm.

Dr Kulvarn Atwal, head teacher and author of *The Thinking School*,[19] has made mastery the norm at his school in London. Every term, every staff member is entitled to the following:

- Paid MA study
- Collaborative action research
- Coaching & mentoring
- Peer learning & lesson study
- Collaborative planning
- Coaching
- Choice in their learning.[20]

This represents a very different school culture to that which most of us have known and one which has the potential to generate exponential results, especially as we resolve to reward effort not ability, and grit not talent.

How could you incorporate some of these opportunities for mastery into your performance management systems as well as in your week-to-week practice? Aim to become much more savvy and innovative by finding ways to measure what really counts rather than the standard performance measures. Make goals people focused, not data focused. Place humans at the heart of your improvement plan.

19 K. Atwal, *The Thinking School: Developing a Dynamic Learning Community* (Woodbridge: John Catt Educational, 2019).

20 See K. Atwal, Twitter post (13 April 2020). Available at: https://twitter.com/Thinkingschool2/status/1249693212773621761.

Purpose

Take the time as a whole-school community to work out your purpose. Everyone needs to be involved and it should be revisited each year. You need to identify a purpose statement that is coherent for everybody who works in the school, from the cleaners to the site team to the pastoral staff. It needs to be displayed and referenced all the time. It is your *raison d'être*. It is your why. It is what you get up for in the morning.

Your purpose needs to be exciting and aspirational, audacious and 'hairy' enough to motivate everyone in the school community. It needs to cast people's minds and vision beyond the day-to-day and the here-and-now. It needs to be bigger than now. Your purpose also needs to be people focused.

Yes, you want to improve results – but what for?

Yes, you want to improve behaviour – but what for?

Yes, you want to improve the progress of disadvantaged children – but what for?

What is the purpose of these aims? These are goals – these are not the purpose. They are not your why.

Finding your why as a school or department has huge power to generate passion and motivation as well as to drive innovation and creativity. This is key to tapping into the intrinsic motivation that, as we have seen, is the most powerful driver of everyone in your team.

Try this at a team meeting in the near future:

1 Ask everyone in your school/team why they do the job they do. See what comes up.

2 Get them to write down no more than two sentences to express what they think this school/department is for.

3 Collate these and collectively identify the common themes. Write these on sticky notes.

4 Collectively rank these themes, discuss them and arrange them in a way that makes sense to everyone.

5 Chew on them for a few days, then revisit the activity and see if you can arrive at a consensus.

6 Formulate your conclusions into a purpose statement which you can display and utilise to shape everything you do.

This activity can be extended and developed and is often helped along by having an external facilitator. But however you do it, make time to clarify your purpose. Once you have that you can identify the exciting and ambitious goals that will transform your outcomes.

The one thing your team want most

In his TED Talk 'What Makes Us Feel Good About Our Work?', Dan Ariely of Duke University describes some studies he has carried out into human motivation.[21] Participants were given a simple, short task in return for US$3. Then they were invited to do another – this time for US$2.40. Then another for even less and so on. The study aimed to find out how long participants would continue with the task given three different variables:

1 When the work was looked at and scanned by an overseer and then put into a pile.

2 When the work was not looked at by the overseer and put straight into a pile.

3 When the work was not looked at by the overseer and put directly into a shredder.

Even though the extrinsic reward was the same in all cases, the participants continued the tasks much longer in scenario 1 than in scenario 3. Fairly predictable. What was interesting, however, was the response of participants in scenario 2, which we might expect to have been somewhere in-between. In fact, the results were identical to those in scenario 3. In other words, work being ignored has exactly the same negative effect on morale and motivation as deliberately destroying it.

21 D. Ariely, What Makes Us Feel Good About Our Work? [video], *TED.com* (October 2012). Available at: https://www.ted.com/talks/dan_ariely_what_makes_us_feel_good_about_our_work.

There is one thing everyone wants above all else: acknowledgement. Learn how to give it and you will be an effective leader. Acknowledgement is the difference between a thriving organisation and a flailing one: if the people you lead feel like their contribution, their sacrifice and their skill set is recognised, they will give and give and give. I think this challenges a commonly held assumption about human nature (more on this in the next chapter) – the assumption that we are basically selfish creatures. I don't think the evidence for this holds up. We have an innate desire to give, to contribute to the wellbeing of others, to make a difference. But we also have an acute sense of justice. When our efforts go unnoticed, when our sacrifices are unrecognised, when our investment is not appreciated, we are incensed and demoralised. It's as if it has been put in the shredder. It's unfair. It's not that we did it in order to be thanked – we didn't. And it's not that we will stop doing it if we are not thanked – we won't. But, oh, what a difference it makes when someone acknowledges it!

On many occasions I have marvelled and been moved by the leaving speeches at the end of the summer term when teachers retire or move on. The tributes can be incredibly powerful and make you feel like you work in a wonderful place. How very sad it is, though, that all that recognition is saved up and withheld until the very last hour of the very last day of a teacher's career.

If you want to transform your staff engagement and build a thriving school, teach and model the importance of acknowledgement in your everyday dealings with your colleagues. They will want to work harder and better than ever before.

Chapter 9

Your Worldview and Leadership Style

How do you see people? How do you feel about people? I don't mean the ones you like and love; I mean your default approach to human beings as a whole. Your assumptions about people will unquestionably be affecting the way you lead them.

Cultural indoctrination is a very powerful thing. There are certain beliefs or ideas that can permeate the public consciousness and have further reaching effects than we would ever imagine. Take patriarchy, for example. The belief that women are inferior to men has infiltrated every social structure imaginable. It has shaped our politics, architecture, religions, education systems, class system, family life and all our social interactions to such an extent that we barely notice it.

Just ten minutes after being born, cognitive neuroscientist Gina Rippon's daughter was already experiencing gender bias. England were playing against Poland in a group match during the 1986 FIFA World Cup and Gary Lineker had scored a hat-trick. Nine babies were born that day, Rippon recalls, eight of whom were called Gary: 'The nurse handed her neighbour a "blue-wrapped Gary" with approval – he had "a cracking pair of lungs". Rippon's own daughter (making exactly the same sound) was passed over with an audible tutting. "She's the noisiest of the lot – not very ladylike," the nurse told her.'[1] The nurse probably didn't regard herself as sexist, but her prejudice came out nonetheless, no doubt a product of years of cultural indoctrination.

I remember when I was 20 years old sitting in a pub having a conversation with a couple of female university classmates about men using the phrase, 'Don't be such a girl'. I was adamantly defending its use and was somehow able to hold this view while at the same time asserting that it was in no way sexist and that I was definitely a feminist. The alarming

1 D. Robson, The Sexist Myths That Won't Die, *BBC Future* (1 October 2009). Available at: https://www.bbc.com/future/article/20190930-the-sexist-myths-about-gender-stereotypes-that-wont-die.

thing is that I could see no contradiction in my position. Such is the power of the status quo to skew our thinking.

Cultural indoctrination can affect our expectations and assumptions in many different ways, which brings me to a centuries-old and deeply held belief that has permeated thinking in the Western Christianised world: the doctrine of original sin. This too has implications for the biases we unconsciously manifest in our approach to leadership.

Christian theology on original sin

St Augustine (354–430 AD) is the theologian most associated with the doctrine of original sin and arguably did more to ensure its propagation than anyone else. The 'original sin' in Christian theology was, of course, that of Adam and Eve in the second Genesis creation story which led, in Augustine's interpretation, to the fall of man and humanity's banishment from the Garden of Eden into a world of suffering and struggle (Genesis 2–3).

Augustine, and thereby mainstream Christianity as a whole, has fairly universally (there are exceptions) taught that all human beings are born with a sinful nature: an inherent bias towards sin and evil that they cannot control or overcome.[2] All humans everywhere, both individually and as an entire species, are in need of being 'saved' – to be delivered from this malevolent power which works within us to bring about chaos and divert us away from good. The only means of this 'salvation', according to traditional Christian teaching, is the grace of God.

You may hold this belief or you may not, but its impact cannot be understated. Two consequences, to which I have already alluded, spring to mind immediately:

1 The notion of sin or 'falling short' necessarily assumes the reality of a perfect standard to which we should aspire yet cannot achieve. This undoubtedly leads people to an endless striving to be better and a sense that nothing is ever good enough.

2 Augustine, *Confessions*, tr. R. S. Pine-Coffin (London: Penguin, 2002), Book 1, Ch. 7, Sec. 11.

2 If all humans are sinful and innately tend towards selfishness, laziness and discord, then fundamentally we cannot trust them. Indeed, we would be foolish to do so. People need to be supervised, checked up on and shepherded; like sheep, people will go astray if we do not establish constraints, boundaries, structures and sanctions to keep them on track. This must necessarily lead to top-down, paternalistic, hierarchical and restrictive systems of government and leadership which are designed to control people, limit their freedom and make them compliant. Furthermore, it leads to the justification that such leadership systems are for our own good and in our own interests.

Do you, as a leader, subscribe to this view? Even unconsciously? Do you somewhere deep down inside think that people are basically bad? Do you subscribe to the idea in William Golding's *Lord of the Flies* that, left to their own devices, people are lazy, self-absorbed, nihilistic, lawless and ultimately self-destructive? Do you believe that people need governance of the controlling sort in order to save them from themselves? If you do subscribe to this view (and I will readily admit that it is not without evidence), then it will inevitably affect the way you lead those in your care.

While this is admittedly a big subject, I would like to offer just three pieces of anecdotal evidence which might suggest that what we, as a culture, have believed about human nature for so many centuries might not be the case.

1 I have already referred to the evidently intrinsic motivation to contribute to the wellbeing of others as evidenced by the reduction in blood donors when a self-serving incentive was introduced. But there is evidence of the desire to do and be good in many different contexts. Perhaps the greatest example of the innate goodness of human beings is their capacity to act entirely selflessly, even sacrificially, in raising children. Even if many enter into it accidentally or for the wrong reasons, there are myriad examples of men and women who, on the birth of their child, discover depths of love, compassion and empathy that they never knew they had. It is the number one life-changing experience that both forces us to grow up and obliges us to put our own needs, perspectives, desires

and wishes firmly to one side and to live, literally, for someone else. It is both beautiful and remarkable.

2 The *Lord of the Flies* narrative of 'the darkness of man's heart' doesn't seem to bear out in practice. Historian Rutger Bregman writes of the real life 'Lord of the Flies' when six school boys were discovered on a desert island in 1966 having been shipwrecked for 15 months. Captain Peter Warner, who discovered the lost boys, wrote in his memoir: 'The boys had set up a small commune with food garden, hollowed-out tree trunks to store rainwater, a gymnasium with curious weights, a badminton court, chicken pens and a permanent fire, all from handiwork, an old knife blade and much determination.'[3] In contrast with Golding's lost boys who fought over the fire, those in the real-life scenario worked together to keep their fire going for over a year. They overcame hunger, thirst, injury and failure, and proved the resourcefulness, resilience and loyalty of human beings when they collaborated and leant on each other.

3 Then there is the story of humanity: the relentless pursuit of freedom and justice in the face of overwhelming odds and oppression. The march towards freedom and justice is well documented throughout human history – whether in the songs of the civil rights movement, or the cause of the abolitionists to put an end to slavery, or the plight of the suffragettes demanding gender equality, or the insistence of the trade union movement on fair treatment for all, or, further back in time, the Protestant Reformation, the Peasants' Revolt, the English Civil War – the examples are endless. Arguably, there has been a slow but steady progression towards greater freedom and justice – towards good. And, notably, this progression has been the determined movement of the majority, not the minority; it has been the powerful and elite minority that has wielded its power so relentlessly for ill. It is people power that has been the driver of a freer, fairer society.

3 R. Bregman, The Real Lord of the Flies: What Happened When Six Boys Were Shipwrecked for 15 Months, *The Guardian* (9 May 2020). Available at: https://www.theguardian.com/books/2020/may/09/the-real-lord-of-the-flies-what-happened-when-six-boys-were-shipwrecked-for-15-months.

Of course, you may point to exceptions in all these examples – the donors who took the money, the twisted parents who abused their own kids, those who have stood firmly in the way of freedom and justice – but they are just that: exceptions. There is good evidence to suggest that humans are basically good. And when individuals do behave badly, it is not due to an innate tendency for evil but often as a result of unimaginable suffering, trauma or abuse to which they were exposed very early in life which distorted their true self beyond recognition.

People are good, which means – assuming you are not shafting them, mistreating them or exploiting them – that you *can* trust them. Now, if that is the case then our whole approach to leadership needs a rethink.

Dysfunctional leadership

In line with the work of Douglas McGregor on Theory X and Theory Y (see Chapter 8), Table 9.1 shows the difference between top-down, controlling leadership motivated by distrust and a negative view of people versus collaborative, innovative leadership motivated by trust and belief in the inherent value and good of people. Be honest with yourself: which do you tend towards? Which is more appealing to you? Which would you rather have as your own boss?

Table 9.1. The command-and-control leader versus the innovative leader

Source: Paul Sloane and Innovation Management, The Innovative Leader vs. the Command-and-Control Leader, *Innovation Management* (30 September 2009). Available at: https://innovationmanagement.se/imtool-articles/the-innovative-leader-vs-the-command-and-control-leader.

The command-and-control leader ...	The innovative leader ...
Leads from the front.	Leads from the side.
Directs.	Inspires.
Checks and controls.	Trusts and delegates.

The command-and-control leader …	The innovative leader …
Improves effectiveness and efficiency.	Finds new approaches.
Thinks she/he knows best (and often does).	Harnesses the abilities of others.
Has a strong sense of direction and purpose.	Has a clear vision and communicates it.
Prioritises operational over strategic issues.	Prioritises strategic over operational issues.
Gives directions and orders.	Asks questions and invites suggestions.
Treats staff as subordinates.	Treats staff as colleagues.
Is decisive, often without prior consultation.	Ponders and solicits input before making decisions.
Builds a team who can execute policy and implement plans.	Builds a team who can create and innovate.
Instructs.	Empowers.
Hires based on experience, track record and qualifications.	Hires based on attitude, creativity and latent capabilities.
Discourages dissent.	Encourages constructive dissent.
Cares about results above all.	Cares about ideas, people and the vision.
Promotes him/herself as the leader and figurehead.	Shares exposure and prestige with the team.
Encourages action, activity and work.	Encourages ideas, innovation and fun.
Rewards performance.	Rewards entrepreneurial action.

The command-and-control leader ...	The innovative leader ...
Is numbers-orientated and analytical.	Is ideas-orientated, analytical and intuitive.
Sees technology as a means to do things better, faster and cheaper.	Sees technology as a means to do things entirely differently.
Minimises risk.	Takes calculated risks.
Abhors failure.	Is comfortable with failure.

A top-down leadership approach generates a working environment that is fundamentally at odds with staff living and working well. Cross-reference the hallmarks of command-and-control leadership with the teachers' dozen and you find that one is directly contrary to the other. The ingredients of a healthy, happy working environment are very difficult to foster and sustain if underlying everything we do is a distrust of the teams and individuals we lead.

In contrast, the right-hand column of traits sounds like an enviable working environment and an organisation that is going places – one where growth and innovation can shape a very different future. But that is the point: to achieve a collaborative culture you have to remove the constraints, and that means you have to release control. For many, this will sound scary at best and utterly terrifying at worst. If you have lived and worked all your life to high standards, if you have a clear and preferred way of doing things and, furthermore, if you are under pressure yourself from higher powers that will hold you accountable, how could you possibly nurture the kind of work environment described above?

Accountability

The answer is balance. I am not advocating a free-for-all – to take your hands entirely off the reins and hope for the best. However, I am suggesting that you, like most people, probably have a few control issues and they may well be hindering you from leading a great team. So the first thing is to check your default position.

This is mine:

> I want something done. I know I will do it well. I want it done well. If I give it to someone else to do, either they won't do it as well or, in the time it will take me to help them do it in the way I want it done, I could have done it myself. So, I may as well do it myself and they can work on something else that doesn't matter as much.

Sounds horrible when I read it back – both arrogant and patronising – but I know that it's my default position, and I don't think I'm alone.

The first thing is obvious: bin the false economy straight away. Yes, it may take longer this time to coach, model and assist someone else to learn rather than do it yourself, but in the long term you will save yourself years and accomplish far more in less time. We know this, of course; it's just hard to do – especially for controlling perfectionists.

I know I can't do everything, but this still leaves me with a problem: how do I make sure that stuff is done to the standard I want? The default answer is monitoring. Give my team a tick list, a set of criteria or expectations, and then measure their performance in relation to that and promise a reward if they do it well, while threatening negative consequences if they don't. Which unfortunately walks us straight into the problem we have right now and undermines everything we have learned about motivation, engagement and trust. Not to mention the fact that it won't work. My way is *not* the only way. There are a multitude of ways to achieve a goal. The more prescriptive we are about the method, the more we limit the ultimate outcome.

The alternative I propose is the ROWE approach (discussed in Chapter 6). It is not that we ditch accountability; rather we make people accountable for the outcome and allow them much greater freedom and autonomy about the methodology. It is about the destination, not which route you take. As leaders, we provide the tools, the environment, the support and the inspiration to enable our people to do what they do best. And we believe in them to do it.

But what happens if I'm not happy with what they come back with? Or the outcome isn't up to scratch in my view? There are a few possibilities here, but start with yourself – self-reflect and ask for feedback.

- Did I communicate the vision effectively?
- Did I provide the necessary time and resources?
- Did I demand too much too soon with inadequate guidance?
- Was I too prescriptive?
- Is my view of the outcome shared by others? (Is the outcome not up to scratch, or is it just that it's not what I had in my mind, but in fact meets the brief and is liked by everyone else?)

To honestly appraise yourself as a leader on all these questions takes a high level of openness, strength and self-assuredness.

Now we get to the crux of the matter: is there sufficient trust in your team between team members, between the leader and the team, and between the team and the leader? Again, the same questions apply in the classroom with the young people you teach:

- Do they know you are on their side?
- Do you know that they are on board with your leadership?
- Do you all know that you are in it together, not just for yourself?

If the answer to any of those questions is no, then forget criticising the work of the team and the standards you think they haven't met because the most important fact is that *you* haven't done *your* job properly as a leader. First and foremost, your job is to build a team that works and which is bound together by trust.

Trust is the essential ingredient in social capital, which is arguably the most important capital of all – far more important than financial capital. As social scientist Francis Fukuyama puts it, 'social capital is a capability that arises from the prevalence of trust in a society'.[4] Its potential is limitless. The strength of a wall is not derived from the strength of the bricks but by the strength of the mortar that holds the bricks together. Trust is the mortar, the glue, the fundamental ingredient of an effective team, without which all you have is a group of individuals. That trust binds teammates together, but even more importantly it binds you to the team and the team to you. And they will not trust you if you cannot show weakness and vulnerability and do not genuinely lean on them. They won't trust you if you don't trust them. Trust is reciprocal.

Situational leadership

One of the challenges of effective leadership is knowing when to trust those we work with and how much to trust them. Hersey and Blanchard's concept of situational leadership is useful here: that different contexts require different leadership approaches.[5] Figure 9.1 shows how this can be an uncomfortable though necessary journey.

The basic idea is that we need to balance our leadership style with the competence level and development of the individuals we lead. It is entirely appropriate to start off in a more directive mode, but it is counterproductive to stay in this mode. We need to move from directing to coaching to supporting to delegating. At each stage, the amount of control we exert should decrease in line with the growing competence of those we lead. The skill is to utilise the appropriate approach at the appropriate time.

4 F. Fukuyama, *Trust: Social Virtues and the Creation of Prosperity* (New York: Simon & Schuster, 1996), p. 26.

5 M. Longoria, What is the Situational Leadership Theory?, *Tough Nickel* (29 May 2020). Available at: https://toughnickel.com/business/What-is-the-Situational-Leadership-Theory.

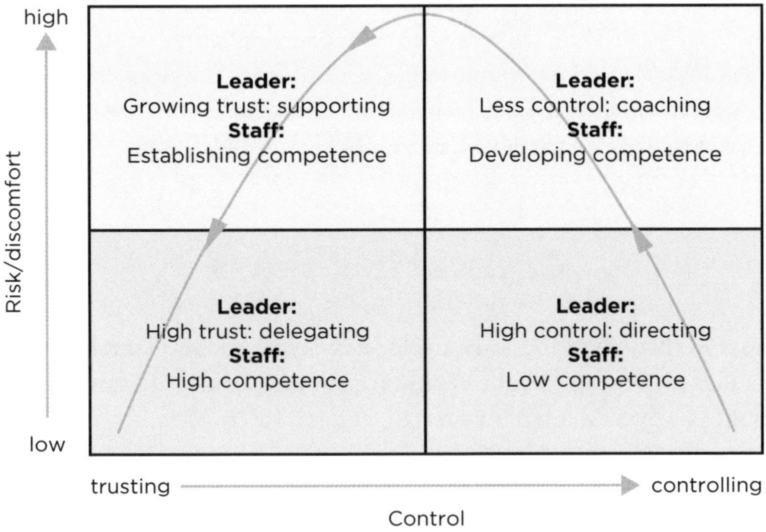

Figure 9.1. The leadership journey

Adapted from the Hersey-Blanchard model. *Source*: M. Longoria, What is the Situational Leadership Theory?, *Tough Nickel* (29 May 2020). Available at: https://toughnickel.com/business/What-is-the-Situational-Leadership-Theory.

To use another parenting analogy, we all want to get to the place where our children can feed themselves. However, it is patently absurd to give a 6-month-old a spoon and say, 'Okay, I trust you – give it your best shot.' Your trust is misplaced. Initially, you offer your toddler a spoon to hold which they will wave around a bit while you continue to feed them. Gradually, you may guide them to find their mouth with their spoon – just a few times, though, because otherwise dinner would never end. Then the time comes when they don't want to take the food from you and they want to do it themselves. But you know they aren't ready – at least not to the standard you would like. They can do it, but it's going to be carnage! Half of the food won't make it to their mouth and will end up on the floor, on the high chair, on their own face and perhaps some of it on yours. For those of us with obsessive-compulsive tendencies this is not a happy situation.

But it is necessary. Some of us give in to the temptation to take back the spoon and just say no, perhaps because we can't stand the mess or we can't cope with not being needed. Others are entirely relaxed with this scenario. The fact is, if you take back the spoon, you delay the time until they master the skill. So it is with all leadership activities. If you truly want to enable and grow your team, and thereby multiply your impact and productivity, you have to become comfortable with mess and you have to become comfortable with not being needed.

Embracing mess

I am told that when you learn to ride a unicycle, the very first lesson you are taught is how to fall off. Wouldn't it be great if we could master that lesson? If we could learn how to fall, and fall safely, then nothing would stop us. The problem is that we have embraced a negative attitude to failure – and no wonder given the definition of sin (falling short of perfection) and the notion of original sin (our innate bias towards failure) embedded firmly in our psyche. Most people would agree that failure is to be avoided.

Except that it's not true. Failure is how we learn. In *Bounce*, Matthew Syed explores the concept of growth and fixed mindsets already discussed in relation to Carol Dweck.[6] But what I like is the title of his book and the concept behind it – namely, that success is not something we achieve via a smooth, unhindered trajectory. Instead, we bounce our way there – we have a go, fall down, get up, have a better go, fall down, get up, go differently, fall down again ... With each failure there is learning, development, resilience and experience, and each time we are making progress in incremental steps towards our vision. Each failure is not a negative but a step closer to the goal. Thomas Edison famously had many thousands of failed attempts prior to patenting the technology for the incandescent light bulb. On one occasion he was asked: 'Isn't it a shame that with the tremendous amount of work you have done you haven't been able to get any results?' Edison replied: 'Results! Why, man, I have gotten a lot of results! I know several thousand things that won't work.'[7]

6 M. Syed, *Bounce: The Myth of Talent and the Power of Practice* (London: Fourth Estate, 2011).
7 F. L. Dyer and T. C. Martin, *Edison: His Life and Inventions*, vol. 2 (New York: Harper & Brothers, 1910), pp. 615–616.

That is an entirely different approach. (In fact, Edison stole the technology, but my point is the same: one way or another Edison had resolved to make a light bulb and he didn't allow 'failures' to hinder him; rather they helped him.) Our role as leaders (and teachers), if we are to see the kind of progress we aspire to, is to create a safe-to-fail working environment. A context in which the courage and creativity to have a go and do something differently is esteemed more highly than efficiently and reliably doing the same old, same old.

The famous Parable of the Talents (or the Parable of the Bags of Gold) makes the same point in Matthew 25:14–30. After delegating various degrees of responsibility to three employees (situational leadership in action), the 'master' returns to take account of the outcome (ROWE!). The most junior employee gives his account:

> Then the man who had received one bag of gold came. 'Master,' he said, '*I knew that you are a hard man,* harvesting where you have not sown and gathering where you have not scattered seed. *So I was afraid and went out and hid your gold in the ground.* See, here is what belongs to you.'
>
> His master replied, 'You wicked, lazy servant! So you knew that I harvest where I have not sown and gather where I have not scattered seed? Well then, you should have put my money on deposit with the bankers, so that when I returned I would have received it back with interest.
>
> 'So take the bag of gold from him and give it to the one who has ten bags. *For whoever has will be given more, and they will have an abundance. Whoever does not have, even what they have will be taken from them.*'[8]

The final verse here summarises the Matthew effect: those who have will be given more. The question is, why? Certainly, the master in this story could be deemed responsible for not having created an adequately safe-to-fail work environment, or we could blame the employee for being excessively risk averse, but either way the point remains that fear of failure inhibits growth. When, as leaders or employees, we embrace the risk

8 See https://www.biblegateway.com/passage/?search=Matthew+25%3A14-30&version=NIV. Italics mine.

of failure and the potential mess it can create, we set ourselves up for an exciting and fruitful future.

Embracing change

As well as becoming comfortable with mess, the other component of brave leadership is becoming comfortable with not being needed. Are you secure enough in your identity to be happy for those in your team to become better than you in certain disciplines, perhaps going further or accomplishing more than you, safe in the knowledge that you, as their mentor, provided the context and direction that enabled them to fly?

As I write, my eldest daughter has just today turned 18. I've seen this day in my mind's eye for some time and I've been dreading it. Of course, nothing significant has changed on this particular day; rather, the past year and the year ahead have been and will be a period of transition. There are so many things for which she no longer needs me. However, I know that this is good and that had I clung to my controlling instincts it would have led to one of two outcomes. Either I would have limited her potential by creating an excessive dependency on me, or I would have provoked a rebellion that would damage our relationship as she pulled away from me. Both possibilities – stifle their growth or lose them – are played out in schools and organisations around the world every day.

In coping with this transition, I have learned that the better approach is to get comfortable with change. It's not that she doesn't need me any more, it's that she needs me in a different way. Yes, in a less dependent, less central, less intensive way, but no less important or significant. The dynamic has and will continue to change.

Change is good. There are many seasons to our lives, not just four. Each season has blessings and frustrations. Enjoy the blessings of the season you are in, but also embrace the changing seasons in the knowledge that they do not represent an ending or demise but a natural cycle of growth. Winter is necessary. It is not less valid or vital than spring or summer.

The growth and maturing of your teams and ventures is natural and good. The effective farmer reads the seasons and works with them to his or her advantage. Twelve months of relentless harvest would be horrendous and lead to an early grave.

Meaningful praise

Throughout this process of nurture and development, the leader's role is to provide feedback and advice. We know this and aspire to this in the classroom too: the evidence is clear that feedback is the most significant factor affecting progress. How ironic, then, that we don't prioritise quality feedback in our staff teams and leadership structures. How much we acknowledge and offer feedback to those we lead has a massive effect on their motivation and can help to establish a safe-to-fail work environment which emphasises incremental growth rather than a fixed mindset.

Here are six rules for 'wise praise' from Professor Barry Hymer:[9]

1 'Praise the effort, not the "ability".' Praising ability reinforces a fixed mindset and undermines perseverance.

2 'Praise in specifics, not generalities.' If you want to see the behaviour repeated and improved, people need to know exactly what it was they did well. Vague praise is void of content.

3 'Praise privately.' Affirming someone's contribution can be counterproductive when done publicly, either leading to embarrassment for the individual or resentment from others.

4 'Praise authentically, and not too much.' Gushing words used liberally lose their impact and credibility.

5 'Praise "now that", not "if then".' Praise and reward offered after the event doesn't undermine the intrinsic motivation of the individual. 'If then' leads back to extrinsic carrots, which stifle creativity.

9 B. Hymer, How to Encourage Chessplayers (or Why Feedback Trumps Praise and Reward). Speech delivered at the 4th London Chess Conference, Kensington Olympia, 10 December 2016. Programme materials available at: https://londonchessconference.com/wp-content/uploads/2017/02/Hymer-Praise.pdf.

6 'Praise behaviour, not the child.' Praising behaviour provides constructive feedback on what a person did well rather than reinforcing entity theory.

What I have sought to demonstrate in this chapter is that trusting people and creating a more positive, innovative and productive work culture does not mean throwing out all accountability or quality assurance. It means being open to new ways of doing things and it means being willing to feel uncomfortable and take risks. I have no doubt that the long-term impact of this approach will be exponentially greater than perpetuating our current hierarchical and excessively controlling systems. I also have no doubt that the working environments we nurture by believing in people and investing in them will be happy, healthy, thriving and exciting. The human march to greater freedom and justice will continue. Here's to being a part of it!

Chapter 10

The Wheel of Leadership: Being a Balanced Leader

In Chapter 1, I introduced the wheel of life – the components that need to remain in balance if the wheel is to keep on turning. I developed this idea with my wheel of teaching – the essentials that cannot be ignored if we are to keep teaching and keep teaching well. Similarly, leadership is multifaceted, and if you don't keep things in balance, you will easily veer off course and cause harm to yourself and those you lead, so here is my wheel of leadership (Figure 10.1).

Figure 10.1. The wheel of leadership

These eight components matter, and just as with the wheel of teaching, what matters most is that they are balanced rather than that a few of them are functioning 'perfectly'. Have a go at rating your leadership on each of the spokes as you did before. Here is mine at the time of my breakdown:

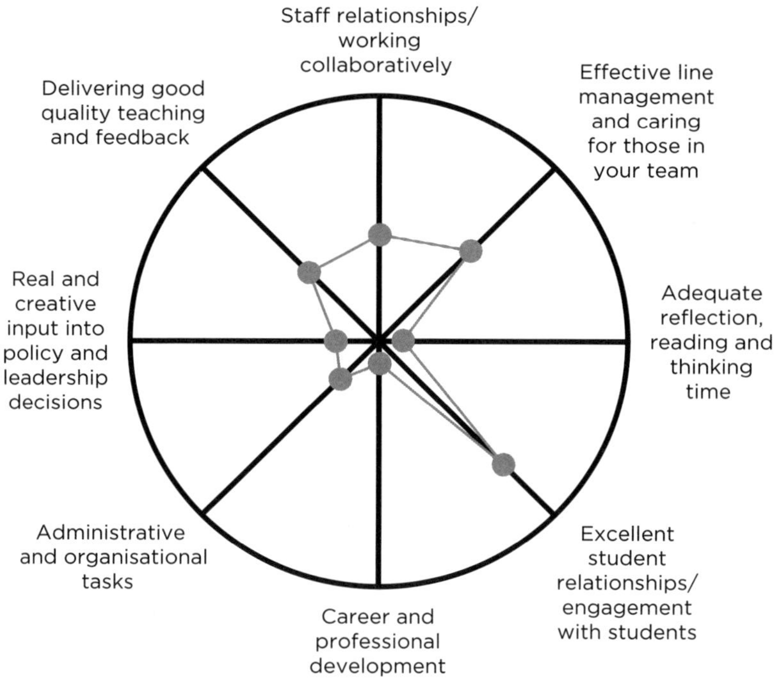

Figure 10.2. My wheel of leadership at the point of breakdown

Not good! There were essentially two things keeping me going: my students, whom I cared about deeply and had such a great relationship with, and those middle leaders I was line managing, whom I was trying my best to support and protect through a very difficult time. Everything else was on a downhill slide and had been for a while.

Let's have a look at each component in turn and explore why each one is essential.

Delivering good quality teaching and feedback

Most leaders in education are great classroom practitioners and this is usually one of the key reasons why they find themselves in a leadership position. However, since this is taken as a given and responsibilities in school multiply, it is extremely easy to get lazy about delivering high quality lessons.

As a leader, now with less contact time, you might find yourself without your own classroom. You will be coming from meetings or addressing day-to-day issues and then entering someone else's classroom, carrying a set of books, logging on to a different computer and preparing to launch into the delivery of an engaging lesson when your head may well be very much elsewhere. Of course, you know what you are teaching and you have got your resources ready beforehand, but it's extremely easy to get into a rut of delivering the same stuff in the same way. You haven't got the time to think afresh about how to make this lesson great or how to apply it to this particular class of students: you are on autopilot. For many leaders, their autopilot teaching mode means they haven't really developed as a practitioner for some time.

This is an issue of integrity – the quality of being whole and entire. Like a stick of Blackpool rock, no matter where you bite it, it has the word 'Blackpool' running all the way through it. It isn't Blackpool on the outside but Bognor on the inside. Who you are in front of those you lead needs to be the same as who you are behind closed doors, whether at home or on the football pitch, and definitely in the classroom. This is because:

- As a leader you should lead. It is difficult to lead teachers with integrity, push them on and help them to develop if you are not practising what you preach.
- As a leader you are probably expected to observe and appraise other teachers and/or their feedback to students. It is disingenuous to pass judgement on others if you are not demonstrating good practice yourself. You will feel like a fraud and lose credibility.

- Your ability to lead effectively in the classroom will affect your confidence and capacity to lead effectively outside the classroom. Every leader in education is (or should be) primarily a teacher, and every teacher is also a leader.

If you neglect your teaching, it will undermine your credibility and confidence as a leader. It is not a sustainable way to operate.

Action point

- Self-assess your teaching and feedback at the moment. What percentage of your lessons would you feel confident and proud of? When did you last try something new in the classroom? Read or attend something new on effective teaching and learning.

Staff relationships/working collaboratively

The psychological needs of belonging and feeling understood are hugely affected by the extent to which you feel valued as part of a team and feel comfortable leaning on the expertise of others when necessary.

Quick question: do you like and respect those you work closely with? If the answer is no, then the clock is already ticking. It is not healthy or sustainable to be working closely on a daily basis with people who either undermine you or whom you don't respect and value.

Here are some questions to help you to evaluate the strength and warmth of your working relationships:

- How often do you talk about non-work related matters?
- Do you know what is going on with each other's families/kids/other pressures?
- Is the team Christmas meal an ordeal or something you look forward to?

- Is the Christmas meal the only time in the year when you see each other in a non-work capacity?
- Are your meetings punctuated with laughter and friendly banter?
- Are birthdays and achievements acknowledged and marked?
- Do you dread team meetings or do you look forward to them?
- Do you find team meetings productive and effective or a waste of time?
- If your team knew what was going on in your head during the meeting would they be surprised, amused or offended?
- Are your contributions invited, considered and valued in team meetings?
- Does this team of people enable you to do your best work or do you feel stifled, undervalued and misunderstood?
- How often do you go home and moan to your husband/wife/partner about those you work with closely?

I could go on but these are a good starter. You are only as good as those you work with. If you feel like you are pulling against them, or they are pulling against you, then something needs to give – or else you need to find another team with whom you can work. It will be a major source of stress and will make you ill if you do not address it.

Action point

- Invite all those you work with closely to answer the questions above anonymously. What do the results tell you about the temperature of your working relationships? Have a discussion about the results.

Effective line management and caring for those in your team

Effective line management is a two-way thing. When it's good, it's good for you as well as those you lead; when it's bad, it's bad for both of you. Refer back to the discussion on employee engagement and situational leadership and control in Chapters 8 and 9. An effective leader draws the best out of those they lead and enables them, while an ineffective leader controls those they lead and debilitates them. The knock-on effect on both of you is direct:

Table 10.1. Controlling versus enabling leadership

Leader	Team
Controlling	Disabled
Enabling	Enabled

How does this affect workload and all those spinning plates?

Table 10.2. Effects of controlling versus enabling leadership #1

Leader	Team	Effect
Controlling	Disabled	**Low impact**
High workload	*High pressure*	
Enabling	Enabled	**High impact**
Healthy workload	*High competence*	

It is that simple. And yet I, for one, spent years doing and controlling far too much rather than enabling and developing others. I will add a couple more rows to this table just to spell it out more clearly:

Table 10.3. Effects of controlling versus enabling leadership #2

<table>
<tr><th>Leader</th><th>Team</th><th>Effect</th></tr>
<tr><td>Controlling</td><td>Disabled</td><td rowspan="2">Low impact</td></tr>
<tr><td>High workload</td><td>High pressure</td></tr>
<tr><td>Task focused</td><td>Devalued – a resource</td><td rowspan="2">Low innovation</td></tr>
<tr><td>Dysfunctional relationships</td><td>Low engagement</td></tr>
<tr><td>Enabling</td><td>Enabled</td><td rowspan="2">High impact</td></tr>
<tr><td>Healthy workload</td><td>High competence</td></tr>
<tr><td>Person focused</td><td>Valued – a partner</td><td rowspan="2">High innovation</td></tr>
<tr><td>Healthy relationships</td><td>High engagement</td></tr>
</table>

Simply put, the more you invest in developing those you lead and fostering a caring and collaborative work environment, the more that will translate into better outcomes for both you and your team – not to mention the students you are all intending to influence.

Action point

- Are you controlling and doing too much? Ask your team to rate how much they feel cared for, listened to and developed by you. Be prepared to act on the feedback.

Adequate reflection, reading and thinking time

Learning is not just what you sell; it is what you do. As soon as you stop doing it your integrity is undermined: you are selling something you don't believe in. You became a teacher (at least in part) because you believed in education and its power to change a life and thereby change the world. But did you then stop or slow your own learning? I certainly did. If we, as teachers, really believe in education – and believe in it not just for its efficacy in plugging the gaps in the capitalist machine but for its own sake – then how come we don't do it more?

Once I achieved qualified teacher status, I was never again encouraged to read another book on teaching and learning, or enrolled in another seminar on helping children to learn, or involved in one single leadership-level discussion about current (or any) thinking on behaviour management, education philosophy or how to motivate people – all of which have direct pertinence to what we all do as teachers on a daily basis. Surely, we don't really believe that we know everything there is to know about teaching, learning and education by the end of our teacher training?

Early on, I was sufficiently interested and insufficiently burnt out that I read some books of my own volition. They inspired me and made me want to be a better teacher, to change the system and to inspire others. Because that is what learning does – it inspires us and pushes us and enthuses us. We grow. And the desire to share that growth with others is what fuelled our desire to be teachers in the first place. This is so important that it should not be regarded as something only the 'keenies' do for bedtime reading. It should not be regarded as a luxury *if* you have the time. It should be part of what we do and what we are paid for.

As leaders we should all be involved in a programme of learning, reading and discussing to develop ourselves, each other, our practice and our schools. If we stop learning and pushing ourselves intellectually and practically, then we start regressing. We can't equip the next generation for the future if we are merely peddling the world we grew up in.

Action point

- The next SLT meeting agenda? Collectively read something new beforehand, then meet up and discuss!

Excellent student relationships/ engagement with students

The number one person in any school that I like to talk to are heads of sixth form. Why? Because they get to experience both worlds. As members of the SLT (in most schools), they tend to understand and appreciate all the pressures and frustrations of school leadership and system management, but at the same time they are hands-on and engaged with the day-to-day and longer term needs of young people. Head teachers have too often lost contact with students. They don't mean to, and it's entirely understandable because the job is immense. But, in my view, many are impoverished and less effective for missing out on that daily, life-at-the-chalk-face experience of helping students, one by one, through the daunting, difficult and messy journey of adolescence.

Every school leader needs to be working face to face with students. Not teaching a lesson or two here and there, but having your own class which you take through a whole course. And, if possible, running an extra- or co-curricular activity that gives you the chance to forge healthy relationships with students beyond the classroom – interactions that will keep you firmly in touch with the everyday reality of being a young person in the 21st century and that will provide you with the privilege of being a student's number one go-to adult when the going and the studying gets tough.

There is no such thing as a good teacher who has no students. No matter how many other things you have to do in a day, nothing is more important than continuing to be the teacher you set out to be. If you don't retain this aspect of being a leader, then very easily, and without realising it, students start to become data and young people become products, then school becomes a factory and teachers become an assembly line, and the dream of education dies.

Action point

- Take on a class, club or sports team and throw your all into those students.

Career and professional development

I discussed professional development in Chapter 2, so I won't repeat myself here. The key point is everyone needs to be moving towards mastery. It's part of being human to want to grow and develop, so where is your career going?

As we all know, the peculiarities of the education system often don't help. Many teachers who aspire to senior leadership also say, 'But I don't want to be a head. Maybe a deputy – that would suit me.' So a leader reaches their leadership goal and then stops there for the rest of their career. Maybe they move sideways or take on a different role within the SLT, and maybe this provides them with the sense of a new challenge, but it is more or less the same bag, just a different flavour. It isn't aspirational. And once you have fulfilled every single SLT role, then what?

We need to keep on developing. Always. Stagnation is a poison. But we don't need to associate developing with climbing a hierarchy. At the time of my breakdown I had engaged in zero professional development for three years. I was doing my job, and enjoying my job, for much of that time. My aspirations were being met through new and innovative projects for the school, but I wasn't developing as a practitioner or as a leader – at least, not in a deliberate sense – and, importantly, I had no one pushing me forward. I was firmly in control of my own development. This can be a problem because as human beings, even those of us who relish a challenge, we have an inbuilt bias towards our comfort zone and the kinds of activities we like and an aversion towards discomfort. Even if I challenge myself, I will do so in a way that I enjoy and that fits with what I want to do.

As teachers, we constantly set our students assignments that they fundamentally don't want to do. But it is an assignment and we require them to have a crack at it regardless of whether they want to or not. We do this because we know that it's good for them to try things they think they won't enjoy, and it's good for them to feel discomfort and then realise it's not so bad after all.

The same is true for you, which is why you need a teacher, a mentor or a line manager who is drawing you out of your comfort zone and pushing you to be better. The term 'line manager' is unhelpful if taken too literally. A good line manager is not just someone who gives you directives and to whom you report when you're done. A good line manager is a leader and a coach.

Who is coaching you? Who is urging you on? Who is pushing you to reach farther and higher? Does your line manager know what skills and experience you want to develop over the next year? Is there a plan in place for that? Have they challenged you about what you want and required you to do some things you don't want to do? Do you have a vivid picture of where you will be professionally in one year, three years or five years from now?

Action point

- Arrange to discuss your professional development with your line manager. Allow them to do a 360-degree appraisal and discuss your priority areas for development. Make a plan. Do the same for those you line manage.

Administrative and organisational tasks

As a leader you are a master organiser, so don't dumb down your achievements. You wouldn't be doing the job you are doing if you were not a master organiser. That doesn't mean you couldn't get better, but give yourself some credit: you manage a colossal number of big and little jobs that would leave much of the population utterly overwhelmed – and that's usually before period 1!

Most of us encounter two key issues when it comes to organisation:

1 **What needs doing.** The to-do list is never ending. The pace of school life, especially with the advent of email and other 'life-improving' technologies, seems only to be getting faster. Undoubtedly, there is a problem with workload, but we can often work smarter and cut out the unnecessary paperwork and bureaucracy. However, it is likely that the void will soon be filled because nature abhors a vacuum. As soon as you find a way to speed up the UCAS application system or automate the duty rota, some other task will absorb your administrative time. More significant, then, is how you respond.

2 **The way you respond.** You spend as much time on administrative tasks as you choose to – that is a fact. You are in control. You know this because there are some days when you don't do any admin. Whether due to your teaching load, meetings, an INSET, a day off sick or unforeseen circumstances, you get to the end of a day without reading or responding to a single email. And the world doesn't stop. Yes, your inbox is fuller the next morning, but as you go through your messages you will find that you can delete lots of them because they have already been dealt with or answered without your input.

   The fact that you can leave admin alone for one day at least demonstrates that you don't need to do it every day. You are choosing to do it every day, and that is important to notice because it will shape your approach to all admin. First, accept that you are in control of your admin time. Stop saying, 'I've just got to ...' No, you don't. You can choose whether and when to respond. Second, recognise and remember that sometimes you are an admin junkie: an inbox full of emails = people need me = dopamine spike.

So how can we address these two issues? Once you accept that you are in control, you can change the way you do admin forever. As a leader, it is your job to get out in front of the conversation and control it both in terms of time and content. Here are some suggestions:

- Send out information with adequate notice. By planning the release of information, you are controlling the timescale and managing anxieties. Recognise that many people get worried if they don't feel they have enough warning of changes. Make your expectations clear – what is needed and by when.

- Pre-empt questions and queries. A huge amount of emails could be avoided if we held off hitting 'send' and just reread the message or got a colleague to read it first and tell us what questions immediately spring to mind. This could be your biggest time-saver. Either rehash your message or add some FAQs with answers.
- Invite responses or questions. People need to feel that you are approachable and that you value their input but ...
- Clearly state when you will be free for queries. Fix a time when you will be available in person or online, and then set aside all responses in a folder until that time and deal with them in one go. Don't be dragged in by the temptation to respond to every email question. You are in control; however, ...
- Manage expectations. Obviously, you don't want people to think you are rude or ignoring them, so when you invite queries or questions, state at the same time when you will respond: 'I will get back to your query by Monday.'
- Wherever possible, reinforce the same messages in person, whether in a briefing or a meeting. Keep it face to face whenever you can.

Accepting that you are in control enables you to start running the show rather than letting the show run you. When it comes to admin and organisational tasks, you need to keep the purpose firmly in your mind. How are the tasks you need to do today going to improve the life of staff or students? Are you doing this for you or them? Stop letting your inbox run your life; get clarity over your purpose and use email as a tool to help you achieve it.

Action point

- Set and stick to fixed times of day for email and admin. Lead the conversations.

Real and creative input into policy and leadership decisions

Last, but by no means least, you need to own what you are implementing as a leader. This is important not only for the sake of your own integrity but also in order to be effective. You will not be successful if you do not believe in what you are asking your people to do. As soon as you feel disenfranchised, resentment will develop and you will not be able to do your best work. For this reason, clear communication between leaders is essential. If decisions have been made by the few without the input or sign-off from others in the team, then implementation will stall.

This was a major factor for me. As things deteriorated, I felt out of the loop, but I was still expected to be on board with policy decisions that I had not been consulted on. I became disengaged and found myself torn between my commitment and allegiance to those I managed and my sense of duty not to undermine other leaders. This was partly a communication issue but it was also an ideology issue. There were core differences between my philosophy and approach to education and that of other people in the team – and it is not an uncommon problem. If the team is not aligned ideologically (which doesn't need to mean identical but it does mean not contradictory), then it isn't going to be successful. It is like three people on a football team attempting to score in their own goal.

Ideology is important to all of us, but when does it ever get discussed? Are we pulling in the same direction towards the same goal? Do we each know what role we are playing? Have we all just got our heads down or are we communicating with each other? These are obvious but important questions.

Action point

- Discuss ideology as a team. Revisit it at least once a year and make time for an annual team development day to check you are working well together (see Chapter 11).

Leadership is all about balance. Which of these eight elements do you need to give some attention to? Each one has the potential to undermine your wellbeing if you ignore it.

Chapter 11

The Game-Changing Index: A Framework for Leading Dynamic Teams

When I was considering applying for a senior leadership post, I was given the opportunity to attend a one-day training course for aspiring or new senior leaders. It was the only formal training I was ever able to access. I have no idea who the trainer was, but I would like to credit him with two pieces of wisdom which struck me on the day and have stayed with me ever since. They are key to leading people effectively.

The first was a lyric from the 1982 hit by Fun Boy Three and Bananarama: 'It ain't what you do it's the way that you do it, and that's what gets results.' To some extent this is what I have been exploring throughout Part II on leadership. Leading anything is going to involve interaction with people, and people are strange and complicated creatures whose moods and whims are constantly changing. Whether you succeed or fail will be down to your students (whether they engage), your staff (whether they stay and follow), your students' parents and the community (whether they trust you). The way you present yourself to and interact with these people is critical. Undoubtedly, you have a fantastic team of staff and a school full of students with phenomenal potential, but if you can't motivate them and draw out their best, then their potential won't be realised. It's not what you do, it's the way that you do it.

The second point is related to the first. 'As a leader,' he said, 'if you're going to be effective in getting where you want to go, first you need to get the right people on the bus. Next, get the wrong people off the bus. Third, get the right people in the right seats.'[1] That is the way I remember it and how it struck me at the time, but I'm aware that it could be misinterpreted, so let me qualify first of all what I don't mean. When I refer to the 'wrong people', I certainly don't mean that in any ontological

1 I have since discovered that this concept comes from Jim Collins, *Good to Great: Why Some Companies Make the Leap … and Others Don't* (London: Random House, 2001).

sense. I believe wholeheartedly in the intrinsic value of every individual and in the potential of all to realise a unique destiny. And I also don't mean that leaders should engage in underhanded tactics to get rid of certain members of staff. (I remember hearing of a head who every day put a printout of job vacancies in other schools into the pigeonhole of a staff member he was trying to get rid of.) Bullying behaviour creates a culture of distrust, fear and one-upmanship and is entirely unacceptable.

What I do mean is this:

1 **Get the right people on the bus.** The 'right people' means people who want to get to the same destination as you. That is pretty much why people ride on the same bus. If everyone on the bus is fully committed to where you are going, you can really make some ground. What I certainly don't mean by 'right people' is people like you – as we shall see ...

2 **Get the wrong people off the bus**. If a bus is going north and some passengers want to go south, then they need to get off the bus! This is what I mean by 'wrong people'. If some of your team are constantly pulling in a different direction (as opposed to a different perspective), then it will be almost impossible to create a positive, healthy working environment.

3 **Get the right people in the right seats.** This is critical and has a bearing on the other two. If people are not in the right roles, then (a) they will not be maximally effective, (b) they will undermine the effectiveness of others and (c) they will slow or stunt the progress of a perfectly good team. I would hold that, in most cases – especially in the teaching profession, where there is a fairly clear ultimate objective – people who are underperforming are doing so because they are not in the right 'seat'. Their role is not aligned with who they are and therefore they are inhibited from doing their best work.

The first and second points both relate to direction and purpose. I referred in Chapter 6 to Simon Sinek's Golden Circle: what, how and why. Sinek suggests that 'People don't buy what you do, they buy *why* you do it.'[2] He is coming from a marketing background but his point is

2 S. Sinek, *Start with Why*, p. 42.

universally applicable. To make any kind of rapid progress, your people need to be on board with your destination, and that means they need to be crystal clear about why you are going there. Give proper time and attention to this from the outset and revisit it regularly. It will save you hours – or even weeks – of time and headaches.

Do you know your why? Most people can tell you *what* they do and they can tell you *how* they do it, but many don't have clarity over *why* they do it. Communicating your why to your staff and students is what provides the alignment, the collective momentum and the emotional wind that gives your school its soul. What is your why? And are you doing what you do because you believe in it? If it is just a job then you won't stay the course. When a better paid job comes along, you will take it, which means you are not committed to what you are doing. And if you are not committed, why should anyone else be?

Furthermore, if you don't believe in what you are doing, then your students will see that too – you lose authenticity. No one was ever inspired by box-ticking – doing something for the sake of it. Does your team know why they are doing what they are doing? Do they believe in it? When your school lives and breathes your why, you give your staff and students more than just a product or service, you give them a motive: a reason to invest, to engage and to follow.

The power of diversity

Matthew Syed analyses the significance of diversity in his book *Rebel Ideas*. Syed refers to perspective blindness: the fact that we all have a subjective view of the world and therefore a skewed perspective on reality. He describes a speech by David Foster Wallace which began with the story of two fish out for a morning swim. They encounter two older fish who duly greet them and politely ask, 'How's the water?' The two younger fish swim on for a bit until one says to the other, 'What the hell is water?'[3] This example makes a very salient point: that we each live within a context or mode of thinking, informed by an experience, an education and a set of influences, which together produce inherent bias.

3 M. Syed, *Rebel Ideas: The Power of Diverse Thinking* (London: John Murray, 2019), p. 31.

Usually, it is only someone different to us who can help us to see reality more clearly. Furthermore, when we gather teams of people around us who all share the same background, experience, education and so on, we end up with a collective blindness that doesn't merely stunt our progress but can be dangerous for our organisations and society as a whole.

Syed also cites a study at Columbia Business School in which teams were given the task of solving a murder mystery. In half the cases, the groups were composed of four friends. The other half were composed of three friends and a stranger. The result? The teams with a stranger consistently and significantly outperformed the teams without one. They also found the task more cognitively demanding as they were forced to engage with different perspectives and think more carefully in order to justify their own perspectives. They were able to see their own blind spots, which enabled them to find more effective solutions collectively.[4]

This has huge implications for the way we build and organise teams. Our natural tendency might be to hire people who are like us – we may even have an inherent tendency to do so (i.e. birds of a feather flock together) – but in a society which historically favours white, middle-class males, we thereby find ourselves blindly perpetuating the status quo. This type of homophily is everywhere, and if we aren't careful our systems and schools reinforce it further. Syed quotes a senior executive from a major bank:

> She told me how painful it was to see the company hire all these great college kids – all sorts of backgrounds; all sorts of ideas brimming in their heads – only to watch them gradually remoulded to 'fit' the culture of the organisation. They came with unique insights and voices. She heard those voices fade, unless it was to echo the company's 'accepted' way of thinking.[5]

As educators, we may believe that we actively seek to challenge our students' thinking. However, without realising it we ourselves conform to the culture of our schools, of our SLT, of our faculties. If, instead, we actively seek out diversity – and recognise, value and develop the varying strengths of our team members – then we will find ourselves far

4 Syed, *Rebel Ideas*, pp. 36–37.
5 Syed, *Rebel Ideas*, p. 74.

more adequately equipped to innovate, problem-solve and create a better future. And we will also be far more stimulated and engaged in the task.

The Game-Changing Index

This concept of recognising and valuing the varied contributions that different people can contribute leads me to the Game-Changing Index (GCI), which is a brilliant framework for identifying what constitutes a dynamic team and how to build one.

This assessment tool 'identifies individual and collective impact and how people contribute to the achievement of organisational goals'.[6] In other words, it isolates the ways in which an individual is likely to make the optimal impact within a team or organisation. This is distinct from a personality test. Personality tests can be useful and provide an insight into the way we understand the world and our motivations. The GCI, however, explores the ways we would prefer to make our own unique contribution.

The original study, led by clinical psychologist Dr John Mervyn-Smith, was designed to find out what makes a 'Game Changer' – those individuals who can drive transformational change, who approach a problem from an entirely different angle (think Dick Fosbury who revolutionised the high jump with his Fosbury Flop). Dr Mervyn-Smith's study found that Game Changers differentiate themselves when it comes to two particular constructs: imagination and obsession. They are the kinds of people who can generate imaginative ideas and view problems from outside the box. They will also have an obsessive drive to share their ideas and see them become reality. Game Changers take risks because they see the potential for loss in inaction – in not doing something – rather than action.

However, Game Changers also need others around them to realise their ideas. There is no such thing as a 'hero innovator'. For real change to occur we need game-changing teams: teams committed to breaking new ground and forging new realities, teams that recognise the value of each

6 J. Mervyn-Smith and N. Ott, *Coaching Me Coaching You … Ahaa* (London: GC Index, 2018), p. 24.

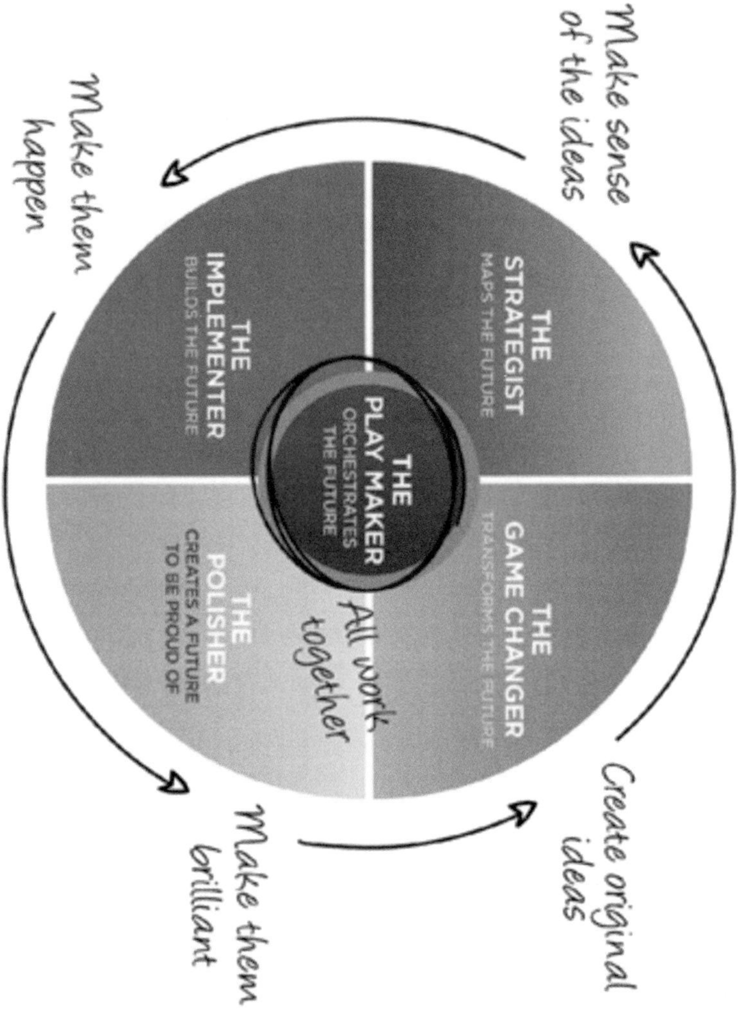

Figure 11.1. The aligned game-changing team

member and, critically, teams that enable each member to do their best work while drawing on and understanding the contribution of everyone else in the team.

Dr Mervyn-Smith identified four other team roles: Implementer, Strategist, Play Maker and Polisher (Figure 11.1).

Balance and diversity versus homophily

Most people have two strong proclivities: tendencies or inclinations that bring a distinct contribution to a task or leadership. Ideally, then, a dynamic team is one where there is a balance of these proclivities within the group or where the mix is suited to or aligned with the nature of the task. For example, a team full of Implementers may feel a degree of discomfort when working on a task which requires constant innovation or in a reactive job environment where it is very difficult to work through a list of tasks and tick them off. In contrast, Implementers are likely to feel more at home when performing a task with established expectations, parameters and clear outcomes.

That said, we should be careful about boxing people in too readily or using this model too prescriptively. Every Implementer is different and a person's profile should always be interpreted as a whole, as we shall see. In a school context, we often have the added challenge of a long-established system and expected outcomes that are beyond the control of the average leadership team. Each school is part of the big wheel of education, which is highly politicised and the product of a long-entrenched culture of hierarchical leadership structures and a post-industrial, mechanistic view of organisational structures. We can therefore unwittingly squeeze people into preconceived ideas of role and end up undermining their potential and productivity.

The founders of the GCI describe their underpinning philosophy in the following way:

> Human beings strive to be potent in their world. You only need to watch a toddler learning to walk to see this, the determination to get up, again and again, after falling down. The drive for potency

> and at times, mastery, is evident … What is clear is that people don't go to work to feel impotent. People thrive when they have a clarity of role and responsibility that allows them to make a valued contribution and impact … When natural inclinations are recognised, harnessed and focussed in the right way, people are at their most potent and valued at work.[7]

This goes to the heart of building mentally healthy working environments. Notwithstanding the staff perks, gym memberships, pension schemes and well-intentioned workload policies, if what is expected of you on a day-to-day basis is out of kilter with who you are as a person, then genuine wellbeing is likely to elude you. There will be an ongoing incongruity that damages your emotional wellbeing. As we saw in the introduction: 'Happiness is when what you think, what you say and what you do are in harmony.' I believe there is good reason to utilise the insights of the GCI to re-evaluate the way we do school at the moment, and think about how we lead our teams to ensure that we create school cultures that maximise and develop the contributions of each staff member.

Here is a brief summary of each team role.[8]

The Strategist

Strategists see patterns and trends. At their best, Strategists ask why and look for links between events and data. They like to see how the pieces of the jigsaw fit together and therefore always have an eye on the bigger picture. They tend to be logical and analytical. Strategists like to make sense of their world and are not so comfortable with chaos or arbitrariness. As leaders, they bring optimism and energy by formulating plans of action that help people to feel potent.

---

7 Mervyn-Smith and Ott, *Coaching Me Coaching You … Ahaa*, pp. 19–20.
8 This section has been adapted (with permission) from Mervyn-Smith and Ott, *Coaching Me Coaching You … Ahaa*, pp. 42–51.

The Game Changer

At their best, Game Changers see possibilities and potential that others don't. They engage with excitement about what might be possible. Their contribution to the world is that of transformational change rather than incremental change: they see what might be rather than wanting to improve or change what is. Game Changers have a need for creative expression and uncensored thinking; they rule things in rather than ruling them out. They don't feel constrained by what has gone before and can become obsessed with how things should be. Being free to express themselves is vital to their sense of wellbeing. As leaders, their single-minded nature may be seen as not being open to influence, but they lead through the power of ideas.

The Polisher

Polishers, at their best, embody the philosophy and practice of continuous improvement. They seek to set the standard for excellence within their role and organisation. They can take products, processes and procedures and constantly seek to improve them. Within any Polisher is a perfectionist nature. They derive energy and satisfaction from taking solutions and developing them to the point of excellence. Polishers will struggle to accept 'good enough'. They will be determined, tenacious and optimistic.

The Implementer

Implementers, at their best, get things done – they deliver. Their philosophy and practice is of practical, pragmatic problem-solving. They will often have a reputation as a safe pair of hands, as someone who can be relied on to get things done in a dependable way. They are outcome focused. In teams they will bring task-focused energy and urgency. Implementers are typically driven by the satisfaction that comes from tangible achievements. As leaders, Implementers will lead by example and demonstrate resilience, but they will also rely on others for ideas and direction.

The Play Maker

Play Makers, at their best, invest in their relationships at work. Their focus is on getting things done through the strength of their relationships and shared endeavour. They enable rather than delegate and take pleasure in seeing others shine. They are orchestrators and facilitators who like to get the very best from others. Play Makers are instinctive people gatherers who are happy for others to be in the spotlight. They tend to have a high degree of emotional intelligence and know what makes other people tick. Their inclination is to seek harmony in groups and manage conflict in a way that produces cohesion.

These brief summaries provide a flavour of the differences people bring to a team and just how important those differences can be. However, it is important to note the following:

- Each role can have a positive or negative expression. Without self-awareness and development, individuals with these defining characteristics can be very difficult to work with. We each have a responsibility to develop and broaden our skill set to be the best version of ourselves and to beware of how our tendencies can come across to others.
- To some extent we all need to develop our skills in all five of these roles. For example, it is not just the Play Maker's job to be emotionally intelligent and enable those they lead; every leader has a responsibility to do this. It is not just the Implementer's job to get things done; we all need to be more effective at realising targets.
- Leaders come in all shapes and sizes. Typically, people might associate leadership with the role of the Strategist or Play Maker. In fact, someone with any variation of these proclivities may be in a leadership position and be a very effective leader. But their tendencies will shape what kind of leader they are and how well they lead those in their teams (see Figure 11.2).

The GCI helps to identify not so much what job you should do, but rather what kind of activity and focus within a given job will energise and excite you rather than debilitate and frustrate you. It might

Figure 11.2. Multidimensional leadership

be interesting to reflect on leaders you know of and what their multidimensional leadership style might be. An example of a charismatic leader might be Richard Branson, while Gandhi might be more of a leader as coach, James Dyson an inventive leader, and so on.

Application

In this section, I will explore how the GCI helped me and what I think its implications might be for the way we lead in school.

My profile (note: 10 is the highest score in any one role and 1 is the lowest) is displayed in Figure 11.3.

When GCI co-founder Nathan Ott saw my profile, the first thing he said was, 'Gosh – how did you stay in education for so long with a profile like that?' He had no idea how apt his statement was! This was about a year and a half after my breakdown.

I have a low Implementer score. For me, this means that I struggle with being task focused, especially if I don't believe in the purpose of the task. I very quickly get bored or frustrated when performing the same jobs, even when doing them well, if I am not moving forward towards a bigger goal. Tasks that essentially maintain the status quo are utterly debilitating.

I have a low Play Maker score too. I have developed my emotional intelligence considerably over the years and practised most of what I have preached in this book, but I cannot avoid the fact that I am more energised and excited by the future, and by polishing new ideas, than I am about developing other people. That doesn't mean I don't do it; it's just that I have to discipline myself to remember to do it and seek help from others in doing so.

My two highest proclivities are Strategist and Polisher, and I also have a high Game Changer score. As a Strategist/Game Changer I have spent my life asking why. From pre-school onwards, I was climbing what I shouldn't climb, crossing boundaries, arguing with authority and questioning rules. If I saw no purpose in a rule, it seemed obvious to me to challenge it or ignore it. Later on, I would sit in SLT meetings thinking,

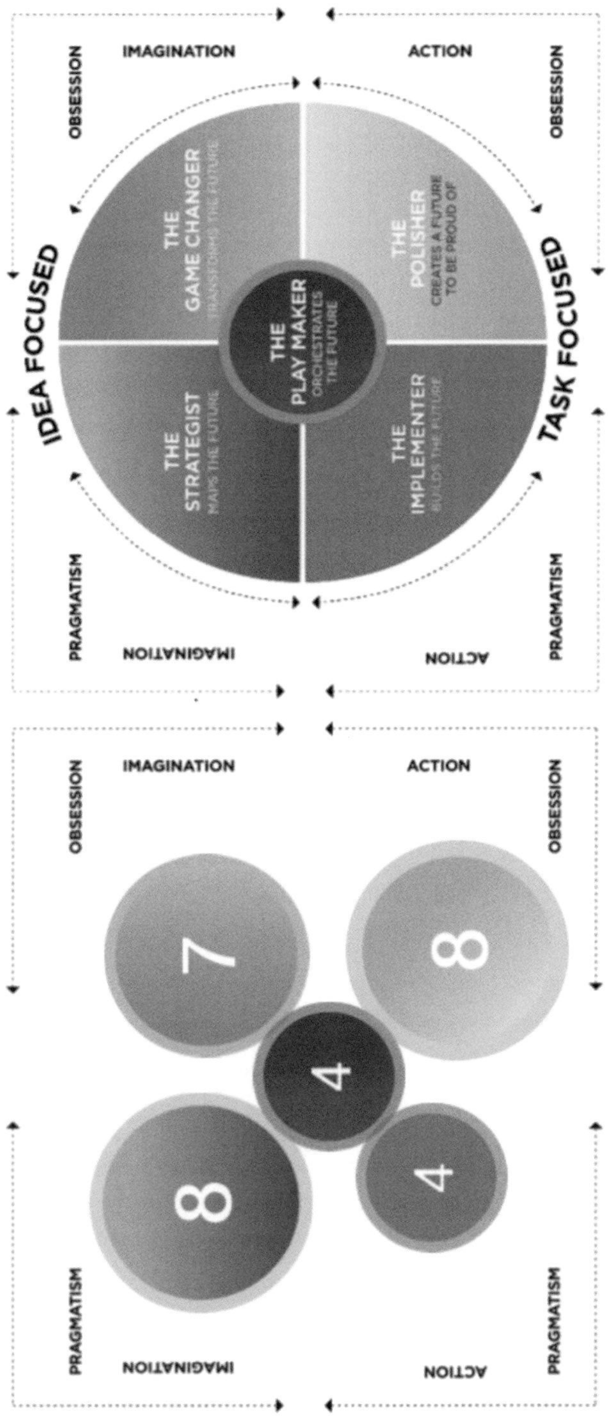

Figure 11.3. My GCI profile

'Why are we doing this? Why don't we do it like that? Why don't we change it all? Why can't we change this? Why are we doing that?' I would be looking at the big picture – at where we wanted to get to. If the purpose was unclear, or if I couldn't see how the task in front of me contributed to that purpose, I would zone out from boredom and frustration. I was excited to lead on whole-school initiatives like the Rights Respecting Schools Award, student voice and the personal, social, health and economic (PSHE) education programme. I could see the purpose and I loved bringing various aspects together in a plan. I also enjoyed the rare opportunity to brainstorm new possibilities or ideas.

All my life I have been labelled as disruptive, argumentative, rebellious, opinionated, difficult and even heretical. These are all very negative terms. I never sought to be disruptive or rebellious. I was just seeing the world differently. I was pursuing the truth as I saw it with passion and fervour. I couldn't understand why people saw things differently. Fundamentally, I valued freedom, so any attempt to confine, stifle or limit that freedom, without good reason, was met with resistance.

As a Polisher, I am relentlessly committed to excellence, to the point that I have often found it difficult to trust others with projects I care about. In the past, as a teacher and leader my Polisher nature led me to take on too much and control too much. I sought to reach an unattainable standard; in part the product of my religious upbringing but also this was in my nature. Unfortunately, I would then be unswervingly harsh with myself if I did not meet this standard.

In short, I was living out my GCI profile but without the self-awareness, understanding or guidance in place to utilise my strengths for the best and mitigate my weaknesses.

Now take this profile and place it within the education system we have in the UK:

- The Groundhog Day cycle of the academic year: new classes, parents' evenings, reporting deadlines, marking and feedback cycle, revision and exam prep, planning for next year, summer holidays.
- A system that measures (properly) only one narrow aspect of what we do.
- A stringently timetabled day from which no one can deviate.

- A stringently timetabled year with zero flexibility.
- Leadership that, in my experience, is concentrated on perpetuating the status quo – albeit in the hope of improved outcomes – but with little or no appetite for real, systemic change.
- A system so politicised that new directives and changes are not only ever changing but are usually thought up by politicians rather than teachers and educationalists.
- An approach to target setting and data that is logically incoherent and therefore unattainable. Unless as a school you get your 'best results ever' you have failed, and since no school can logically continue to get the 'best results ever' year on year, we are all doomed to fail repeatedly.

I am not suggesting that someone with a profile like mine should not be a teacher. My point is that every teacher is different and every leader is different. An Implementer/Polisher teacher is going to be very different to a Game Changer/Play Maker teacher. But very often our schemes of work, specifications, timetables, feedback policies and meeting schedules do not allow for this. Similarly, a Strategist/Implementer head teacher is going to be very different to a Game Changer/Polisher head teacher.

There are other implications for teaching and leading:

- Strategist teachers will struggle to get on board with short-sighted directives or approaches that lack a robust rationale. Disparate initiatives or practices that lack clarity and direction will generate frustration and disconnection. A lack of opportunity to express or question leadership will lead to low engagement.
- Game Changer teachers are likely to get demoralised very quickly if required to do things in a certain way or conform to set processes. They don't want to run their classroom in the same way every day or churn out the same stuff. Given insufficient freedom they are likely to go rogue or find unhelpful ways to express their creative energy.
- Polisher teachers are likely to struggle with the sheer breadth of the teaching role because it prevents any one role or task being completed to a sufficiently high standard. Polishers will work

long into the night to try to cope with this tension and are prime candidates for burnout or leaving the profession.

- Implementer teachers may thrive on the busyness of the role but are likely to be frustrated by the reactive nature of school life and the difficulty of seeing many tasks through to a concrete conclusion. The intangibles of working with people are various, so without meaningful measures of progress and acknowledgment of the varied aspects of teaching, Implementers will gravitate towards tasks they can see the effects of (like writing a scheme of work) and avoid the more nebulous ones (like chatting with a student after the lesson).
- Play Maker teachers are likely to struggle if the team dynamic or atmosphere is lacking. Locked away in a classroom all day without opportunities for interaction with colleagues or enriching staff relationships, Play Makers will find their enthusiasm draining away. Excessive administrative tasks or a focus on process rather than outcome will chip away at their energy levels.

No matter what our position in a team or school, there are a number of implications for how we go about what we do. First, we need to understand each other. This means having self-awareness of ourselves as individuals and as line managers, understanding what energises and excites us and those we lead, recognising what tasks and aspects of the role will bring frustration, maximising the interrelation of the different proclivities in the team and celebrating those differences. We need to move away from a simplistic understanding of equality as everyone doing the same amount of the same stuff, to everyone being expected to add value to the team while also acknowledging that we all bring different skills.

Second, we need to adopt a personalised approach to teaching. We talk of personalised learning (i.e. adapting learning to meet the needs of each individual student) but in recent years, often in the name of 'raising standards', there has been a move away from personalised teaching. We should allow teachers to teach and feed back in the way that best suits them. This doesn't necessarily mean the abandonment of all generic policies and procedures, but it does mean a fundamental acceptance that one size does not and never will fit all. To do this effectively and avoid carnage, we will need to take a situational leadership approach. Some teachers want the certainty and security of being told what to do, when to do it and how to do it, and that is fine. But if we adopt that same approach with other teachers, we will kill the very lifeblood of their passion and lose them from the profession, either literally or emotionally. One way or another, they will disengage.

Third, we should be designing our teams around the people we have, not the tasks that need to be done. Occasionally I have seen SLT job opportunities advertised like this:

> Post: Deputy head teacher
>
> Responsibilities: To be agreed in light of experience and skill set of the successful applicant and in discussion with the head teacher.

This is the way we need to go. But it is not the simplest way to go, and it is why many don't go that way. The simplest thing to do when your deputy head pastoral leaves is to advertise for a replacement deputy head pastoral. But no matter who you appoint, they won't be the same – and nor should they be. You invite headaches down the road if, from the very outset, you fail to look at the person in front of you, identify their skill set and proclivities, and design a job that will utilise them in achieving your outcomes.

I recommend that we look seriously at the organisational design of our schools. It might be a useful exercise to contemplate what a leadership team would look like based on the proclivities identified by the GCI. Compare the task-based leadership model in Figure 11.4 with the person-focused leadership model in Figure 11.5.

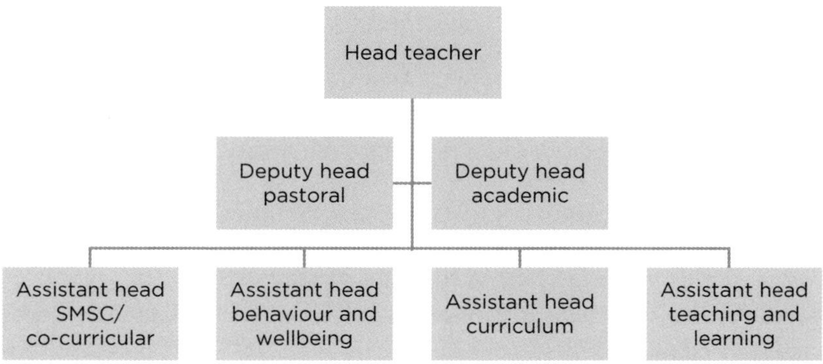

Figure 11.4. Task-based leadership model

Figure 11.5. Person-focused leadership model

The person-focused model is, of course, an oversimplification. The fact is that every area of school life needs creativity and innovation as well as organisation and quality assurance. My purpose here is to raise the question of what a leadership team might look like if we abandoned hierarchy (even the word 'head' is unhelpfully autocratic and top down) and replaced it with flat, person-focused structures. By focusing tasks around people, rather than people around tasks, perhaps we could create staff teams that flourish and take our schools in directions we never previously dreamed possible. The way it is now is not the way it has to be.

Regardless of which way you go with these ideas, I recommend using an assessment tool like the GCI as part of your recruitment process so that you can appoint and discuss the job in question with a candidate's profile in mind.

Back to my bus analogy: if the right people (those on board with your destination and purpose) are in the right seats (released to do what they do best), then your team is going to change the game. And it will be a massively enjoyable ride!

Chapter 12

Managing Chimps: Keys to Effective Leadership

'All behaviour is communication.' I came across this statement while assessing a special school for Unicef's Rights Respecting Schools Award. Mountjoy School in Dorset caters for children aged 4–18 with severe learning difficulties. Many of the students are unable to communicate verbally – however, at Mountjoy this does not impede their right to 'express their views, feelings and wishes in all matters affecting them, and to have their views considered and taken seriously'.[1] Instead, the school proactively 'listens' to the non-verbal communication of all its students, recognising that all behaviour is communication.

When a child behaves in a way that is unacceptable, instead of addressing the external behaviour and imposing a disciplinary measure, staff are trained to seek to identify what the child is trying to communicate by his or her behaviour, however inappropriately, and address this. For example, when a child was in distress and exhibiting violent behaviour, he was asked where he would like to go to calm down and which toy he would like to take with him. His voice was not denied and, by giving him some control and respecting his rights, he was able to regain his composure and staff were able to identify that his agitation was prompted whenever he felt unsafe. His behaviour was an unconscious attempt to control his environment.

What a shame that we don't readily take the same approach in all our dealings with other people. It is well documented that only 7% of communication is verbal, and of the 93% that is non-verbal, 38% is tone of voice and 55% is body language – our behaviour.[2] Just as the folding of the arms or legs during conversation can communicate defensiveness or discomfort, so when staff or students are regularly late, for example,

1 Article 12 of the UN Convention on the Rights of the Child – see https://www.unicef.org.uk/what-we-do/un-convention-child-rights.

2 N. Belludi, Albert Mehrabian's 7-38-55 Rule of Personal Communication, *Right Attitudes* (4 October 2008). Available at: https://www.rightattitudes.com/2008/10/04/7-38-55-rule-personal-communication.

they are communicating something. It might be that they are expressing disengagement or disorganisation or perhaps something more serious, such as that they are not coping with a dysfunctional home life. The knack of a great leader and teacher is to read between the lines of behaviour and address the causal factors, rather than merely sanctioning the symptom.

Sanctions will motivate up to a point; however, deterrents seldom change attitudes at a core level. They may achieve compliance but never engagement. And that is what you really want, whether as a teacher or a leader: for your people to be engaged, to be with you, to be fully on board with your mission, whatever that may be.

Parenting is again a great analogy for all our relationships. When my kids are wilful or rude or ignore my wishes, they are not trying to be obnoxious. They are not getting a kick just out of irritating me. Their behaviour is communication. My daughter's occasional rudeness and seeming inability to see my point of view is not maliciously motivated; it is an expression of the fact that she feels constrained, is desperate for some freedom and thinks that I can't see her point of view. My youngest son is often loud and annoying to his brother and sister, not because this is his aim in life but because he is seeking to assert himself and find affirmation as the youngest in the family. In both cases, the 'cure' is unlikely to be sanctions; rather, it is to help them find what they are looking for in a positive way.

Basically, what people communicate through their behaviour is the extent to which their six psychological needs are being met. It is your job as a leader, then, to create a safe and inclusive school culture that seeks to acknowledge and, if possible, address those psychological needs. Fundamentally, people feel safe where there is trust. Your effectiveness as a leader will be in direct proportion to the degree to which you are trusted by those who follow you.

The essential characteristics of a leader

In *The Leadership Challenge*, James Kouzes and Barry Posner summarise the conclusions of a data-gathering exercise which took place over two decades and six continents into the characteristics of admired leaders. Consistently over time, four traits have received over 50% of the votes: for people to follow someone willingly that leader must be honest, forward-looking, competent and inspiring.[3]

- **Honesty.** The extent to which people believe you correlates directly with the extent to which they believe *in* you. How transparent are you with those you lead? Do they know that you are a person of your word? People tend to mirror each other and will be as open with you as you are with them. Nobody wants to be taken for a mug. Dishonesty will generate distrust.
- **Forward-looking.** The whole point of following a leader is because you have some confidence that they know which way they are going. Do you have clarity about your direction and purpose? Leaders who fail to communicate their vision and are caught up with the day-to-day will lose the commitment of their followers.
- **Competence.** People want to know that you have experience and expertise that qualifies you to lead. Do those who follow you have confidence in your capabilities to do your job well? Are you in control (in a good way)?
- **Inspiration.** People will willingly follow, and even die for, someone who inspires them. This usually comes down to the degree of passion and self-sacrifice they exhibit. The example of Jesus washing his disciples' feet is a timeless example of inspirational leadership.[4] People who challenge norms and assumptions by demonstrating humility and service for others ignite passion in others. Bottom line: do people want to be like you in some regard?

3 J. M. Kouzes and B. Z. Posner, *The Leadership Challenge: How to Make Extraordinary Things Happen in Organizations* (San Francisco, CA: Jossey-Bass, 2003), p. 25.
4 See John 13:1–17.

All four of these characteristics relate to the credibility of the leader and how much he or she is trusted. Trusted to tell the truth. Trusted to know where they are going. Trusted to know what they are doing. Trusted to overcome the struggles and obstacles ahead. A lack of trust in any of these areas generates anxiety and undermines our sense of wellbeing.

So, how do we build trust? Frances Frei and Anne Morriss of Harvard Business School identify three key components to trust:[5]

1 **Empathy.** If I don't feel that you understand and identify with my perspective, and if I don't feel that you have really listened, then I am unlikely to trust you.

2 **Authenticity.** If I don't feel you are being your authentic self, if I feel like this is an act and there is a lack of integrity, then I won't trust you.

3 **Logic.** If I don't get why you are doing what you are doing or you have not communicated your logic and reasoning to me effectively, then I will be less likely to trust you.

Nailing these three components requires some serious self-understanding about how we all function as emotional beings.

You, your chimp and all the chimps around you

Steve Peters, in his brilliant book *The Chimp Paradox*, explains in simple terms how the human brain works.[6] He refers to the three main psychological 'brains' as:

1 The human (the frontal lobes) – the rational centre.

2 The chimp (the limbic system or amygdala) – the emotional centre.

5 F. Frei and A. Morriss, Begin with Trust, *Harvard Business Review* (May–June 2020). Available at: https://hbr.org/2020/05/begin-with-trust.

6 S. Peters, *The Chimp Paradox: The Mind Management Programme to Help You Achieve Success, Confidence and Happiness* (London: Random House, 2012), chs 1–2. This chapter represents a very brief summary of Steve Peters' insights – I recommend that you read his book in full.

3 The computer (the parietal lobe) – the information centre.

The human and the chimp developed in the womb. The computer consists of all the thoughts and information we have uploaded into our brain since birth.

Peters suggests that the 'chimp', your emotional hard drive, is preprogrammed to respond to situations emotionally. The feelings generated in the limbic system can be extremely powerful and often overwhelming. They have the power to hijack all other aspects of the brain and body. They trigger our inherent survival instincts of fight, flight or freeze. We all have a chimp which thinks very differently to the human. It cannot rationalise or consider (that is what the human does). It reacts. In threatening situations the chimp can keep us alive, but in the day-to-day running of a school or classroom (or family) the chimp is usually unhelpful. It is like a child and should not be trusted to make decisions. It jumps to conclusions, it sees things in black and white, it is paranoid, irrational and lacks perspective. It also has certain compelling drives that shape its responses, such as territory, power, ego, sex and parental instinct. In short, the chimp must be managed.

The human, on the other hand, is evidence based, rational, understands context, perspective and grey areas, and is capable of reaching balanced judgements. Problems arise because the chimp and the human have different agendas which are not always aligned. Additionally, if we don't have this self-awareness then we can find ourselves hijacked by the chimp, making decisions based on emotion without recognising it and being blind to other people's perspectives. This is a recipe for disaster and will result in highly dysfunctional teams.

There are three steps to managing your chimp:[7]

1 **Recognise who is in charge.** Peters observes: 'The golden rule is that whenever you have feelings, thoughts or behaviours that you do not want or welcome, then you are being hijacked by your chimp.'[8] Very simply, ask yourself, 'Do I want these feelings or thoughts? Do I want to be behaving this way?' If the answer is no, then you are in chimp mode.

7 Peters, *The Chimp Paradox*, ch. 3.
8 Peters, *The Chimp Paradox*, p. 40.

2 **Understand and accept how the brain works.** All information goes to the chimp first. If new information upsets the chimp then it is likely to react in line with its survival instincts and basic drives. The chimp will make an offer, a suggestion on how to respond, but it's down to the human to either accept or reject that offer. The human is responsible for the chimp. You cannot blame your chimp or change your chimp, but you can manage it.

3 **Nurture then manage the chimp.** Nurturing the chimp means creating opportunities for the chimp's needs to be met and an environment in which the chimp feels safe and valued. Sport, food, space and acknowledgement all help to achieve this. As we have already seen, the critical factor in establishing a safe, positive and nurturing environment is leadership.

This way of understanding how the brain works is hugely helpful on an individual level in terms of managing our own emotions and responses to everyday situations. It has certainly helped me to recognise why I am feeling certain things at certain times and how to prevent my emotions (my chimp) from leading me towards unhealthy behaviours and damaging my relationships. However, since everyone has a chimp, we are interacting all day, every day with other chimps. Understanding how the chimp works and how to manage it, therefore, will undoubtedly make us more trusted and effective leaders. Recognising when you are dealing with a person's chimp and when you are dealing with their human will affect your response. In addition, keeping your own chimp in check will help those you lead to feel safe and avoid destructive confrontations in school with both students and staff.

Nurturing and managing chimps

I have already discussed at length the sort of working environment conducive to helping people do their best work. The environment and culture we create goes a long way to helping the chimp feel secure and providing an outlet for emotion when necessary. These environmental and structural factors form the 'cage' (think back to Rat Park in Chapter 5). If the cage is nurturing and provides adequately for most of our needs, if it feels safe and secure, then when an unforeseen event takes place we are more likely to cope better and manage our chimp response. If the cage is not nurturing, then we find ourselves living in a more or less constant state of alert. Anxiety is at the fore and our chimp is not just ready and waiting to react, it is actually seeking out threat proactively. Our stress bucket capacity is reduced and we may turn to unhealthy coping mechanisms in order to self-medicate.

Take Richard, for example. Richard is a newly qualified teacher who has not been adequately nurtured. Not only is he trying to adapt quickly to a whole raft of systems and procedures with which he is unfamiliar, but his line manager often seems grumpy. Richard is struggling with behaviour in some of his classes, the atmosphere in the faculty office is unfriendly, he has had no feedback on his progress so far, and certain programs on his computer aren't working but the ICT technician has been rather curt and said that he won't be able to get to it until next week. And, to top it all, a member of SLT 'drops in' on his lesson with a Year 9 bottom-set with whom he is struggling.

The lack of a supportive environment means that the SLT drop-in makes Richard's chimp scream with anxiety and head home feeling all sorts of emotions: he is upset, annoyed with Year 9, frustrated with himself and angry with the ICT technician. He believes he is failing, useless, disliked and so on. These emotions might be expressed later on in the reckless way he drives or at home with his partner. Or he may snap at or react sharply to Jenny. Jenny is a fellow NQT in a much more nurturing team who seems to be managing much better than Richard. In turn, Jenny's chimp reacts: 'How dare you snap at me? I haven't done anything wrong!' She makes a throwaway comment, 'Maybe you should be a bit more organised!' and walks off. Now, two chimps are upset and this will have a knock-on effect on the way they each deal with all the other people and challenges that come their way that day. I'll call this the 'chimp effect'.

The implications for a workplace requiring a high degree of personal interaction (like a school) is huge. Certainly, we can minimise the chimp effect by giving time and attention to developing nurturing cultures and environments which address people's basic needs. However, even in the most supportive environment there will be circumstances that aggravate the chimp in each of us. As a leader, it is your job to both manage your own chimp and the chimps in your team by exercising, boxing and feeding the chimp.

Exercise the chimp

Exercising the chimp means providing an appropriate opportunity for the chimp to express its emotions without interruption or judgement. This can be done in your scheduled line meetings, but it will also require you to be sufficiently emotionally aware to pick up on tone, body language and comments, as well as checking in on those you lead whenever you have an inkling that something isn't right – or just checking in as a matter of daily routine. Asking astute questions will usually tease out what may be troubling someone. Some of the issues will be addressed just by listening and others you may be able to solve on their behalf. Key questions include:

- How was your day?
- Tell me how your Year [X] was today.
- Tell me how you're feeling about …
- On a scale of 1–10, how on top of things do you feel?
- Have you got everything you need for tomorrow?
- Is there anything else that would be helpful for me to do/for you to have?

You will need to ask some of these questions more than once because the chimp will want to know that you definitely care before it tells you the truth. Richard's chimp, for example, probably needs to be reassured that none of his answers will be used against him. Remember, the chimp is particularly sensitive to threat, so Richard doesn't want to appear weak unless he feels safe. Once the chimp has shared its emotion, it will be in a much calmer state to engage with its own human and your human. Be careful not to take Richard's rant personally; some of what he says might rouse your own chimp if you feel that some of his assertions are unfair. Let him exercise his chimp fully.

Box the chimp

To put the chimp back in its box, the human can use facts, truth and logic. Having listened to Richard expressing how he feels, you are in a place to respond and he is in a place to engage. You can now confront him with three 'truths':

> It's very early days in your teaching career. The head teacher commented to me just the other day how well you have settled in. I overheard one of your students saying that they really liked your lessons.

These are all facts that Richard needs to hear, especially from you as his line manager or mentor.

> No one finds the first year of teaching easy. There's a huge amount to learn and no one expects you to get everything right first time. Give yourself time.

This makes sense to Richard. He can see that he is putting undue pressure on himself.

> You will get more confident in all of these areas as time goes on. The SLT drop-in was routine and she knows that class is a difficult one. We can work together on strategies to manage them.

Richard's chimp is now firmly boxed. His emotions are back in check. He can see the light ahead and feels more in control. His human is able to reinforce this perspective and the balance that he has heard from you. He feels understood and acknowledged. He is in a much stronger position to plan and teach well the next day.

Feed the chimp bananas

Bananas are either distractions or rewards. They don't usually solve the problem but they can be useful for managing the chimp.

First, we can employ distractions, or rapid patterns of actions, that thwart negative thinking. In many ways schools offer endless distraction: the pace of the school day means that many little things that might have been big things for your chimp are put to one side. However, the danger is that these niggles build over time, and if the underlying causes are not addressed then at some point it will have an adverse impact on our overall emotional wellbeing and ability to perform effectively.

Second, we can reward or praise. Again, this won't tackle the underlying issue. But if we can create a culture in which we affirm more than we criticise and we acknowledge effort and outcomes more explicitly and regularly, then the chimp will be able to wait longer (at least until the next line meeting) in order to say what it really thinks, without this undermining wellbeing and performance in the meantime.

Building trust

Let me return to my statement at the outset of this chapter: all behaviour is communication. Hopefully this makes more sense in light of the understanding we now have about the chimp. How we read those we lead is essential for the wellbeing of our teams and schools. Hopefully, this insight also reinforces the three components of trust identified by Frei and Morriss and how you can foster each one:[9]

1 **Empathy.** Your commitment to hear and understand the concerns and anxieties of those you lead is essential. You need to listen so that your colleagues can exercise their chimp without fear of judgement or interruption in a safe and accepting environment.

2 **Authenticity.** Your honesty and openness about your own strengths and weaknesses, as well as your commitment to be open about your own feelings (your chimp) in an appropriate manner, means that those you lead can relate to you. It makes you approachable. It means they offload on you appropriately, rather than internalising it and then offloading it inappropriately in the staffroom or at home. Your willingness to acknowledge your own shortcomings is crucial if your competency is to be recognised. This may seem like a contradiction but it isn't. Many mistakenly believe that in order to be seen as competent they must show no weaknesses and appear invincible. The problem is that you do have

9 Frei and Morriss, Begin with Trust.

weaknesses and you are not invincible, which means that on some days and in some respects you are not going to be able to pull off a convincing display of competence. If you have over-egged your ability in a certain area people will see it, and that will undermine their confidence in your competence in all areas, since they now do not trust you to be honest.

3 **Logic.** Frei and Morriss point out that there are two issues here: the quality of your logic and the communication of your logic. If you are taking a certain course of action, provided that your chimp has not hijacked you, probably there are sound reasons for your decision. Whether people trust you, therefore, will usually come down to whether you have communicated your reasoning with them and done so in a manner that acknowledges their natural chimp instincts and reactions. I remember an email being sent to my department announcing that their classrooms were now going to be reassigned to the psychology department and they would be rehoused in a different block. Some staff members would not have their own classroom or would have to share their classroom with other teachers. This is bad leadership – not because it wasn't the right decision, but because the logic behind the decision was not communicated or explained. As chimps we instinctively feel protective of our space – therefore if our chimp is already feeling insecure, any decision that feels unjust will feed the confirmation bias instinct and get added to the list of injustices suffered.

   There are two ways to go about communicating logic effectively: (1) tell the story – with all the twists and turns, pitfalls and problems that lead to the conclusion or decision, or (2) start with the decision – but then lay out clearly the evidence or reasons for it. Both are effective in that the recipient understands why the decision was made (and is clear that it wasn't made for other, more sinister reasons). Essential to both approaches is empathy.

So, empathy, authenticity and logic work in harmony to establish trust. You can't be an effective leader unless you trust and build trust.

Part III

School – How to Change the World One School at a Time

So far, we have explored personal wellbeing in Part I and how we can each take responsibility for our own emotional wellbeing, think in more constructive ways, and approach teaching and leading differently in order to develop a more balanced, healthy and sustainable working life within the teaching profession. In Part II, we examined our approach to leadership and the centrality of effective, person-centred, emotionally literate leadership in changing the culture of our schools, such that we mould sustainable environments with high levels of staff engagement.

Just as we cannot properly address student wellbeing without addressing staff wellbeing, neither can we address staff wellbeing without rethinking the whole educational picture. These issues are not separate and distinct – they are interrelated facets of the whole. The positive effect on students of a healthy, enthusiastic and engaged teacher is obvious. But if the system, the vehicle for the delivery of education, doesn't support the wellbeing of both students and staff in the long term, then both will suffer. A car engine may be running perfectly, but if all four tyres are flat then the amount of petrol and revs expended will be far greater to get that car up a hill and the lifespan of the engine will be all too quickly reduced.

In Part III, we will look at the way we do school at the macro level – some of the constraints and barriers inherent in the education system we have inherited, but also, more importantly, how and why we could and should challenge and seek to change things. As I stated in Chapter 1, there is always a temptation to blame those above us and passively accept the status quo. This is easier than the alternative, which is to take the time to identify what we can change and what we can't change, and accept the challenge to change the things we can. I would suggest that, in most cases, we can change, or at least modify, far more than we think at first glance. We need to accept responsibility. Yes, there are legal and systemic constraints laid down by government, but there is a huge amount of potential to achieve good outcomes in a myriad of different ways, if only we could give ourselves permission to imagine different ways of doing things.

We will start with a summary of the changing world of work and its implications for what we do and how we do it, and from there move to suggest possible ways to rethink schools, such that we begin to reshape it with wellbeing and sustainability at its heart.

Chapter 13

The Future of Work and the Challenge for Education

What will the workplace of the future look like for our students?

- According to some predictors, 65% of the jobs that our current students will do in the future don't yet exist.[1]
- The average student leaving school in 2015 might have as many as 40 different jobs in 10 totally different career paths.[2]
- Some 74% of finance leaders plan to move their previously on-site workforce to permanently remote positions post-COVID-19.[3]
- The future landscape for stock traders will make coding as important as writing an English sentence.[4]
- Given today's rate of technological progress, we will experience approximately 20,000 years of progress in the 21st century.[5]

The question these predictions raise is whether the education we are providing for our students will prepare them for these not-yet-existent roles in a global job market in which fast-paced change and technological advance is the norm. This world is not in the future, it is already here.

1 World Economic Forum, *The Future of Jobs* (2016), ch. 1. Available at: https://reports.weforum.org/future-of-jobs-2016/chapter-1-the-future-of-jobs-and-skills.

2 P. Harris, How Many Jobs Should You Expect to Hold in Your Lifetime?, *Workopolis* (8 October 2015). Available at: https://careers.workopolis.com/advice/how-many-jobs-should-you-expect-to-hold-in-your-lifetime.

3 A. Parungao, The Future of Remote Work After COVID-19: 3 Common Predictions, *Eko* (27 April 2020). Available at: https://www.ekoapp.com/blog/the-future-of-remote-work-after-covid-19-3-common-predictions.

4 J. Kelly, How to Future-Proof Your Career in a Fast-Changing, Unforgiving Global Job Market, *Forbes* (24 September 2019). Available at: https://www.forbes.com/sites/jackkelly/2019/09/24/how-to-future-proof-your-career-in-a-fast-changing-unforgiving-global-job-market/#543f1fb13d83.

5 D. Butler, Tomorrow's World, *Nature*, 530 (2016): 399–401. Available at: https://www.nature.com/news/polopoly_fs/1.19431!/menu/main/topColumns/topLeftColumn/pdf/530398a.pdf?origin=ppub.

According to the World Economic Forum, 'In many industries and countries, the most in-demand occupations or specialties did not exist ten or even five years ago, and the pace of change is set to accelerate.'[6]

Throughout history, the education system has been developed with a country's economy in mind. What jobs need doing? What skills are needed to fulfil those jobs? Then school young people to provide for those needs. It is a simple equation. Except our education system in the UK hasn't kept up with the pace of change.

Daniel Pink discusses this in *A Whole New Mind*, where he makes the persuasive argument that 'right-brainers will rule the future'.[7] According to recent neuroscience research, the right hemisphere of the brain processes our creativity, emotion, empathy and artistry, and the left hemisphere is responsible for our analysis, information processing, recall and logic. There is a difference of opinion as to whether one side of the brain is more dominant in different people, but, either way, Pink makes the case that it is the skills and aptitudes associated with the right brain that will prove to be increasingly important in the future job market.

He traces the development of jobs and education through three distinct eras:[8]

1. The industrial age

During the 19th century, profits and careers were built on the manual labour of the workforce. Factories and industry relied on large numbers of workers doing relatively menial tasks on assembly lines and in mines. These jobs have disappeared as technology and automation have increased – machines can now fulfil these roles more economically, reliably and accurately.

6 World Economic Forum, *The Future of Jobs*, ch. 1.

7 D. Pink, *A Whole New Mind: Why Right-Brainers Will Rule the Future* (New York: Marshall Cavendish, 2008).

8 Pink, *A Whole New Mind*, pp. 48–49.

2. The information age

This is the age of knowledge workers which dovetailed with increased education in the 20th century. Blue- and white-collar workers became the backbone of the economy as workers now traded on their learning and know-how, whether in management, industry or the growing public sector. This era brought us right up into the computer age. These jobs require classic left-brained thinking: logic, analysis, function, systems, strategy, communications. Our education system prepared young people well for this, schooling them in mathematics, science, analysis, deduction and business, and assessing them on their ability to exercise left-brained skills: knowledge, memorising, recall, writing, comparing, contrasting, equations and functions.

However, with the incredibly rapid evolution of the computer age and the exponential increase in the computational capacity of new technologies, we now find ourselves in an age where the majority of these knowledge-based jobs can now be fulfilled by technology – increasingly cheaply and with greater accuracy than humans. Couple this with the fact that even if we do want a human to do the analysis and system coordination, we can certainly find someone who can do it more cheaply, and perhaps even better, by drawing from the increasingly highly educated workforce in China or India. As a result, these left-brained, knowledge- and analysis-based jobs are on the way out in Britain and every other economically developed country. Cars and vans will soon no longer require drivers, data does not require a human analyst, shops don't need checkout assistants and banks don't need cashiers.

3. The conceptual age

Today, the volume of jobs and careers in design, creative arts, innovation and entrepreneurship are increasing – and being invented – by the day. These are right-brained jobs which utilise the creativity, art, lateral thinking, innovation and people skills of a left-brained workforce. Critically, this is a workforce that will have to adapt, change and rethink on a regular basis because the pace of technological change and adaptation is so rapid.

Some recent statistics from the United States are revealing:[9]

- The number of graphic designers has increased ten-fold in a decade.
- Graphic designers outnumber chemical engineers by four to one.
- Since 1970, 30% more people are earning a living by writing and 50% more people by composing or performing music.
- More Americans work in arts, entertainment and design than work as lawyers, accountants and auditors.

In his book *The Creative Economy* John Howkins notes:[10]

- In the UK, the creative sector produces US$200 billion of goods and services a year.
- In 15 years this sector will be worth US$6.1 trillion internationally.

During the information age, the education system adapted and grew to produce the knowledge workers the job market required. However, it is continuing to produce students equipped for an age that has largely already passed, preparing them for the world *we* grew up in and not the one *they* are growing up in. Whereas the sequence of events leading from the industrial age to the information age was relatively slow, allowing education to change with it, the transition we are witnessing now is on a completely different level. Far from starting to adapt, education has arguably taken a step backwards. Recent Conservative governments have focused on typically left-brained subjects, like science, technology, engineering and mathematics, and sidelined the arts, design, vocational skills and creativity. They have also increased the emphasis on assessment by traditional examinations which require students to memorise copious amounts of information, regurgitate facts and record their left-brained, computational ability using a wooden or plastic writing stick within an arbitrary time frame. Young people are being forced to acquire skills they are unlikely to need once their formal education is over and they enter the real world, when they will discover just how ill-prepared they are.

---

9 Pink, *A Whole New Mind*, p. 55.

10 J. Howkins, *The Creative Economy: How People Make Money from Ideas* (London: Penguin, 2001), p. 116.

I am not arguing for a wholesale removal of traditional subjects or that academic education has no place. It's not either/or; it's both/and. However, I see exceptionally little time, thought or investment being made in schools to address the changing job market and prepare young people for working life. Admittedly, planning a curriculum for a world that doesn't yet exist is not a straightforward task, but that is why prioritising life skills and character development is so essential: resilience, adaptability, social skills, teamwork, problem-solving, speaking skills, empathy, awareness, decision-making, self-belief, self-respect, self-discipline, aspiration, respect for human rights and the values of compassion, generosity, equality and inclusivism.

This type of education cannot be peripheral; it cannot be a bolt-on. These skills are core if we want our students to survive in the future. If we want them to thrive, then we need to go even further:

> In a world tossed by Abundance, Asia and Automation, in which L- [left-brain] Directed Thinking remains necessary but no longer efficient we must become proficient in R- [right-brain] Directed Thinking and master aptitudes that are high concept and high touch. We must perform work that overseas knowledge workers can't do cheaper, that computers can't do faster, and that satisfies the aesthetic, spiritual and emotional demands of a prosperous time.[11]

Across the UK as a whole, the number of new companies registered in 2019 rose by 5.7% to over 660,000 – a record high.[12] This figure has been rising year on year, and yet the average student will leave school after 14 years of compulsory education without one single hour of input on how to start a business.

Changes are also occurring in the structure of the economy, leading to expanding job opportunities in previously less significant or

11 Pink, *A Whole New Mind*, p. 61.

12 M. O'Dwyer, London Drives Increase in Number of New UK Startups, *City AM* (14 January 2019). Available at: https://www.cityam.com/london-drives-increase-number-new-uk-startups.

non-existent industries. The Open Business Council reports that the five fastest growing job sectors in the UK over the past few years are:

- Transport and logistics: the number of road freight logistics firms founded in the UK skyrocketed by 229% between 2012 and 2016.
- Fintech (financial technology): according to a London Stock Exchange survey, fintech companies are predicting growth of 88% between 2018 and 2021.
- Construction: typically a cyclical area of production, the sector has seen the number of businesses in the industry grow by 10% between 2016 and 2018.
- Digital marketing and advertising: this sector marked its 21st consecutive quarter of growth at the beginning of 2019.
- Energy: the UK government was planning for 15% of all energy consumption to come from renewable resources by 2020. It is estimated that the UK's renewables industry could support up to 400,000 jobs by the end of 2020.[13]

According to Indeed, of the top eight fastest growing jobs in the UK in 2019, three were in IT/tech, three in design and two in people management.[14]

Does the education we are providing for our students prepare them to thrive in this job market? Are our careers programmes central or peripheral? Does our curriculum develop the skill sets necessary to access and advance in this rapidly changing world?

To be clear, I am not arguing for an entirely functional approach to education. I am not proposing that schools exist merely to fill job vacancies and keep the economic machine turning. However, I certainly believe that preparedness for the workplace is a central part of the education we should be offering, and that we are doing our students a disservice if we fail to equip them adequately.

13 Open Business Council, Working in the UK: The Top 5 Fastest-Growing Sectors (25 February 2020). Available at: https://www.openbusinesscouncil.org/working-in-the-uk-the-top-5-fastest-growing-sectors.

14 C. Taylor, These Are the Fastest Growing Jobs and Sectors in the UK, Researchers Say, *CNBC* (17 May 2019). Available at: https://www.cnbc.com/2019/05/17/these-are-the-uks-fastest-growing-jobs-and-sectors-researchers-say.html.

I am all for education for its own sake. I believe in the value of learning as an independent activity – growing our minds, considering new perspectives, learning about the world in which we live and understanding ourselves as a species. All academic disciplines are to be valued and nurtured. Our students would undoubtedly be impoverished by a lack of knowledge of history, linguistics or physics. But I also think that we have got the balance wrong, and it isn't fair on the students in our care.

Furthermore, the education we offer is insufficiently connected to the world of work – the application and implications of knowledge and understanding for the real world is deficient. Additionally, we have placed undue emphasis on knowledge and understanding while ignoring the development of the skills, aptitudes and character qualities necessary to enjoy success not only in work but also in life.

Education needs to take seriously the development of young people's EQ as well as their IQ, their emotional intelligence as well as their academic development. Daniel Goleman, the author of *Emotional Intelligence*, cites a study in which engineers were rated by their peers as to their relative success. This was then correlated with their IQ as well as their EQ. The study showed that there was zero correlation between their success and their IQ, whereas EQ correlated very highly.[15] In fact, the percentage of career success that can be traced back to IQ is just 4–10%. That's all! IQ may open up certain career paths but, according to Goleman, progression within any career is largely down to imagination, joyfulness and social dexterity, along with effort and practice.[16]

This is directly related to growing schools that are committed to the wellbeing of all, because it speaks to the concept of balance as being integral to everything we do: balance in our education of students, balance in our school systems, balance in our care and nurture of the whole person, whether staff or student.

15 D. Goleman, Emotional Intelligence at Work: Why IQ Isn't Everything [video] (2018). Available at: https://www.youtube.com/watch?v=7ngIFlmRRPQ.

16 Pink, *A Whole New Mind*, p. 58.

Developing students for a brave new world

In light of recent changes to the world of work, it is interesting to note how some businesses are adapting the way they recruit. Instructive in this regard is the relatively well-developed approach of global professional services giant PwC. The firm operates in 152 nations and runs its own apprenticeships and degree programmes in addition to providing a huge array of career opportunities. PwC's Employability Hub clearly explains what they look for in candidates, as well as outlining their recruitment process, which notably does not at any point ask for a CV.[17]

PwC have identified five essentials or attributes which form the type of professional they seek:[18]

1 **Whole leadership:** the ability 'to lead yourself and others, regardless of your grade, by making a real difference in the work you do. This means delivering results in a responsible, authentic, resilient, inclusive and passionate way.'

2 **Technical capabilities:** the ability to 'apply a range of technical capabilities to deliver quality and value for our clients and PwC'.

3 **Business acumen:** business knowledge and awareness, or the 'willingness to learn about business, and … bring innovation, and fresh thinking, to create distinctive value for our clients and PwC'.

4 **Global acumen:** the need to 'operate and collaborate effectively, with a mind-set that transcends geographic and cultural boundaries' in a 'continually complex and changing world'.

5 **Relationship:** being 'skilled at building relationships of high value which are genuine and rooted in trust' and the ability to 'communicate with confidence'.

PwC 'use this framework to recruit, develop and assess our people at all grades and in all areas of our business, because all of our people need to be authentic and inclusive leaders'.

17 See https://www.pwc.co.uk/careers/student-jobs/employability.html.
18 See https://www.pwc.co.uk/careers/student-jobs/apply/the-skills-we-look-for.html.

I find this is truly insightful and forward-looking. What concerns me is that our students have no idea that this is how they will be judged by future employers and therefore they are unprepared to evidence and demonstrate these attributes. Instead, we ask them to compile CVs and personal statements in much the same way as I did when I was at school. And we certainly lead them to believe that their GCSEs and A levels are the most important factor in their future success and failure. This is just not the case. Natural selection attests to this: 'it is not the most intellectual of the species that survives; it is not the strongest that survives; but the species that survives is the one that is able best to adapt and adjust to the changing environment in which it finds itself'.[19] And yet *responding to change* or the skills associated with it isn't on the curriculum.

School improvement organisation PiXL have identified five key skills that they suggest will give students 'the edge' in life and work: leadership, organisation, resilience, initiative and communication (LORIC). Their Edge programme provides schools with a mechanism to help students develop the skills that will prepare them for success.[20]

Clearly, these represent just a few examples, but there are common themes here which I believe are currently being overlooked by the provision we offer in our schools.

Recruiter sentiment studies also demonstrate huge changes in the way recruitment works: 90% of recruiters now believe the labour market is candidate-driven.[21] In other words, recruiters don't pick talent any more; rather, talent picks them! Savvy candidates know what they want from an employer and are proficient at making themselves attractive. In recognition of this, firms are hiring recruitment agencies to give them a makeover in order to make them more appealing to the high-calibre candidates they need to fill the new positions they are creating. This understanding of the job market is missing from many of our school careers programmes.

19 Leon Megginson allegedly summarising Darwin's *Origin of Species*: L. C. Megginson, Lessons from Europe for American Business, *Southwestern Social Science Quarterly*, 44(1) (1963): 3–13 at 4.

20 See https://www.pixl.org.uk/edge or the following video for a quick summary: https://www.youtube.com/watch?v=fLvGRRwU534.

21 MRI Network, *Recruiter Sentiment Study: 2015 2nd Half* (2015), p. 3. Available at: https://www.mrinetwork.com/media/1036/2015_recruiter_sentiment_study_2nd_half.pdf.

Angela Duckworth's research further reinforces this need for the development of non-academic qualities. She identifies the need for people to develop grit.[22] According to her research, grit is the most critical factor in determining success – that is, the degree of passion and perseverance for a given pursuit. Her Grit Scale predicted who succeeded, and who didn't, better than any other measure following extensive studies within education, sales and the military.[23] Grit predicts success better than IQ, better than aptitude tests, better than SAT scores and better than prior experience.

Duckworth has also written about the impact of self-discipline on success: the ability to control impulses and delay gratification. She has found that the extent to which a person can delay gratification is directly related to their success in all areas of life.[24] The link between grit and self-discipline is evident: am I willing and determined to persevere with a task or a dream even when I don't feel like it? This is yet another area of education and personal development that we give very little attention to in schools in any deliberate or focused way.

The following attributes all have huge significance for success and progression in any job or career, but also in life:

- Communication skills
- Problem-solving
- Teamwork
- Initiative
- Independent thinking
- Empathy
- Emotional literacy
- Evaluation

22 A. L. Duckworth, *Grit: The Power of Passion and Perseverance* (London: Vermillion, 2016), pp. 10–12.

23 You can try the Grit Scale yourself at: https://angeladuckworth.com/grit-scale.

24 A. L. Duckworth and M. E. P. Seligman, Self-Discipline Outdoes IQ in Predicting Academic Performance of Adolescents, *Psychological Science*, 16(2) (2005): 939–944. Available at: https://www.academia.edu/5466301/Self-Discipline_Outdoes_IQ_in_Predicting_Academic_Performance_of_Adolescents.

- Confidence
- Motor skills

These are present in our current educational set-up, but not explicitly so. They are skills regarded as somewhat peripheral to the main business of school – we hope our students will pick them up along the way. We may see some of them as being within the remit of parents but, of course, those with inadequate parenting lose out. I would argue that they are all integral to a holistic and well-rounded education.

In recent years, I have been helping to develop these aspects of learning by delivering a programme in secondary schools derived from the Game-Changing Index (detailed in Chapter 11). The Young People Index uses the same assessment tool to help students develop the self-awareness and employability skills needed to make sound decisions about their future pathways and excel in their chosen careers. It has been moving to see students recognise the unique contribution they each have to offer as individuals, regardless of their academic attainment. The programme aims to enable young people to be 'aware of their own individual strengths and skills so they can not only see the value they add in the classroom or in society but are also able to make more informed choices about their future'.[25] Again, my point is that this kind of education should not be an add-on but core to what we do.

Finally, where in our curriculum do we take seriously our duty to prepare young people for everyday life? The implementation of the new statutory guidance for PSHE, *Relationships Education, Relationships and Sex Education (RSE) and Health Education*, at last goes some way to recognising the necessity of education for life and not just for work.[26] It affirms the need for comprehensive education around adolescent mental health, healthy relationships and sexual health, health and wellbeing in general, as well as education around equality and inclusivity in society. Making this mandatory is long overdue, but many would argue that the guidance does not go far enough. Critically, in most schools I have come across, the plan so far at Key Stage 4 is to attempt to roll this out via a few more 'drop-down days' and the tutor programme. Essential and potentially

25 See https://www.youngpeopleindex.com.

26 Department for Education, *Relationships Education, Relationships and Sex Education (RSE) and Health Education* (25 July 2019). Available at: https://www.gov.uk/government/publications/relationships-education-relationships-and-sex-education-rse-and-health-education.

life-altering education delivered by non-specialists in 15-minute slots is not good enough.

For reasons I cannot fathom, this essential education still lies at the periphery of most schools' agendas. And this in spite of the overwhelming evidence that students who enjoy good mental and physical health, positive relationships and emotional wellbeing achieve higher academic attainment and make faster progress.[27]

I don't think we will ever truly build schools that cater adequately for the wellbeing of all students unless we address the skewed nature of our current system and seek to establish balance. This means adequately nurturing and developing the whole child, not just the left brain of the child. In the process, we will necessarily prepare the teachers and leaders of the future to continue the trend and weave balance and holism into everything they do.

Are you up for the challenge?

27 Public Health England, *The Link Between Pupil Health and Wellbeing and Attainment: A Briefing for Head Teachers, Governors and Staff in Education Settings* (November 2014). Available at: https://assets.publishing.service.gov.uk/government/uploads/system/uploads/attachment_data/file/370686/HT_briefing_layoutvFINALvii.pdf.

Chapter 14

A Rights Respecting Foundation: Beginning with the End in Mind

Unicef UK launched the Rights Respecting Schools Award in 2004. Since then, over 5,000 UK schools have engaged with the award and worked towards becoming accredited as a Rights Respecting School. Some 1.6 million children in the UK currently attend a Rights Respecting School.[1] In my view, it is unquestionably the most effective vehicle for whole-school improvement that I have encountered, offering a coherent, robust and powerful basis for rethinking everything we do in schools.

The award is based on the UN Convention on the Rights of the Child (CRC), which was first drafted in 1989 and has since become the most widely ratified human rights treaty in history. It was enshrined into law in the UK in 1991. Remarkably, however, in my experience most teachers have neither heard of it nor read it. The CRC has 54 articles – in contrast to the Universal Declaration of Human Rights (UDHR), which has 30 – and was drawn up in response to the recognition that there are vulnerabilities and needs specific and peculiar to childhood which require the protection and provision of adults. For example, the very young are unable to feed and clothe themselves. They depend on adults to do that for them. Children of all ages are more vulnerable to abuse and coercion and lack the knowledge and power to protect themselves. The CRC recognises that, as adults, we are all 'duty bearers'. It is our duty to ensure that children of all ages have the essentials they need to survive, develop and flourish in order to grow up and realise their potential to be outstanding global citizens.

I have led two large secondary schools to achieve the Rights Respecting Schools Award and continue to work with other schools to support them on their rights-respecting journeys. I usually begin my work with school leaders. I provide them with an outline of a person and ask them

1 See https://www.unicef.org.uk/rights-respecting-schools/the-rrsa/about-the-rrsa.

to label it with their thoughts on what would make an outstanding global citizen. Figure 14.1 is an example of what frequently emerges.

Figure 14.1. An outstanding global citizen

This is a useful exercise to do with your staff or leadership team. A broad consensus is reached very quickly – there tends to be little, if any, disagreement. Most look at their outstanding global citizen and agree that this is what we, as teachers, are trying to produce. This is why we are here. This is why we are teachers. It is the ultimate goal of education.

In this light, consider Article 29 of the CRC, which provides a masterful summary of the goals of education:

> Education should develop the child's personality, talents and mental and physical abilities to their fullest potential; develop

> respect for human rights and fundamental freedoms; respect for the child's parents, his or her own cultural identity, language and values, for the national values of the country in which the child is living, and from which he or she originates, and for civilizations different from his or her own. Education should prepare the child for responsible life in a free society, in the spirit of understanding, peace, tolerance, equality of sexes, and friendship among all peoples, ethnic, national and religious groups and develop respect for the natural environment.[2]

Brilliant! If we have some clarity and agreement about our goal, then the question of how we get there becomes much more focused.

Beginning with the end in mind

We make a fundamental mistake when we fail to start with the end in mind. We create endless diversions for ourselves, we run around in circles and undermine our own efforts, we work at cross purposes and end up shooting ourselves in the foot. If we begin squarely with the end in mind and use that end as a measure – a bar by which we critique and assess everything we do – then we will be far more successful. The problems emerge when we start with a task or a process rather than an outcome. Like a team of footballers who can't agree on which goal they are aiming at – chaos.

The Rights Respecting Schools Award is not an additional extra. Rather, it proposes that the rights of the child should underpin everything we do and thereby means that we adopt an outcome-focused, children's rights-based approach to education. This then forms a foundation for both why and how we go about educating young people and preparing them for the future.

2 Paraphrased from Unicef, *The United Nations Convention on the Rights of the Child* (20 November 1989). Available at: https://downloads.unicef.org.uk/wp-content/uploads/2016/08/unicef-convention-rights-child-uncrc.pdf?_ga=2.86970783.641093437.1591280497-612875821.1591280497. If you haven't already done so, have a look at the summary version of the CRC – it will be useful to do so before you read on: https://www.unicef.org.uk/what-we-do/un-convention-child-rights.

> Unicef works with schools in the UK to create safe and inspiring places to learn, where children are respected, their talents are nurtured and they are able to thrive. Our Rights Respecting Schools Award embeds these values in daily school life and gives children the best chance to lead happy, healthy lives and to be responsible, active citizens.[3]

As I stated in the introduction, we are not aiming to develop good geographers or good mathematicians, but good human beings. That is, people who know and understand their rights and respect the rights of others. Everything else is secondary and subordinate to this aim. All of the rights of the child, some of which are more pertinent to our role as educators than others, sit within this framework.

A first-class academic education is obviously integral to this objective, as acknowledged in Article 29 on pages 208–209: the development of every child's talents and mental and physical abilities to their fullest potential. But not only this: also integral is the development of the child's relationship with, and respect for, the wider world (parents, culture, the environment) together with preparedness for responsible life in a free society. Quite simply, the development of the whole child.

I believe that the CRC provides a coherent rationale for every single thing we do in school (Table 14.1). What the Rights Respecting Schools Award successfully achieves is to tie all these threads of education together around one basic, unifying idea: that everyone's rights (including those of adults) should be known and respected.

Table 14.1. School life linked to the CRC

Aspect	Detail
Ethos	The intrinsic value of every child, the purpose of education, aspiration for all. (Articles 2, 28, 29)

3 See https://www.unicef.org.uk/rights-respecting-schools/the-rrsa/about-the-rrsa.

Aspect	Detail
Achievement and progress	The breadth of education and the challenge to achieve, including cultural and artistic development. (Articles 28, 29, 31)
Safeguarding/ bullying	The right to protection from all kinds of abuse; non-discrimination and the duty to blow the whistle. (Articles 2, 19)
Behaviour and relationships	Respect for the rights of all. The rights to an environment that enables learning. (Articles 1, 2, 12, 19, 28)
Pastoral systems/ student wellbeing	The right to healthcare, safety, wellbeing and support. (Articles 3, 6, 19, 24, 27, 39)
Pupil premium, SEND, additional educational needs and looked-after children	Explicit affirmation of the rights of disadvantaged or vulnerable students. (Articles 1, 2, 22, 23, 25, 26, 27, 30)
Career education, information, advice and guidance	The right to develop to full potential and access reliable information. (Articles 6, 17, 29)
Spiritual, moral, social and cultural development/ tolerance	The right to freedom of expression and the right to freedom of thought and belief and respect for the rights and freedoms of others. (Articles 2, 13, 14)
Racism/prejudice	Rights of refugees, disabled and minority groups. (Articles 2, 22, 23, 30)
Student voice	The right to have a say and participate. (Articles 12, 13, 14)

Aspect	Detail
Global citizenship and charity initiatives	The rights of all (not just those in the West), touching on child soldiers/labourers/exploitation/torture. (Articles 6, 24, 27, 32, 36, 37, 38)
PSHE/drugs/child sexual exploitation education	The right to information, protection from drug abuse and exploitation. (Articles 6, 33, 34)
Parental engagement	The responsibilities of parents and support for parents. (Articles 5, 18)
Extracurricular	The importance of cultural development, leisure time and play: protecting the distinctive qualities of childhood and the importance of strong social connections. (Articles 15, 31)
British values	The rule of law, democracy, individual liberty, mutual respect and tolerance – these are universal values that are abundantly evidenced when rights are respected. (Articles 1, 2)

So:

- *Why* do we not tolerate bullying? Because everyone has the right to be safe (Article 19).
- *Why* do we provide first-class teaching and learning? Because everyone has the right to an education (Article 29).
- *Why* do we ensure our school is inclusive, fully accessible and adapts learning to meet the needs of all students? Because these rights apply to everyone regardless of abilities (Article 2).
- *Why* do we have a vibrant and developed student voice? Because children have the right to a say when adults are making decisions that affect them (Article 12).

- *Why* do we have a robust and comprehensive careers programme? Because children have a right to be developed to their full potential and a right to reliable information (Articles 6 and 17).
- *Why* do we teach religious education? Because every child has the right to think and believe what they choose and practise their religion (Article 14), and because education should encourage respect for other cultures (Article 29).

This rationale is hugely useful and effective in drawing together staff and students around a common ethos and value-set that affirms the dignity, worth and value of every human and which is inclusive and accessible to those of all faiths and none. It also provides an accessible framework for students for many of the rules and sanctions that, at times, may appear arbitrary or unfair – for example:

- *Why* am I receiving a detention? Because everyone has a right to learn and your disruptive behaviour is preventing others from enjoying that right. As your teacher (duty bearer), I'm responsible for ensuring that everyone in the class can access their right to a good quality education.
- *Why* are we not allowed to run in the corridor? Because everyone has the right to be safe and we have a duty to prevent harm.

Very quickly, the language and accompanying understanding of rights explicitly becomes part of what we do, why we do it and how we do it.

Critical to effectively implementing a children's rights-based education is to understand from the outset that rights are unconditional. At first glance, many schools like the idea of linking rights with responsibilities. However, while the concept of responsibility is an important one, it is not a prerequisite. Children do not have the right to be protected from violence only if they behave themselves. Children do not have a right to an education only if they bring a pen with them to school. They have these rights because they are children, period. They are unconditional and universal, just as your human rights are unconditional and universal.

Children don't lose their right to learn because they swear at the teacher – although this does raise an important point: namely, that rights sometimes need to be balanced. There is a proviso to all the rights in the CRC (which applies also to the UDHR), which is this: since all of the rights in both treaties apply to everyone (Article 1), an individual is only entitled to fully exercise all of his or her rights provided that doing so does not hinder or prevent others from enjoying their rights. This is why restrictions and sanctions must at times be imposed both in society and in school in order to protect and balance the rights of everyone.

I will prepare you now for the smart alec in Year 9 who will interrupt your lesson, disrupt others and think he is being clever to respond to your warning by saying, 'Er, Miss, I have a right to have a say. I'm exercising my rights. You can't stop me.' This is your chance to educate him about what being rights respecting means: everyone else in the class has a right to learn and as the teacher you have a duty to ensure that they do!

As staff and students gradually come to understand what rights respecting means, it begins to take on a deeper meaning: I have rights, but so does the person next to me, and actually my rights will be better enjoyed when everyone else's rights are respected too. Suddenly we have the building blocks of a flourishing and positive school community in which wellbeing is valued, protected and embedded.

But are rights essentially just made up?

There will be some reading this book who buy into the view that the concept of human rights is a man-made concept – an idea, ideology or belief that has no more evidential basis or validity than any other belief or ideology, whether religious or secular. So why would we use it to underpin our education system? I believe that this is to misunderstand the basis of human rights and the robust rationale behind them.

The notion of human rights was a long time coming and developed over hundreds of years, but the reason they have had such widespread acceptance and appeal is that they align with a scientific, post-Enlightenment worldview: naturalism and empiricism. Naturalism starts first and foremost with the natural world, and empiricism with what we can know through the senses by observation and experience, then further through logic and deduction. Naturalism has a long and eminent history, arguably beginning with Aristotle (sometimes referred to as the first Western scientist) and followed by such influential thinkers as St Thomas Aquinas, Immanuel Kant, Jeremy Bentham and modern-day philosopher Peter Vardy. Naturalism holds that we can deduce what actions or behaviours are better or worse by looking at facts, evidence and studying nature. This is the tradition on which human rights are based.

For example, it is not made-up that humans require adequate food and water in order to survive and flourish. This is a biological fact, therefore it is a right. It is not made-up that humans require some rest and relaxation time in order to remain healthy and well. This is a biologically verified need, therefore it is a right. It is not simply an opinion that humans, if coerced, silenced or prevented from self-expression or social interaction, suffer mentally and physically. This is an evidence-based psychological need, therefore these freedoms are rights.

All basic human rights are grounded in verifiable and universal needs. Those that aren't based on need are derived from the concepts of fairness and justice. I don't believe that you could find a human anywhere on the planet who would believe that being blamed and punished for something they did not do could be called fair or just. No one. Justice is a universally accepted and acknowledged idea regardless of culture or religious belief.

The concept of rights rests on these two bases: survival and fairness. Upholding and defending the universality and unconditionality of these rights should, in my view, be at the heart of our education system. They are fundamental to the survival, development and flourishing of the human race. They are the building blocks for a better world.

Becoming a Rights Respecting School

There are three strands to the Rights Respecting Schools Award:

1 Teaching and learning about rights, as set out in the CRC.

2 Teaching and learning through rights – an approach that models rights-respecting attitudes and values based on dignity, respect, equality and participation.

3 Teaching and learning for rights – being empowered to exercise rights and promote the rights of others locally and globally.

Schools that register for the award then work towards achieving Bronze: Rights Committed, Silver: Rights Aware and then Gold: Rights Respecting. Embedding knowledge and respect for rights is not a quick fix, especially in a larger school. It involves a culture change which usually takes a number of years. It is not necessarily about changing everything you do or even doing lots of new things, since much of what many schools currently do is rights respecting, just not explicitly so. The award therefore helps to cohere all that you do by making the implicit explicit, by providing an underpinning rationale based on rights and by developing the way you go about doing what you do. Of course, it does mean being willing to ask important and difficult questions about some of our policies and practices, and should, if really effective, lead to a remodelled, refreshed and decidedly improved education.

All the problems in society, with the possible exception of natural disasters, are caused by the choices and actions of individuals – whether domestic abuse or drunken violence, segregation or war, drug misuse or exploitation, inequality or the gender pay gap. And in the UK (if not in every country), all these people went to school. We had them for 12 or 14 years. We had them for five days a week. We had the chance to enlighten and inspire them to be rights-respecting citizens who would leave our care equipped to live rich, full and healthy lives, empowered to make their own unique and positive contribution to the world. With many thousands we have failed.

Of course, life is complex and difficult, and unforeseen circumstances will befall us that the greatest education in the world cannot prepare us for, but I believe that we can do better than we are currently doing. We can start with the end in mind and coalesce around that vision, and from there deliver an education that grows thinking, reflective, socially conscious and respectful human beings, nurtured by schools in which every staff member and student is valued and cared for.

According to a Unicef Impact Report in 2018, some of the quantifiable impacts of a rights-respecting approach to education include:

- Children know about their rights and support the rights of others locally and globally:
    - 82% of children and young people at Gold schools say they are taught about their rights, a rise of 40% from before work began.
- Children feel happier in themselves:
    - 78% of children and young people at Gold schools say they feel happy in themselves, an increase of 5% from before work began.
- Children feel safe in school:
    - 82% of children and young people in Gold schools say they feel safe in school, an increase of 6% since before work began.
    - 93% of head teachers in Gold schools report a noticeable reduction in exclusions and bullying, an increase of 23% from Silver.
- Children are engaged in their education:
    - 99% of adults in Gold schools report high levels of pupil engagement, an increase of 8% from before work began.
- Adults have positive relationships and enjoy their job:
    - 98% of adults in Gold schools report enjoying their work, this is up 4% from before work began.
    - 98% of adults in Gold schools report feeling respected by children and young people, this is up 4% from before work began.
    - 99% of adults in Gold schools report respectful relationships between other adults, this is an increase of 5% from before work began.[4]

4 Unicef, *Impact Report 2018: Creating Active & Engaged Citizens* (2018), p. 2. Available at: https://www.unicef.org.uk/rights-respecting-schools/wp-content/uploads/sites/4/2019/06/Summary-Impact-Report-2018_Final.pdf.

The last bullet point is instructive for our discussion here: Rights Respecting Schools tend to generate a healthier, more positive and respectful working environment for everyone. And, of course, if we as teachers are happier and enjoying our work, then our teaching will be better as well.

Here are some further impacts from my own assessments of Rights Respecting Schools.

A primary school in an area of high social deprivation in South Bristol reported that they run a Year 5 visit to a local mosque as part of their religious education provision. Unfortunately, resistance from parents was such that the majority of parents refused permission for them to attend. One year later, after engaging with the Rights Respecting Schools Award, they ran the trip again. This time only one student was refused permission. I asked the head why she thought this was. She said, 'Because the children *want* to go!' This is striking. This is transformational education impacting on the community: the awareness, understanding and respect of primary schoolchildren influencing the attitudes, preconceptions and prejudices of their parents.

At a secondary school in Dorset, I asked a group of students about the prevalence of homophobic language in the school. They said, 'It doesn't happen.' I was sceptical – I've spent a lot of years around secondary school students. I said, 'But if you heard someone say "Don't be gay", would it be addressed by the teacher?' I was trying to ascertain if staff actively challenged prejudicial behaviour and attitudes. But their response again caught me off guard: 'Well, everyone else in the class would react and say, "You can't say that!" Everyone would be outraged, so it doesn't happen.' This school has addressed the issue of homophobia proactively in a range of ways, and the ethos embraced by the school is fundamentally rights respecting.

Another moving example of rights respecting in action was an experience I organised as part of our rights-respecting journey at my school in the South West. I arranged an exchange with a school in Tower Hamlets in London. Central Foundation Girls' School is a comprehensive state school which, due to its catchment, is 99% non-white and 97% Muslim. We took 15 of our students from Poole (96% white) to visit the school for a day, join in with their lessons and take part in a collaborative session with 15 of their students to work on producing a charter for creating a more harmonious society. A few weeks later, 15 students from Tower Hamlets visited Poole; some had never been out of the borough of Tower Hamlets before.

Both days were moving and striking. As our students got out of the minibus and mixed with the students in Tower Hamlets, the vast majority wearing the school uniform hijab, they were essentially mobbed! The London students gathered around them asking about their uniform, exchanging Instagram addresses, wanting to know about Dorset and their lives there. Our students were visibly taken aback by the friendliness of the welcome they received. As the day progressed, it was as if stereotypes and prejudices perceptibly crumbled as our students recognised that the presentation of Muslims they had encountered in the media was wrong. They quickly realised what they had in common with their new-found friends and that what unites us is far greater and stronger than what divides us. I came home feeling that this was the most important day of my life. If only everyone could do something like this!

I wrote in Chapter 5 about the impact on our own mental health of having purpose and achieving. The implications for our engagement levels, excitement levels and energy levels are huge when we truly believe in what we are doing and are unified in the way we approach it. From my own experience, I know that I was never more motivated to go to school and work long, hard hours than when I really sensed that my work was making a difference, when my contribution was changing things and helping other people. When we re-personalise education, and keep the child and the rights of the child at the centre, then that powerful, altruistic, intrinsic motivator of self-actualisation comes to the fore and makes life not merely bearable or tolerable but exciting and energising.

The wheel of education

Elsewhere I have used the wheel as a metaphor for sustainable and balanced progress. Given the content of the previous two chapters, I want to propose here a wheel of education that could be a starting point for redesigning what we do every day in school and the way we go about it.

Figure 14.2 has five spokes and at the hub are the rights of the child, which underpin everything:

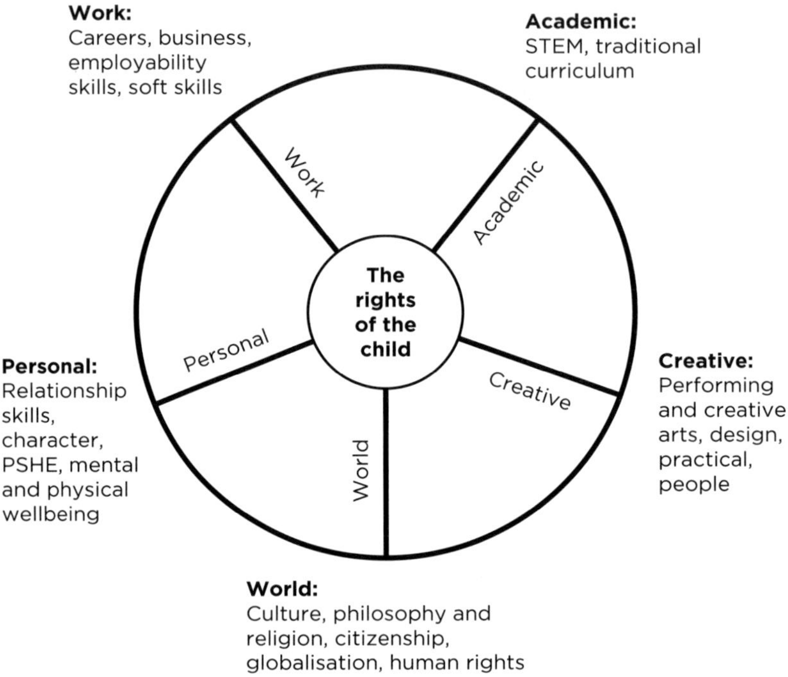

Figure 14.2. The wheel of education

Holistic education, or some variation of it, is not merely an idea. It is a right. It is not a privilege; it is what children are entitled to. And it is our duty as adults to provide it. I am not suggesting that that we try to slot these different aspects into our existing framework, but rather that we reshape our system and provision to deliver a truly rights-respecting education that successfully produces outstanding global citizens of whom we can be truly proud.

Chapter 15

The Measuring Conundrum and a Possible Route Map for Change

A well-known cartoon depicts a scene in which six animals are lined up expectantly in front of a teacher's desk: a monkey, a penguin, an elephant, a goldfish, a seal and a dog. The teacher explains what's going to happen: "For a fair selection everybody has to take the same exam. Now, please climb that tree." The point is clear: to have one measure for everyone in order to be fair, isn't fair!

Let's return to the McNamara fallacy: that we tend to measure what can be easily measured, which leads us to disregard what cannot be easily measured. Or, worse, to presume that what cannot be easily measured isn't important or doesn't exist. In the context of education, this is very apt. What can we easily measure in schools? Exam results. And so this is what we measure. The problem is that using one fairly simplistic measure never tells the whole truth

It is very difficult to quantify the impact of a teacher's smile and nurture of his tutees each morning; or the significance of the extra two minutes at the end of a lesson when a personal word with a student lifts their day and realigns their trajectory; or the impact of a one-to-one with the student counsellor; or the effect of an inspirational assembly which sparked an idea, a dream or a new way of thinking; or the motivational significance and sense of belonging generated by being part of an afterschool club or team. And because these things are difficult to measure, generally speaking we don't attempt to do so and consequently don't place much value on them. They end up relegated to the periphery of school life rather than lying at its core.

One thing is fairly certain: the fixation with judging schools on such narrow data severely impoverishes our students' education. There is little drive among most school leaders to put any significant investment of either time or money into the kind of initiatives that develop students personally, emotionally, morally and socially. This is principally because of the way we currently assess schools and a ruthlessly short-term and short-sighted approach to accountability.

Real change does not happen overnight. It can't and it shouldn't – not where people are concerned. However, the relentless pressure placed on head teachers (and politicians) to deliver results, and deliver them fast, results in a race to the bottom: the quickest route to the greatest gain on the most simplistic measure possible. Hence, we have created a school culture driven by Year 6 SATs and Year 11 GCSEs. In many schools it is not an exaggeration to say that there is a heavily skewed focus on these two year groups: what strategies and interventions can we put in place to squeeze every smidgen of value possible (and by value I mean data value) from these cohorts? Little wonder, then, that this pressure is projected onto students, who undoubtedly suffer greatly from this immense scrutiny as their teachers, in turn, crack the very whip they themselves resent.

It doesn't take a genius to work out that the resultant 'progress' doesn't equate to real value for the student. The data is misleading, manipulated and arguably fairly irrelevant, especially given our rapidly changing world. It tells employers very little about what a student can actually offer them. It is meaningful only within the synthetic educational world we have created. We know it doesn't tell the whole picture, but we have signed on and given our consent anyway. Until we admit that the data is wrong, and that the measuring methodology which generates it is wrong, we won't change the system.

The current method is lazy and unduly focused on the short term. There is a better way. We have already explored the value of other skills and aptitudes, such as employability, EQ, communication and social skills, relationships, financial acumen and so on – skills which arguably will have greater impact on students' future success in life than academic achievement. But in addressing this imbalance, we must be wary of simplifying matters, for that is what led us into this mess in the first place: one simple measure on which to base our progress judgement.

I do not wish to imply that there is a straightforward solution. There isn't. Nor do I wish to rubbish academic achievement and all the great teaching and learning out there that develops this. My point is that to draw a line between academic achievement and holistic development is a false dichotomy. Human beings are complex creatures and the art of drawing out their potential is not easy. To pretend otherwise is to insult the phenomenal skill of teachers everywhere.

The principle of obliquity

What to do? Let me begin with a lovely idea I came across through an Anglican priest called Ann Morisy: the principle of obliquity.[1]

Imagine you are in a sailing boat. You have a destination in sight but the wind is against you. If you turn the boat towards your destination you will be driven away from it, so the solution is to tack. In order to tack, the sailor directs the boat away from its destination, or at an oblique angle to it (as shown in Figure 15.1).

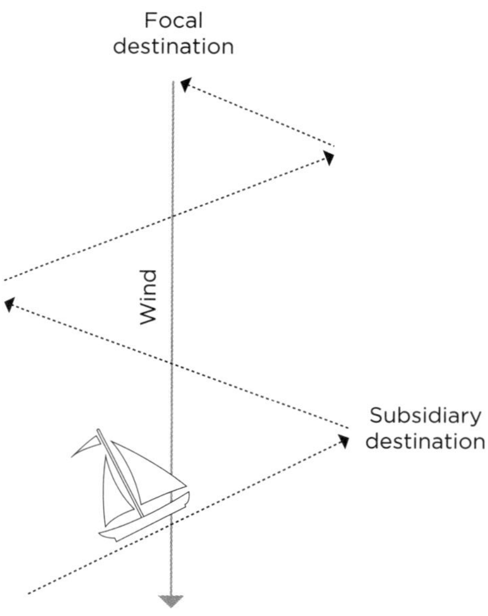

Figure 15.1. Tacking: an oblique approach

1 A. Morisy, *Journeying Out: A New Approach to Christian Mission* (London: Continuum, 2004).

Notice that at no point is the boat aiming directly at its intended destination. It is approaching its intended destination obliquely. Now, in order to tack efficiently, the sailor may set her sights on a secondary landmark or compass bearing which is quite different to the intended destination. The sailor may be deliberately sailing north-east, for example, when her destination is actually north.

Here is the danger: what if the sailor forgets about her ultimate objective? What if she is feeling so comfortable speeding along on her north-easterly course that she forgets, or even chooses (for the sake of ease), to make north-east her new destination? To stop tacking and just go where the wind is taking her? She may get very good at sailing north-east. She may reach the subsidiary landmark she has fixed her gaze upon, but in doing so she will have aborted entirely her focal destination.

Likewise, we did not intend to create a deficient education system – various factors led us to this point. We lost sight of our focal destination and got excessively caught up approaching the subsidiary landmark of ever-increasing academic progress. We need to rediscover that academic progress is not the focal objective; it is a subsidiary one.

For example, Morisy notes that Disneyland employees are not told to go and make money; instead they are encouraged 'to make sure the guests have fun'. Profit is a by-product and, arguably, should remain so if it is to be maximised. George Merck, founder of the most profitable US pharmaceutical company Merck & Co, said, 'We try never to forget that medicine is for the people, it is not for profits. The profits follow, and when we have remembered that, they have never failed to appear.'[2]

Our role as leaders is to make sure that the focal objective is kept clearly to the fore, while organising our actions to enable its fulfilment. The question for us in education, then, is what exactly is our objective? Which brings us back to the topic of the previous chapter: to begin with the end in mind. But is the end measurable?

2 Quoted in Morisy, *Journeying Out*, p. 16.

Triple bottom line accounting

Let me stay with the business analogy for a while longer. The number one measure of success within the capitalist system has long been assumed to be profit. Economist Milton Friedman famously stated: 'there is one and only one social responsibility of business – to use its resources and engage in activities designed to increase its profits'.[3]

This ideology, also known as the trickle-down theory of economics, holds that if businesses make money then everyone benefits through greater employment, more spending power, more tax revenue, better services and so on; literally, greed is good. However, pushed to its logical conclusions the capitalist system has resulted in a host of problems, not least of which is the growing gap between rich and poor, the exploitation of the most vulnerable people in society and the mindless rape of the planet's natural resources. With this in mind, John Elkington proposes an alternative way to measure 'good business': triple bottom line accounting.[4]

The traditional bottom line of financial profit doesn't tell the whole picture. Rather, a good business needs to measure and show progress in its impact on people (the consumer, employees, public) – a people account – and its impact on the environment – a planet account. Three bottom lines, not just one. Increasingly, businesses are realising that being socially responsible actually makes for financial success too. In fact, when these other bottom lines are ignored for the sake of profit (think of the Tesco horsemeat scandal or the VW faked emissions tests) the financial bottom line can be significantly damaged. Again, it is about balancing the short term and long term: for a while both Tesco and VW were getting away with it – reporting 'progress' – until their failure to recognise the longer term implications caught up with them.

When it comes to education, the implications for schools not adequately addressing the holistic development of our students are substantial: a fragmented society, increased criminality, greater poverty, higher rates

3 M. Friedman, The Social Responsibility of Business Is to Increase Its Profits, *New York Times Magazine* (13 September 1970), p. 6. Available at: http://umich.edu/~thecore/doc/Friedman.pdf.

4 J. Elkington, *Cannibals with Forks: The Triple Bottom Line of 21st Century Business* (Bloomington, MN: Capstone, 1997).

of domestic violence, a mental health epidemic, record obesity levels. Oh, wait, that's not the future, that's what we've got now!

It is not going to be easy, of course. Is it even possible or desirable to measure a human being? I made the case earlier in this book that there is no finished product, no 'perfect', just continuance. We are all works in progress. So, I have reservations about drawing a line at some random point in a child's development and judging them to be a success or failure according to flawed mechanism. Certainly, using the blunt instrument of 'average' in order to do so will never be appropriate. Quite apart from the fact that no one is average, whoever wanted to be anyway? The average human has one testicle and one breast! No, much better to affirm the uniqueness of each individual and allow them to identify and pursue their own unique destination. Being prescriptive of an outcome or standard was what got us into trouble in the first place.

My proposal then, is not to measure the outcome, the focal objective, but to devise a robust balance of subsidiary measures which will collectively enable us to tack our way forward for each student in our care.

Which is most successful: Microsoft or Apple? Disney or Sky? Amazon or Facebook? It is impossible to answer because the question begs another: at what? It depends on what the bar is. In reality, these are all singular companies with differing aims and objectives, so to reduce them all to a dollar sign is to miss the point. When we reduce our students to a grade or a number we do them a similar disservice.

A further question: who has been most successful? Bill Gates or Steve Jobs? Walt Disney or Rupert Murdoch? Jeff Bezos or Mark Zuckerberg? Again, the question is a misnomer. Their companies are expressions of themselves. And so it is with teachers: to compare teachers on one or two crude measures devalues them and the teaching profession, and negatively impacts on the incredible human beings they nurture.

To illustrate, I recall seeing an interview with Tiffany Haddish.[5] Tiffany is a successful Hollywood actress but she revealed that she could not read until she was 15 years old. She'd had a tough early life and, alarmingly, had managed to get through to ninth grade without her teachers

5 Doctor Oz, Tiffany Haddish's Drama Teacher Taught Her How to Read [video] (26 August 2019). Available at: https://www.youtube.com/watch?v=EevSKGxQn3I.

realising this. Finally, her drama teacher caught on and put her on the spot one day. Here is what she did: she made Tiffany report to her every single lunchtime for a whole semester until she could read. Tiffany is successful today due in large part to that dedicated and compassionate teacher.

But here's the problem. It struck me as I heard this that in most schools that drama teacher would not have been acknowledged for her extra work. It would not have featured in her performance management appraisal. It would not have contributed to her numeric 'progress' target. She would not have been credited with time in lieu or extra pay. And she may well have been challenged by her superiors because perhaps her latest data drop was not entered on time. Yet she was doing exactly what a great teacher does: investing her time, compassion and expertise in helping her students to make progress – in spite of the school system. Surely, our schools should be enabling teachers to help students, not hindering them, or, worse still, penalising them for doing so.

Rather than measuring one outcome and using it to rate both teachers and students, we need to be measuring the contributing factors that enable students to thrive, while keeping firmly at the forefront of our minds the focal objective of the whole child and his or her unique contribution to the world.

The focal objective of education

I introduced my wheel of education in the last chapter. In triple bottom line accounting neither the profit margin, nor the people account, nor the planet measure tell you about the success of the company as a whole. They each measure progress – whether we are moving forwards and how fast – but in one regard only. In a successful company these different elements will be in balance. If one comes at the expense of another (e.g. profit at the expense of poor pay and conditions or environmental damage) then the company's so-called success is hollow. And it certainly wouldn't be appropriate to compare them to another more ethical company.

In education, we need to measure a child's progress in English and maths, of course. It is necessary to know where they are in order to challenge them further and move them forward. But to measure English and maths in isolation from all other skills and aptitudes, or to impoverish other subjects in order to do so, is unhelpful and possibly immoral.

In *The Second Curve*, Charles Handy distinguishes between the process and the content of education. He refers to his experience of applying for a job in the oil industry, despite knowing nothing about oil. The selection committee said, 'Don't worry. You have a well-trained mind which we can fill with the content you need.' Now, more than ever, information is just a click away and our ability to process it, apply it and use it is the currency of success. Handy says, 'We are all artists in that we are the creators of our own lives. We learn most about life from living, by practice, with help ... Learning without context is hard, and learning without use soon evaporates.'[6] The subsidiary objective has become the focal point. He continues: 'To be effective as schools for life, the schools need to be more like work as it is today, where tasks are increasingly project based, done in groups, where initiative is prized and commitment rewarded.'[7]

Admittedly, much already goes on in schools to address the process of education and the application of skills to the real world. The problem is that, broadly speaking, it is not measured, and so it stays at the periphery. Andreas Schleicher at the Organisation for Economic Co-operation and Development says:

> The world economy no longer pays you for what you know; Google knows everything. The world economy pays you for what you can do with what you know ... the kinds of things that are easy to test and easy to teach are also the kinds of things that are easy to digitise, automate, and outsource.[8]

We need to begin devising ways to measure all the components on the wheel of education.

6 C. Handy, *The Second Curve: Thoughts on Reinventing Society* (London: Random House, 2015), p. 183.

7 Handy, *The Second Curve*, p. 185.

8 Quoted in K. Robinson, *Creative Schools: Revolutionizing Education from the Ground Up* (London: Penguin, 2015), p. 168.

In *Creative Schools*, Ken Robinson compares schools in Finland with their counterparts in the United States. Finland has consistently high standards of achievement on all international measures. He notes that Finland chose not to go down the route of standardisation. Finnish schools give high priority to practical and vocational programmes and the development of creativity. They also collaborate rather than compete, develop close links with parents and the community, and principals have wide discretion in how they run their schools. They have also invested heavily in the training and development of their teachers.[9] Again, the principle of obliquity is evident. High achievement is a necessary by-product of a focal objective which acknowledges the uniqueness and significance of each child and context. Standardised measuring very easily diverts from and undermines progress.

Furthermore, any grading system is necessarily a simplification. It arguably conceals far more than it reveals. Joe Bower, teacher and co-author of *De-testing and De-grading Schools*, goes as far as to say, 'I have come to see grades as schools' drug of choice and we are all addicted ... Grades were originally tools used by teachers, but today teachers are tools used by grades.'[10]

Robinson considers Surrey, a school district in British Columbia, which has done away with letters and numbers altogether. Instead, it uses a portfolio programme called Fresh Grade. Teachers work with students to define individual goals and markers of progress. Success is then defined in relation to these. Teachers feed back to parents continually using photographs of work to provide glimpses into the child's progress. In this system you can't get an A without progress. Rather than being rewarded for reaching an extrinsic standard, students are intrinsically motivated to keep moving forward.[11]

This practice is perfectly in sync with Carol Dweck's research on the distinction between performance goals and learning goals (discussed briefly in Chapter 8). Dweck's research showed that performance goals, such as getting an A in French, inhibited students' ability to apply concepts to

9 Robinson, *Creative Schools*, p. 60.

10 Quoted in Robinson, *Creative Schools*, p. 171. See also J. Bower and P. L. Thomas, *De-testing and De-grading Schools: Authentic Alternatives to Accountability and Standardization* (New York: Peter Lang, 2013).

11 Robinson, *Creative Schools*, p. 179.

new situations, whereas students who were given learning goals scored significantly higher on these novel challenges, as well as working longer and trying more solutions.[12] The implications for measuring progress in any discipline are huge. Performance goals are inferior to learning goals both as motivators and as measures, yet we remain wedded to them. As in British Columbia, we need to be innovative with progress measures that relate to learning rather than performance, and application and process rather than knowledge and content. I have mentioned more than once the potentially damaging effect on our mental health of internalising standards. For me it was an obsession with perfection, but for all of us, the constant comparison with others, exacerbated in our earliest years by being graded, ranked and then praised in relation to abstract standards, can be crushing.

All the standards in our schools are made up. Even though some are more useful than others, they are still essentially arbitrary and arguably do more damage than good. Think back to the cartoon at the start of this chapter. Even if some animals can climb trees better than others, why is it something that needs to be measured? Who suggested that climbing trees is desirable or to be aspired to? The fish is certainly not deficient for not being able to do it. It is a contrived standard.

If we are to take the education of each child seriously, assuming as a given the infinite value and unique potential of each child, then I would argue that we must move away from standardised testing entirely. This is not to say we don't measure. On the contrary, it actually means that we remove the artificial limits that tests inevitably create.

Getting our goals right

Why do we – children, teachers, anyone – get sidetracked and give up? Angela Duckworth cites four basic reasons. She calls them 'buzzkillers':

1 I'm bored (boredom).

2 I don't care (carelessness).

12 Dweck, *Self-Theories*, p. 17.

3 It's too much effort (low aspiration).

4 I don't think I can (pessimism).[13]

These all come down to one thing: wrong goals. If the goal is too high we switch off or won't try (pessimism and low aspiration). If the goal is too low we get bored (boredom). If the goal isn't ours – that is, if it doesn't resonate with our core values and beliefs – we won't care enough (carelessness).

Wrong goals kill motivation, achievement and the sense of purpose which is integral to emotional wellbeing, engagement and flourishing. Right goals are everything. They result in intrinsic motivation, excitement and achievement. Students and staff need to own their goals. If we are going to build schools that are emotionally and mentally healthy, schools in which children really excel, then we must abandon any kind of automated target setting. And I don't think it goes far enough to say, 'Well, we don't tell the students their target grades – they're just for the teacher's data record.' That is just paying lip service. If the numbers are in your markbook, then they remain a bar by which you judge others and others judge you.

Numeric targets are performance goals. The research is conclusive: they inhibit progress. So let's be bold and do away with them, which means doing away with most, even if not all, standardised testing. Instead, we should start with each child and identify:

1 What can or can't you do now?

2 What would you like to be able to do?

3 What might be the next step towards achieving this goal?

4 How will you know when you have been successful in achieving this goal?

This is what we should be measuring and what students and teachers can be held accountable for. What is more, these four questions are

13 Duckworth, *Grit*, p. 90.

applicable to every strand on the wheel of education (which we first encountered in Chapter 14). Here are some examples:

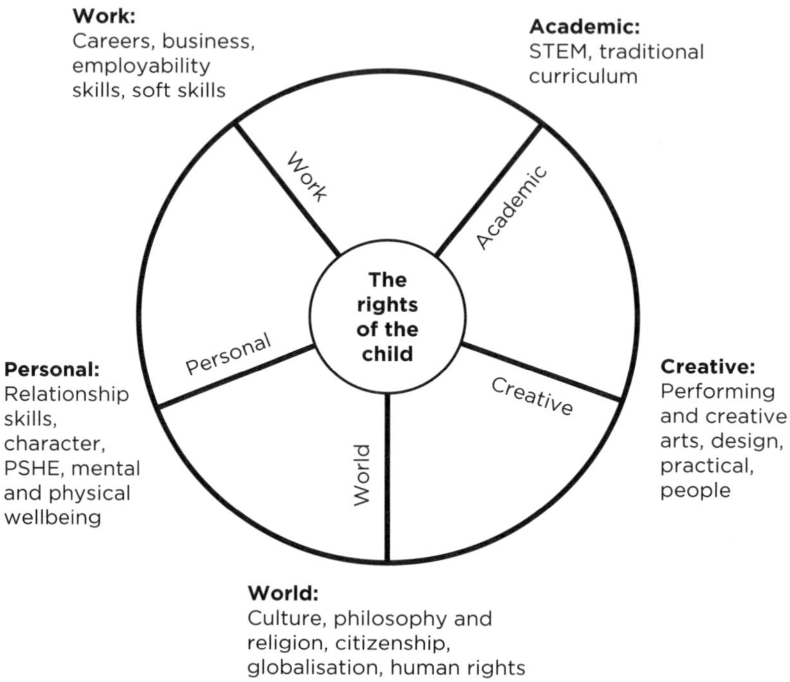

Figure 15.2. The wheel of education

Work

1 **What can or can't you do now?** I can't talk about myself confidently.

2 **What would you like to be able to do?** I would like to be able to talk confidently about myself and my skills in an interview context without feeling embarrassed.

3 **What might be the next step towards achieving this goal?** (This is where the teacher or mentor uses their expertise to identify the knowledge and practice necessary to reach the goal – for example,

there might need to be some education around the application of skills, and literacy would need to be considered and addressed.) A possible first step might be to identify my skill set and then write two personalised paragraphs as if speaking to an interviewer.

4 **How will you know when you have been successful in achieving this goal**? (The teacher and learner break down this goal into its component parts and devise a self-assessment mechanism to measure progress.)

Immediately, it is easy to see the various next steps that will be necessary to build on step 1 and work towards the goal. It is also possible to see how students could make significant progress in their personal presentation skills. They own the goal and they own the process, so given the opportunity they can also own the success criteria. A very simple list might look something like this.

- Eye contact: too little/about right/too much.
- Assertiveness: too timid/about right/too much.
- Clarity: too unclear/about right/a bit patronising.
- Enthusiasm: too apathetic/about right/over the top.
- Conciseness: too little detail/about right/too long-winded.

Alternatively, you could use a numeric scale. You could also pad out the descriptors and make this into a whole-class activity with class-agreed success criteria. The point is if they are owned by the students, they are likely to be far more effective in eliciting progress. Of course, these judgements are subjective, but that is okay because there is no absolute standard – there is just improvement. So, let's measure and affirm the progress made rather than comparing it against the 'perfect' standard which has not yet been reached. This reminds me of my counsellor's advice: 'Face what you've already dug.' This doesn't mean, don't be aspirational. It means keep digging, keep reaching and keep setting goals, but measure the actual progress made and not the abstract distance ahead.

I'm not suggesting anything new here. This is just assessment for learning, which many have written about far more eloquently. But I am proposing that we apply these principles more holistically to all aspects of student development and be bold enough to let them truly drive our assessment at its core.

Personal

1 **What can or can't you do now?** I can't control my anger when my parents argue.

2 **What would you like to be able to do?** I would like to be able to manage my anger so that I don't 'lose it' in future.

3 **What might be the next step towards achieving this goal?** (The teacher or mentor uses their expertise to identify the knowledge and practice necessary to reach the goal. There might be a number of component steps which would link to the scheme of learning.)

- Understand how the mind and emotions function.
- Self-awareness of key triggers.
- Strategies to use in high-pressure situations.
- Practice and self-evaluation.

4 **How will you know when you have been successful in achieving this goal?** (The teacher and learner devise a self-assessment mechanism to measure progress.)

World

1 **What can or can't you do now?** I don't understand why Christians think homosexuality is wrong.

2 **What would you like to be able to do?** I would like to be able to debate with a conservative Catholic and be able to state my reasons for disagreeing with him or her.

3 **What might be the next step towards achieving this goal?** (The teacher or mentor uses their expertise to identify the knowledge

and practice necessary to reach the goal. There might be a number of component steps which would link to the scheme of learning.)

- Understand Catholic ethics.
- Self-awareness of my own beliefs and influences.
- Skills and components of a good argument.
- Practice at making an argument and supporting a conclusion with evidence.

4 **How will you know when you have been successful in achieving this goal?** (The teacher and learner devise a self-assessment mechanism to measure progress.)

I won't labour the point further: there are plenty of examples of success criteria linked to learning goals for both academic and creative subjects. They are used extensively every day in most schools. What I have sought to illustrate here is that we can adopt the same approach with any discipline and use it to measure meaningful progress which excites, motivates and equips students to reach the focal, holistic objective of success in life, rather than the subsidiary objective of a set of GCSE grades.

There is lots more thinking and experimentation to be done in this area. My hope is that this chapter acts as a prompt to further investigation and innovation. If we take a more rounded view of student progress, it will undoubtedly impact on the way we think about teacher accountability for that progress and lead to a more holistic appreciation of the multifaceted role of the teacher and, by extension, schools. So, how about quintuple bottom line accountability for our schools?

Chapter 16

Embedding Wellbeing in School Life

Freud once said, 'We bleed our beliefs through every pore.'[1] It's worth musing on. What beliefs do your activities, interactions and words unconsciously communicate? What about over the past few months or year? What keeps coming through over and over again? And, importantly, are those beliefs positive and constructive or negative and destructive? Over the course of this book, perhaps you have put your finger on a few of both kinds. The skill is to recognise and weed out the destructive ones and replace them with healthier and more positive ones. For better or worse, our experiences have shaped each one of us. The skill we must develop is that of distilling each experience by harnessing the good and discarding the bad.

Case Study – Burton Borough School[2]

Krissi Carter, the principal of Burton Borough School, is an example of a visionary leader who has allowed her experience to positively shape an ethos to school leadership that bleeds wellbeing through every pore. Krissi almost became another casualty of the teaching profession. After just two years as a teacher, she was sleeping for just four hours a night, working relentlessly and had a breakdown. She tells of going to the doctor and being unable to recall even her name, address and phone number. Krissi battled back and found a more sustainable way of living

1 Quoted in I. Gilbert, *Essential Motivation in the Classroom* (Abingdon and New York: Routledge, 2013), p. 101.

2 The content of this chapter is derived from interviews with Krissi Carter and attendance of her TEDx NorwichED talk, 'Badly Behaved or Emotionally Strained?' [video], *TED.com* (July 2019). Available at: https://www.ted.com/talks/krissi_carter_badly_behaved_or_emotionally_
strained.

and teaching; however, over time she became frustrated by an unsustainable system which is letting down both teachers and students.

In one school where she worked as a senior leader, Krissi was spending 22 hours a week 'on patrol'. Many senior leaders will identify with this: time spent walking the corridors, around the school field and grounds, addressing behaviour incidents or providing back-up for other staff struggling with poor behaviour. She asks a very valid question: how can it be a good use of public funds for the most highly paid school staff to be spending their time walking the school grounds in hi-vis jackets with walkie-talkies? Aren't these leaders employed to use their experience and expertise to strategically lead and drive progress forward?

Yet this is the story in many schools – schools which are reactive rather than proactive in their approach to addressing behaviour, pastoral needs and mental wellbeing. We may have very good systems in place to support students once we discover, for example, that they are self-harming (although it is fair to say that most schools are strained to the point of breaking point by the workload this is generating). However, we have not been sufficiently hands-on in providing students (or staff) with the knowledge, tools and strategies they need to manage their own wellbeing, such that they are able to address the causes of mental ill health long before they resort to self-harm or other negative coping mechanisms.

Krissi, by now a head at Burton Borough School, decided to step back from responding to incidents and look again at the data. It was an uncomfortable experience:

> What we discovered was that those most in need of our help, those most vulnerable, those who had mental health and wellbeing issues, those were the ones we were excluding, those were the ones being put in detention, those were the ones being put in isolation. And every single time we did that, we were making them feel more and more rejected and reinforcing that they didn't belong in our school and our community. So they stopped coming to school because school was a horrible place to be.

Krissi draws on research by Professor Kathryn Riley from the UCL Institute of Education on the subject of belonging:

> Belonging is a sense of being somewhere where you can be confident that you will fit in and be safe in your identity. In our volatile world, a sense of belonging provides young people with a springboard which enables them to be and become their best possible selves.
>
> What happens in any school is down to the people in and around it. What makes a school a place are the relationships. What makes a school a place where young people and adults want to be is whether the spaces in the school are transformed into places of belonging and learning.[3]

The drive for this sense of belonging is powerful – we touched on it in Chapter 5 as one of the six basic psychological needs of human beings. Fundamentally, if we are to build schools that help students and staff to thrive, then fostering this sense of belonging – rather than exacerbating feelings of isolation and exclusion – must form the basis of our policies and practice.

On GCSE results day 2018, some students who had formed a campaign group called Education Not Exclusion posted a spoof Tube map on some London Underground trains called The School to Prison Line. It demonstrated powerfully how, beginning with sending students out of class or placing them in detention, a strategy of exclusion leads on to permanent exclusion, prison and an endless loop of reoffending. It also disproportionately negatively impacts on those with special educational needs. Alongside the map they wrote:

> It is the most disadvantaged pupils who are disproportionately punished by the system. We deserve better. We are a group of South London students who believe in empathy not exclusion. We demand a more compassionate education system with a supportive approach to behaviour and discipline.

Krissi has sought to transform Burton Borough School by placing mental health and wellbeing at the heart of everything they do. As a result,

3 K. Riley, M. Coates and S. P. Martinez, *Place & Belonging in Schools: Opening Up Possibilities* (London: UCL Institute of Education, 2018), p. 3. Available at: https://www.ucl.ac.uk/ioe/sites/ioe/files/place-and-belonging-unlocking-possibilities.pdf.

annual school exclusions have reduced from over 100 to single figures, staff attendance has gone from 92% to 98%, staff retention has ceased to be an issue (the school now has unsolicited offers from people looking for teaching jobs) and the school is oversubscribed year on year.

There have been two important and interrelated aspects of the transformation at Burton Borough: the structure of the school pastoral system and investment in, and the development of, staff.

The structure of school

Krissi inherited a common school structure in which heads of year, along with admin support, managed the pastoral wellbeing of students. The heads of year shared an office, which was often empty as staff were teaching or engaged elsewhere. The upshot was that pastoral and wellbeing concerns ended up being reported and shared to a wide range of staff as need arose. Krissi notes that the lines of communication increase exponentially the more people are involved, and this in turn increases the potential for miscommunication, mistakes and ineffective action. With eight people sharing the office, there were 28 lines of communication. Add in SLT and you have 14 people, making for 91 lines of communication! In contrast, if you have three people there are just three lines of communication. Far more efficient!

The first thing Krissi did was to restructure the school system by establishing three 'mini schools', each with their own head and deputy (both SLT) and three supporting staff members (all non-teaching). These five staff members became a 'Wellbeing Hub' with their finger firmly on the pulse of what was going on with each student. Five staff, ten lines of communication, all operating from the same place.

Furthermore, these mini schools were given the autonomy to develop their own name, their own identity, their own colours and their own motto. I have already commented on the significance of autonomy in developing intrinsic motivation (Chapter 8). Krissi speaks of her own journey in 'letting go' of the controls to some extent:

> I'm an only child and a control freak! I struggle with not being in control, but I had to recognise the value of difference and

> draw on that in order to develop something better than what we had. I love Bertrand Russell's quote: 'Do not fear to be eccentric in opinion, for every opinion now accepted was once eccentric.' Our whole school motto, selected by the students, is 'Be the difference'.

For belonging to be a reality we have to embrace difference, in opinion and in expression. This has become central to Burton Borough's approach. The three mini schools are living, breathing expressions of difference within the school – and, crucially, they foster and promote belonging. For example, isolation booths have been removed. If students enter class clearly out of sorts they may be directed to the Wellbeing Hub to address what they are feeling and the reasons why. But being 'directed' to the hub for support is very different to being 'sent' to isolation as a sanction. It doesn't take a genius to see the direct link between isolation (whether in detention or in a booth) and the exacerbation of a student's sense that 'I don't belong', 'I don't fit in here' or 'I'm not wanted here'.

However, this is not to say that Burton Borough has done away with sanctions altogether. Krissi explains that staff seek to be very clear with students that 'an explanation doesn't excuse'. While all sorts of circumstances may explain why a student acts unacceptably or disruptively, that does not excuse such behaviour. Every person is responsible for his or her own actions and responses to situations, but the necessity for sanctions has been reduced significantly due to the emphasis on prevention rather than cure. Krissi says:

> The hubs are such welcoming places, and the support structures so effective, that students now self-refer if something has happened at home or on the way to school. This means that issues are addressed before they get to be behaviour issues in the classroom.

But structure isn't everything. At the heart of Krissi's school makeover has been an explicit and proactive investment in her staff.

Staff wellbeing

If staff are not well, happy, enthusiastic and engaged then their teaching is going to suffer. But more than that, staff need to be collectively on board with changes. Too often a new head or new initiatives (even ones designed to reduce stress) are stress-inducing for staff who already feel overwhelmed. Krissi describes some of the changes that have created an environment for teachers to flourish and, in turn, truly support and nurture the wellbeing of their students:

> We scrapped lesson observations and learning walks and have banned the use of graded lesson judgements like requires improvement or good. Instead we introduced 'Talk for Teaching': teachers and leaders go into each other's lessons and talk about what they see. The conversations are collaborative, constructive and focused on learning. Instead of teachers in the staffroom asking, 'Have you been seen yet?' they are talking about teaching and learning. Staff are disappointed if SLT haven't popped in and seen the good work they are doing!

The school has invested in coaching training for all, so that staff development is now addressed within a coaching culture and individuals are enabled to set and review their own targets in dialogue with their coach. As Krissi observes, 'People don't go to work to do a rubbish job.' If we approach staff development from that starting point, we are in a much stronger position to foster an aspirational teaching culture. Effective development is about knowing your staff, just as effective student development is about knowing your students.

As part of their performance management, every teacher works on their own research project, which they choose in consultation with their coach/line manager. There is an intrinsic valuing of each staff member and what they contribute, as well as a commitment to grow them as professionals and individuals. This is a culture of trust and helpfulness rather than fear and one-upmanship.

This culture was established right at the outset when Krissi and her team reviewed the pay structure in the school and recognised that pay was not commensurate with output, with some staff being paid a disproportionate amount while others, who contributed far more, were being paid much less. Krissi consulted with union reps and made everyone's pay public, including her own, in a move towards complete transparency. Some people took a cut, some received a pay rise and some took on more responsibilities, but overall the move has clearly helped to establish an open culture that rewards effort and outcomes.

Wellbeing is part of the ethos at Burton Borough. Every Monday morning in the staff briefing there is a focus on wellbeing called Mindfulness Monday. The governors are mental health trained, and all staff have been trained in mental and emotional wellbeing to both understand themselves and the students they teach. Staff have also had mindfulness training and many now incorporate mindfulness into their daily lessons beginning with 'stillings' or reflections. Krissi adds, 'It has become part of what we do. The students expect it now.'

There is also ongoing training in the area of language and using language effectively and consistently. Krissi explains that there is a 'no shouting rule' in the school: 'Shouting is usually associated with a loss of control. It generates anxiety and is usually unhelpful. My staff don't shout. All staff know to separate the behaviour from the child in the way they address students and challenge inappropriate behaviour.'

Staff have agreed a no emails after 5.30pm rule, with the proviso that if emails need to be sent after that time, then no response should be expected until the following working day. It is important to note, though, that this decision was reached collaboratively rather than as a directive from the top. This collaborative approach is a hallmark of Krissi's leadership and arguably has been a critical factor in her success in implementing so many changes in such a short time.

Although it has taken some longer than others to adapt to the changes, the staff at Burton Borough seem to be fully on board with seeing themselves as holistic developers and nurturers of students rather than simply as subject specialists. The child comes first, the subject second. This approach to the child flows from a sense of the teacher's own sense of belonging, trust and value. To attempt to revolutionise adolescent wellbeing in any school without first revolutionising the staff culture is short-sighted and ultimately doomed to failure.

What Burton Borough School demonstrates is that another reality is possible, even within the confines of our current educational system.

With some bold leadership and creative thinking, we can redesign what we do and build something sustainable and healthy. Burton Borough is a work in progress, but they are committed to the journey – and that is what matters.

Chapter 17

Brave Thinking: Out of the Cave Ideas for Change and Possibility

As we saw in Chapter 4, Plato's Cave depicts an existence in which people are imprisoned, not by some external force but by their own voluntary acceptance of the reality with which they are presented. The prisoners are prisoners in mind only. The philosopher urges them to escape and discover the truth beyond the world of shadows, but they ridicule, persecute and kill her.

As human beings we seem to be inherently resistant to change. Change represents threat; familiarity brings security and safety. We like what we know. But as the world around us changes, it is our duty to not only adapt and change with it but also to shape and lead the change. Successful companies and movements do just that: they don't wait for a kick up the behind, they forge ahead into the unknown and make the future what they want it to be.

This is the difference between cave thinking and brave thinking. In the cave, we are distracted by what seems to be acceptable, by what seems to be the norm. Accepting these norms is more comfortable and less traumatic than breaking out into an unknown, brave new world. This is captured brilliantly in the film *The Shawshank Redemption* which shows Morgan Freeman's character, Red, released from prison after 50 years of incarceration. He tries to live outside the cave of the institution that has become his home but he finds it too new, too difficult, too scary. There is a moving scene which shows him walking up to the prison gates and asking if he can come back in. He keeps thinking of ways to break his parole so he can be sent back. He has become institutionalised.

It is hard to swim upstream, to go against the flow of the majority, of the familiar, of the accepted. The same idea is captured in Matthew (7:13–14): 'Enter through the narrow gate. For wide is the gate and broad is the road that leads to destruction, and many enter through it. But small is the gate and narrow the road that leads to life, and only a few find it.' It is difficult to be a change-maker but there is life ahead. Doing what everyone else is doing is never a recipe for success. Those who have stood out throughout the ages and changed the world are the ones who have questioned the reality they were handed and were brave enough to try something different. From the Wright Brothers to Martin Luther King Jr and from Jesus to Joan of Arc. Brave thinkers change the world.

Charles Handy in *The Second Curve* posits that all of life can be plotted on a sigmoid curve[1] – like this:

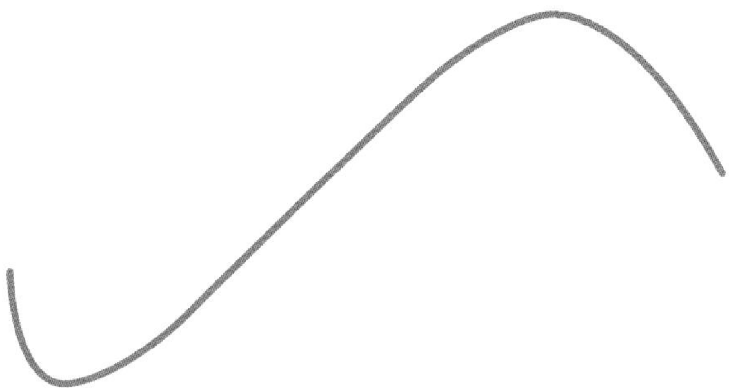

There is an initial investment of expense, study or outlay illustrated by the dip at the start. This is followed by a period of growth and progression, illustrated by the upward trajectory. This progress and growth then starts to peak and plateau, and then begins the inevitable decline into oblivion. Potentially this is your life. This is the life of any and every movement, business or organisation. The average life of a business used to be 60 years; now it's less than 20 years.[2] Sometimes the curve is long (the Roman Empire lasted for over a thousand years), sometimes it's short (like the rise and fall of a reality TV star).

1 Handy, *The Second Curve*, p. 21.

2 M. Sheetz, Technology Killing Off Corporate America: Average Life Span of Companies Under 20 Years, *CNBC* (24 August 2017). Available at: https://www.cnbc.com/2017/08/24/technology-killing-off-corporations-average-lifespan-of-company-under-20-years.html.

Handy's point is this: the secret to longevity, to avoiding that inevitable demise into oblivion, is to begin a second curve and ideally do it *just before* the first begins to plateau. Like this:

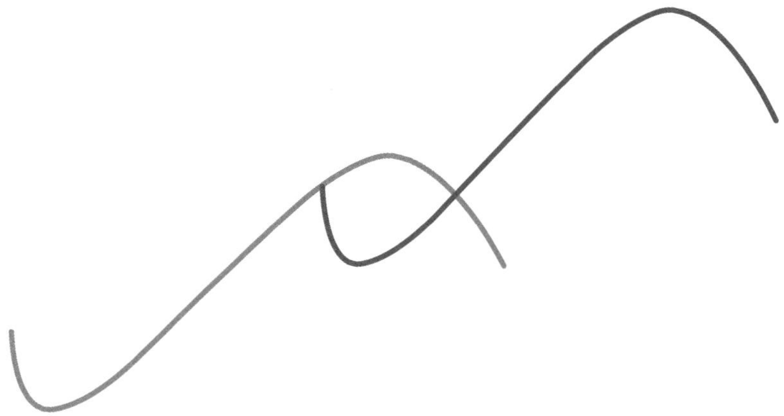

It is much more difficult to begin that new curve if you are already on the decline – self-confidence, resources, creativity and so on are all stretched – although it is possible. Equally, it is also difficult to stick your neck out and go for change when, to many, the status quo seems okay: if it ain't broke, don't fix it. The problem is, sometimes we kid ourselves that it ain't broke for far too long and ignore the truth that is staring us in the face.

The example of companies like Blockbuster Video and Toys 'R' Us is instructive, especially when compared to the likes of Netflix and Amazon. There was a time when it was hard to imagine a town without a Blockbuster Video. Yet when Blockbuster was at its peak, Netflix launched. The original idea was video rental by mail, and it almost never got started because founders Marc Randolph and Reed Hastings couldn't see how to compete with Blockbuster. In its day, Blockbuster had changed how we watch movies. It crushed the market for purchasing videos. Blockbuster led and shaped the market.[3]

Then DVDs came along. Mailing costs were much lower and Netflix were ready. They led and shaped the DVD mail order rental market

3 M. Randolph, *That Will Never Work: The Birth of NETFLIX and the Amazing Life of an Idea* (London: Octopus Publishing, 2019), p. 262.

while everyone else was playing catch-up. Then in the early 2000s came bandwidth that allowed internet streaming and Netflix positioned themselves to take advantage of these technological shifts to look ahead to a future without DVDs or mail. Blockbuster, on the other hand, was stuck with thousands of stores all over the world but with no product to sell in them. Blockbuster failed to start a second curve because it looked as if the first curve was going just fine.

Here is an uncomfortable truth: when it looks like everything is going well, the truth is you have probably already peaked and seeds of change are already germinating. I want to argue that *now* is the time to change our schools and education system. But in order to do this, to begin a new curve, we will need to question everything we do currently. Some questions may lead to seismic shifts and some may result in no change at all – in fact, we may firmly conclude that in some areas we already have the right answer. I'm not suggesting we change everything, just that we question everything, and, in doing so, we throw out the dirty bathwater without harming the baby.

What follows is a fairly random set of questions, working on the assumption that there is no such thing as a stupid question. They are in no particular order. If, as you read through, your instinctive response is negative, I recommend that you pause and just ask yourself why.

Questions about teaching and learning

- What would happen if you gave your teachers totally free rein to simply teach and mark in the way they want, with the proviso that they will be held accountable for the results and progress their students make?
- What would happen if you invited your teachers to redesign their subject curriculum?
- What would happen if you didn't test students so often?

- What if you abandoned grading and numeric targets for all work except public exams? Would it enhance or undermine your outcomes?
- How about actively encouraging staff to come up with their own marking patterns and recording systems, minimising data entry wherever possible and sharing good ideas or systems?
- Do reports need to be written? Could they be verbal instead? Could they be constructive and formative rather than summative? Do they actually aid progress?
- What if we measured everything differently, like the number of times a student has tried something new or encountered a novel or uncomfortable situation? What if we made sure that every student was being pushed outside their comfort zone in new ways every year?
- What if outdoor education was a mandatory part of the curriculum? If mountains, coasteering, kayaking and the benefits of the Duke of Edinburgh's Award were enjoyed by those students who don't have proactive parents as well as those who do? Could every school have their own type of Duke of Edinburgh's Award programme for all students to go through and graduate from? How would this improve student resilience and a broad skill set?
- How about all students engaging with music more? What if we really invested in our music and arts departments and helped every student to feel at home in these parts of the school, not just those who are aided by more hands-on parents outside of school?
- Instead of telling your staff to keep the pressure on in the last few days of term, making sure content and progress doesn't dip, how about doing the opposite? Tell them to take their foot off the gas and have some fun in the classroom, or just give them the option to do so? (I would wager that not much progress happens in the last few days either way!)
- How about saying yes to more educational visits and memorable school trips?

- What about including school clubs and extracurricular activities as contact time for staff and providing time off in lieu or extra payment, while also keeping them optional or voluntary.

Questions about staff development

- How about abandoning all formal lesson observations? What do they prove anyway? Aren't you more interested in what is going on every day in the classroom than what can be pulled out of the bag twice a year?
- How much coaching do your teachers receive? What would their teaching be like if all observation was about collaborative development and mutual learning?
- How much time do you allow for innovation? What if you devoted two INSET days a year to just coming up with a new idea or way of doing things?
- Do you expect all teachers to teach in the same way? Is your approach to staff development personalised?
- What if you did a skill set audit and then rethought your educational provision based on that rather than the other way round, with some teachers delivering video lessons or lectures for multiple classes at a time and others focusing on facilitating individualised learning?
- How about training every teacher in PSHE?
- How about training every staff member in mental health and mindfulness?
- How about starting a master's programme for staff to develop their knowledge and research in areas that will benefit them and the school?
- Why not timetable regular line meetings for all staff and include them as contact time (and protect them from cover)?

- How about providing leadership training every year for all those in or aspiring to leadership roles?
- Could you run or encourage more team awaydays or weekends, or bunch all your training days together and have an inspirational staff week away which sets the agenda and direction – and generates passion and innovation – for the whole year?

Questions about teacher wellbeing

- What if you told your teachers that they shouldn't be working at evenings and weekends, unless they want to do so?
- Could you create a team that shares its resources and planning so effectively that individual teacher planning time is vastly reduced?
- How much teacher time could be saved if sharing and collaborating was properly facilitated and encouraged?
- What if you allowed staff to take 'mental health days' each year, no questions asked?
- What if you encouraged staff to take a sick day pre-emptively rather than when they are on their knees? Would it actually save you money and generate goodwill?
- What if all free periods were genuinely free?
- What if you challenged the busyness culture and rewarded/affirmed outcomes rather than time?
- Could you subsidise lunch or coffee for staff? Would what you get back in goodwill, well-balanced teachers and reduced absenteeism be far more than you spend on provisions?
- What are your communal spaces like? Are they a priority in the budget? What would make them more welcoming, usable and valued?
- When was your last staff social? Do teams socialise together? Could you give a teaching and learning responsibility to a staff social coordinator?

- Have you got a wellbeing lead for staff and another for student wellbeing?
- Could you weave wellbeing into every week/every day? How?
- Why not give total flexibility in free periods so that teachers can use the gym or go home early and organise their time themselves?
- Could you offer a counselling service for all staff or an entitlement to six paid-for sessions of counselling as part of their terms of employment?

Questions about cultural norms

- Why do we need to call teachers Sir, Miss, Mr, Mrs or Ms? Why not lose the formality and use first names?
- Why allow only one piercing in each ear and only a stud earring to be worn in it? What are the actual implications for education of relaxing dress codes?
- Is school uniform really the great equaliser or does it feed into a philosophy of education as the mass production of clones? What about individuality and creative expression? What about asking parents and students themselves?
- Why do male teachers need to wear ties? What does 'smart' mean? Is clothing used to establish power, respect and hierarchy? Should we not be taken seriously because of who we are and what we do and accomplish rather than what we wear?
- Could you rethink parents' evenings and teacher–parent engagement? Could you offer time in lieu of evening commitments or give teachers autonomy over this area so they report back and log contact with parents in other more effective ways? Is everyone in one night the best way to do it?
- Does the school year have to rotate with quite the same degree of repetition? Could we vary the calendar year-on-year and include different things at different times of year?

Questions about logistics and time

- If we stopped using email for non-essential communication, would it make schools run better and help us talk to each other more?
- How much are emails actually read? Is this the best way to communicate? Are there better apps or social media platforms to keep people up to date or filter the important and urgent stuff from the other stuff for them?
- Why use teaching staff for breaktime and lunchtime duty? Is this a good use of their time? How about making it voluntary but for a free lunch instead?
- How about rethinking the timetable? Are we being counterproductive in seeking to squeeze every last drop of value from each hour of the school day? Do all lessons need to be equal in length? What about different kinds of lessons – short ones for condensed content (like TED Talks) and longer ones for application and practice?
- What about having more breaks? Or longer breaks? Or more varied activities during those breaks?
- What about changing the timings of the school day to allow more variety? Late starts some days and early finishes other days, or late finishes and early starts?

Questions about leadership

- How accessible are the SLT? What about starting an SLT surgery once a week so anyone can come and share an idea or a concern without an appointment?
- What if student voice was so central to school life that student reps sat in on governor meetings and SLT meetings, not as spectators but because they are genuinely part of the decision-making process?
- What if every school policy was ratified by student committees?

- What if the SLT wasn't called the SLT? How about dropping the word 'head', 'senior' and 'middle' from our vocabulary and just calling them 'lead teachers', 'team leaders' and the 'leadership team' instead? Does the reinforcement of hierarchy help or hinder?
- How about using a tool like the GCI as part of the recruitment process, so we don't end up with a school full of Implementers and no Creative Thinkers?
- How about involving teachers more in the recruitment of those they will be working with?
- Could you judge each request for time off or early finish on its merits and not worry about 'setting a precedent'? Would people understand if a single mother of three had to leave early or arrive late more often than a single man or woman without children?
- What are your prejudices? We all have prejudices, so it is best to be honest about what they are and how they impact on your attitudes and decision-making and try to do something about them.
- Do you trust those in your team? If not, why not? As a leader do you trust your teachers?
- Could you ask all staff what they think more? Could you invite feedback from staff and team leaders more frequently and report back every single time you ask them?
- Could the reasons for decisions be explained to staff more clearly and more often? Could school leaders be less paternalistic and more transparent and approachable?
- How could you make your middle leaders feel like leaders? How could you facilitate more grassroots innovations and organic change?

Questions about wider impact

- What about seeing your school or department as existing not simply for the education of the students but the betterment of the local community and the world? Could the school have offshoot charity and community projects, political or local care initiatives that utilise the skills and knowledge gained in the classroom and put it to practical use in the real world?
- What if every department had an annual outward-looking community or citizenship focus that it chose and linked to learning?
- Could every department have a careers lead who ensured that employability skills and future pathways were woven into every aspect of your schemes of learning?
- What if every class, every department and every year had rights ambassadors and wellbeing ambassadors? And you trained and empowered them with clear remits and responsibilities?
- What other income streams could be generated if the potential for innovative ideas in the school community was really tapped and the curriculum allowed time for students and staff to work on projects that would produce income for the school as a by-product?
- What if every school had a meaningful relationship with a partner school in a contrasting part of the country or world, and developed a reciprocal relationship with that school?

Questions about ethos and purpose

- What are you trying to achieve? Does everyone know and does everyone believe in your mission, including the site team and cleaning staff?
- What is an educated person? Are we fostering an underlying academic snobbery that esteems academic pathways above practical or vocational pathways?

- What do we mean by 'success'?
- What do we mean by 'talent' and does it even exist? Do we place far too much emphasis on nature than on nurture?
- What are your values? How does your school reflect them? For example, if you believe that family is important, how does your school reflect that value? Do you believe in hierarchy and autocracy, or do you believe in equality and democracy? Does your classroom reflect your beliefs?
- What if we stopped calling students who have benefitted from external private tutoring and proactive parenting 'talented', and instead praised their hard work, effort and practice? And perhaps even acknowledged that the opportunity was made possible by money? What if private music and arts lessons were accessible to all, not just those from wealthy backgrounds?
- What if we developed a vision that was a vision for our students too? So, not just a vision to develop well-rounded individuals ready for life and work, but one that calls on our students to participate in a bigger mission to build a fairer society and challenge injustice? What if the education of our students was clearly framed within that bigger picture and, right from the outset (whether in the private or state sector), we acknowledged that the world is unfair and the education system imperfect, and we actually invited our students to help us change that? Wouldn't that be something quite exciting to be part of?

I could go on. In fact, these questions only scratch the surface. Some of them will strike you as unworkable or unrealistic or maybe even silly. But before you dismiss any of them, I would urge you to answer the question I've posed: why? And if you do choose to reject it as unviable, be clear why you think it isn't viable.

Some of these things would take time to establish. Some are quick wins. Some would roll on from each other. Some might get a given ball rolling and then head off in a totally different direction. Some might be things you could do on a trial basis. You might want to discard the lot, simply because these are my questions and you need to ask your own. Or you may want to invite questions from those in your school community, so they own the questions and ask about what is pertinent to them. However, be prepared for the fact that many teachers and support staff, even though they are unhappy with the status quo, when presented with the challenge to change will resist.

Bear in mind too that, to be effective, changes must be introduced slowly and at the right time. Overwhelming change is counterproductive. Be patient with people, listen, win hearts and minds, give the freedom and autonomy for them to change at their own pace. Be mindful of the oxymoron of legislating that people must become more autonomous!

The philosopher in Plato's Cave was mocked and killed. Change-makers often are. But sometimes the change is realised a generation or two later, so all the more reason to start your journey now.

Chapter 18

The 21st Century Teacher: A Vision for the Future

The education we provide will reflect the teachers who provide it. As we saw in Chapter 7, 'The quality of an education system cannot exceed the quality of its teachers.'[1] If we are truly to work towards a better educational system, then we must get serious about properly growing and developing ourselves as leaders, teachers and support staff, so that we have the knowledge, skills and experience necessary.

However, for the education we provide to be sustainable and authentic, we must recognise our significance as role models. We cannot separate good teaching from a good teacher. The one is an expression of the other: 'A good tree produces good fruit, and a bad tree produces bad fruit. A good tree can't produce bad fruit, and a bad tree can't produce good fruit.'[2] I like the word 'good'. It's so much better than 'perfect'. Good has potential. Good can grow. Perfect is static. You cannot be more perfect or less perfect, only perfect. Perfect cannot grow. Perfect cannot become better. I don't want to be perfect, I want to be good.

I argued in Part I that a good teacher is a balanced teacher. If we do not take seriously the different components of being balanced, then we cannot teach well over the long term, and we cannot nurture and grow young people who are likewise balanced and well-rounded. What we put in is what we will get out. We each have a responsibility to care for ourselves, our own wellbeing, our physical and mental health, our continuing development, our relationships, our psychological needs and our core values. The Bible urges us to 'Love your neighbour,' but first requires

1 Barber and Mourshed, *How the World's Best Performing School Systems Came Out on Top*, p. 19.

2 Matthew 7:17–20 (NLT). See https://www.biblegateway.com/passage/?search=Matthew+7&version=NLT.

that you 'love yourself'.[3] We cannot proficiently and sustainably care for the needs of others until we love ourselves.

In Part II, I emphasised the critical role we each play as leaders to care for, engage and motivate those we lead in order to enable them to be the very best version of themselves. John Dunford of Whole Education says that far too much of what we currently do 'results in valuing what we can measure, instead of trying to measure what we value'.[4] The responsibility of leadership is to value the people we lead above the product they are there to produce. Together we can create schools in which all staff are truly valued. The more we value and enable our teams, the more effective they will be. Again, we all have a responsibility to model this in the way we interact daily with our colleagues and with students. A leader is not defined by rank or position but by influence.

In Part III, I have called for the reshaping of our education system so that it more adequately provides for the holistic development of each and every child. However, this too is inseparable from the wellbeing of teachers: our care for ourselves as well as our care for each other. The potential for change will not be realised by waiting for some ground-breaking legislation to usher in a new era. Rather, it will be realised as each one of us takes up the challenge to think differently, innovate, experiment and lead our classrooms in accordance with our core values, instead of perpetuating a subservience to systems, styles and structures which stifle, limit and constrain. We need to take seriously the full and entire role of a teacher; to value and affirm every component and skill that is in use every day; to acknowledge that skill and expertise, measure it, reward it and develop it further.

The 21st century teacher needs to have a well-developed and developing skill set in the same five areas of education as our students: personal, creative, academic, work and world (see Figure 14.2). If we are not confident and qualified to deliver these components of education, then how can we possibly expect to grow students who are equipped to tackle the challenges ahead and succeed in life?

3 Luke 10:27.

4 J. Dunford, We Should Measure What We Value, Not Value What We Can Measure, *TES* (12 December 2016). Available at: https://www.tes.com/news/we-should-measure-what-we-value-not-value-what-we-can-measure.

Table 18.1. The roles of the 21st century teacher

Aspect of education	Wellbeing	Teacher's role	Component skills and competencies (just for starters …)
Personal	The wheel of life	Personal development mentor	PSHE, mental health awareness, child development, educational psychology, behavioural science, counselling skills, SEND, safeguarding, relationship skills, drugs awareness, identity and gender awareness, sexual health, social media awareness and addiction, communication skills
Creative		Creative inspirer	Emotional intelligence, growth mindset, arts, intuition, interpretation, self-expression, design, self-awareness, empathy, innovation
Academic	The wheel of teaching	Academic expert	Specialist subject knowledge, numeracy and literacy, SEND, current areas of research, research skills, analysis, evaluation, recall, application
Work		Careers guide	Financial awareness, technological advances, the world of work, application processes, higher education options, changing job market, soft skills, leadership skills, team development, interpersonal skills, entrepreneurship, taxation, business studies, marketing
World	The rights of the child	Global guru	Current affairs, religion and philosophy, politics and citizenship, sociology, globalisation, economics, digital communication

I believe that, underpinned by the wellbeing of the teacher and the rights of the child, each teacher fulfils five essential roles: personal development mentor, creative inspirer, academic expert, careers guide and global guru (Table 18.1).

If this sounds like an impressively broad range of skills and knowledge, well, yes it is! But the fact is that most teachers already display this breadth of knowledge and skill every single day. The problem is that it isn't acknowledged, valued, measured or deliberately developed. If we expect teachers to be providing such a phenomenal package of support to young people, then we should adequately equip them for it, recognise and value all aspects of it, and ensure their continued professional development in all of these areas. I would argue, then, for a programme of performance management and CPD matched to these five areas. If we don't measure it, we can't improve it. None of these areas are a bolt-on or added bonus. They are part of what being a teacher means. They don't just 'go with the job' as if some aspects are a regrettable hidden extra that we didn't sign up to; they *are* the job. And for most teachers, they are what we already do.

I have summarised in the following pages what I think each one of these five elements should mean for the average teacher, although this will obviously depend on the age of the students and the setting in which you teach. My hope and plea is that these elements begin to be properly recognised and developed. None of these areas can be learned on the hoof or adequately addressed in a single twilight session. When we explicitly acknowledge what we are each doing every day, plan for it and recognise its significance, we will be in a position to grow a truly groundbreaking education system.

Personal development mentor

Teachers are personal development mentors, period. To recruit a new teacher to the profession, and then dump him or her in the role of tutor or classroom teacher without adequate training and expertise in these highly complex areas is irresponsible. Every teacher is, first and foremost, a relationships, sex and health education teacher.

The 21st century teacher needs to have a comprehensive understanding of child and adolescent mental health and the many and varied factors that contribute to mental ill health. We will know what is going on in the current drug scene and understand the factors leading to addiction. We will know how to pick up on signs of abuse. We will be skilful and confident in liaising with parents and identifying causal factors that might contribute to poor behaviour or progress. We will know about current social media and gaming usage and their potential impacts on young people. We will understand the factors affecting changing attitudes towards gender, sexuality and identity. We will be able to help students navigate childhood and adolescence, to sift through and be discriminating in their consumption of the media, and to make positive and informed decisions.

We will understand all kinds of special educational needs and disabilities and the skills necessary to develop each child in light of these. Fundamental to education is the child and his or her starting point, wherever that may be, and the ability to meet each child at his or her point of need with relevant, accessible learning.

All of this is essential to being a great teacher if we are going to address these issues properly with students, yet I don't know of any school that has yet provided training and development in all of these areas to all of its teachers.

Creative inspirer

I would argue that you don't need to be a creative person – in the sense that most people use the phrase – in order to inspire students to be creative and explore their creativity. The fact is (as we explored in Chapter 13) that the job market is shifting towards right-brain orientated jobs; most left-brain tasks are being increasingly automated. It is not acceptable for us to leave this aspect of education to the art or drama teacher because 'I'm not a creative person'. For one thing, I just don't believe that is true. As human beings we are all incredibly innovative, resourceful and creative people. We use these skills every day in all sorts of circumstances. It is what makes us human. We need to stop defining creativity in the narrow terms we have used previously – this is not just about music, art and drama.

Our creativity is one of the fundamental differences between humans and machines. In his TED Talk 'The Jobs We'll Lose to Machines – and the Ones We Won't', machine learning expert Anthony Goldbloom mentions a study from 2012 which showed that after being fed hundreds of essays, a computer can 'read' and grade them with more accuracy and efficiency than a teacher: 10,000 essays can be marked in a matter of minutes. Does that mean we are out of a job? No. We can automate frequent, high-volume tasks. But innovative thinking – that requires creativity. That is human. What computers can't do, and what every human needs to be able to do, is to tackle novel situations. Goldbloom wishes for his niece: 'May every day bring you a new challenge, if it does then you will stay ahead of the machines.'[5]

There is so much that could be explored on this topic, but suffice to say, this innately human skill and competency can be learned and developed as we start to recognise and value the myriad ways in which creativity is expressed every day, not just in teaching but in life. It is our job as teachers to prompt the creative questions, to provide the problems and the challenges, to create novel situations which require innovative thinking, empathy and interpersonal skills. And as we observe those skills, to affirm and develop them and provide feedback to push students even further.

Academic expert

While I have sought in this book to challenge the imbalance in education, I would not wish to undermine or disparage the vital and significant role of academic education and expertise in human development across the whole range of disciplines. Academic progress in science, medicine, architecture, engineering, philosophy, the humanities, the social sciences, literature and so on have been integral to the progress of the human race and the betterment of the world. I am wholly committed to the discovery of truth in all of these fields, because pushing at the

5 Goldbloom, The Jobs We'll Lose to Machines – and the Ones We Won't.

boundaries of our knowledge and understanding of the world lies at the core of what will help us to survive and adapt as a species and create a better future. In this regard, the 21st century teacher will continue to be one who sows the seeds of curiosity and discovery that will fuel future progress.

As teachers, we should remain committed to developing our subject knowledge and the application of that knowledge. This has long been integral to the role of the university lecturer and we would do well to borrow from their example: not only sharing our knowledge with students but pushing our own knowledge forward by engaging in learning and research. There is exciting potential for our schools to become centres of new ideas, where the curriculum acts as the springboard and not the end point or destination. Schools can be somewhere where we are all engaged in further study and given the freedom to explore new questions within our chosen field rather than confined by a remit to regurgitate the basics year-on-year.

Careers guide

Most of us are currently the worst possible careers guides! Most teachers went to school, to university and then back to school. We know only one job sector, one recruitment process, one post-16 pathway, one income bracket, one pension scheme. Yet we are tasked with preparing students for the world of work, although in practice this is usually left to the careers leader and this whole area of education is pushed to the periphery of school life.

The 21st century teacher will be trained in what the job market is like – the changing trends and necessary skill sets. We will know about the breadth of opportunities currently out there and the sectors that are likely to grow. We will know how technology is transforming the workplace and the implications of automation and globalisation. We will know which skills are most necessary to be successful and we will weave these, along with opportunities to practise them, into our lessons in an explicit and meaningful way. We will know and constantly link our subject specialism to the opportunities and challenges in the workplace. We will not allow our inherent bias towards academic success cloud our guidance and undermine students' access or exposure to the breadth of legitimate career choices available. We will be aspirational. We will encourage a strong work ethic and inspire big dreams and possibilities. We will plant seeds of great ideas and enterprise.

Global guru

The 21st century teacher will know about the world in which they live. We will have a basic handle on current affairs and what is going on internationally. But in order to guide students through the questions that world affairs will inevitably raise, we will need a basic knowledge of world religions and practices and how they impact on society. As teachers, we need to know about and understand the different political ideologies as well as how the political system works in our own country. We need to understand how the ultimate questions of life affect world events and how to explain these in an age-appropriate way.

We need to have thought through our own position and beliefs on these issues in order to be able to present contrasting perspectives in a professional and unbiased manner. I would argue that all education is basically philosophy, or the quest for truth, and all teachers are philosophers – if we did but know it – and our task is to grow the philosophers of the future. Those bold and courageous individuals who will not be content simply to accept their lot in life but who are armed and equipped to challenge the status quo, push at frontiers and create a better society for our children and our children's children.

When written down like this we sound like phenomenal individuals! On paper I might doubt whether such a teacher exists, but in practice I have met so many that I know it is eminently possible to develop a whole movement of them. What is lacking is a determination to nurture more teachers like this and a deliberate and comprehensive CPD programme and appraisal system to continue to develop them.

This is my vision for a truly exciting education, in schools that place proper value on the incredible contribution we can all make. I truly hope that this book has inspired you to realise three things:

1 Why you do, in fact, still *love teaching*, still believe in the educational project and just what an honour and privilege it is to be a teacher.

2 How you can, in fact, *keep teaching*, as you care for and balance your life and passions and properly invest in yourself and your teams.

3 That we can, together, emboldened with passion and determination, change our schools for the better and make them places where hopes are fulfilled and dreams are ignited.

Possible? Definitely!

Appendix:

Whole-School Strategic Plan to Transform Wellbeing

The following template is designed to help leaders begin the process of implementing some of the strategies and ideas in this book. It is not intended to be prescriptive but may help as a checklist as you engage in discussions to change the culture of your school. The stages may take many months or may be completed relatively quickly. The important thing is to go at the right pace for your school and ensure that all consultation and resultant change is real and lasting, not superficial or token.

I wish you and your brilliant colleagues the very best in building schools that truly value every individual and help each and every one of them realise their potential to create a better future.

<table>
<tr><th colspan="5">Stage 1: Audit and investigation</th></tr>
<tr><td colspan="5">Immediately stop all formal lesson observations and book scrutinies.</td></tr>
<tr><td colspan="5">As a leadership team, apologise to your staff for having sometimes got things wrong and accept responsibility. Affirm that you value them and that you are going to listen to them as you work to find a more sustainable way forward.</td></tr>
<tr><td colspan="5">Investigate the Rights Respecting Schools Award/visit a Rights Respecting School.</td></tr>
<tr><td colspan="5">Begin to rethink school leadership structure and job titles.</td></tr>
<tr><th>SLT</th><th>Middle leaders</th><th>All staff</th><th>Departments</th><th>Students</th></tr>
<tr><td>Complete the GCI assessment and arrange a team development day.
Take time to tailor and adapt this strategic plan to your own context.</td><td>Share all plans with middle leaders and invite input.
Carry out the teachers' dozen survey with middle leaders.</td><td>Share initial plans with all staff. Invite input and feedback.
Carry out whole-staff teachers' dozen survey.</td><td>Ask departments to carry out a 4 T's audit.
Invite departments to discuss wellbeing and feed back views and suggestions.</td><td>Invite students to complete a wellbeing survey. There are different ones available – see mentallyhealthyschools.org.uk</td></tr>
<tr><td colspan="5">Determine to be transparent from the start. Share all the data with each group beginning with the SLT, followed by middle leaders, all staff and students. Never share new information with staff and students without your middle leaders being informed beforehand.</td></tr>
<tr><td colspan="5">Arrange a whole-staff INSET day devoted to wellbeing to address the data raised by the audits and begin focusing on wellbeing, mental health and the six psychological needs as a whole-school community.</td></tr>
</table>

Stage 2: Consultation and conversation				
Begin training for senior and middle leaders on effective leadership and management. Remove or postpone other duties to enable this.				
Amend the timetable to protect line meetings. This *cannot* wait until the next academic year. Ensure that staff and middle leaders understand the purpose of prioritising line meetings. Allow middle leaders to maintain control of this time. Trust them. Remove other duties to enable this.				
SLT	Middle leaders	All staff	Departments	Students
Discuss your values and purpose as a leadership team. Begin your rights-respecting school journey.	Consult with middle leaders on values and purpose. Share the Rights Respecting Schools approach and invite feedback.	Begin whole-staff consultation on values and purpose. Introduce the Rights Respecting Schools Award.	Department leads to run a department-specific values and purpose activity. Identify the significance of rights in each subject area.	Run emotional wellbeing training/lessons with students. Ensure that the whole school community becomes more emotionally literate together. Run a consultation with students and develop a school charter.
Report back to staff on outcomes. Collectively draw together the data to formulate or reaffirm a whole-school purpose statement and school charter, as well as department-specific purpose statements which synchronise with the whole-school purpose.				

Stage 3: Policy amendment and future planning				
Continue leadership training for all leaders. Incorporate mental health first aid training as part of this.				
Continue your rights-respecting journey.				
SLT	Middle leaders	All staff	Departments	Students
Discuss and consult on new performance management and leadership structures. Develop staff wellbeing policy. Update sick pay policy and mental health policy.	Consult with middle leaders on all policy changes. Invite input. Offer opportunities to rewrite and update policies.	Begin offering a rolling programme of CPD for staff to opt into on the five areas of the wheel of education. Ask staff what they would like to receive more CPD on. Ensure that *all staff* can engage with consultation and receive feedback.	Make time for discussions on sustainable assessment, data collection, job descriptions, performance management, target setting, etc. Feed back all findings.	Begin a consultation with students about target setting, assessment, feedback and the use of grading. Begin training mental health ambassadors.
Feed back to staff on all changes and discussions. Invite feedback via line managers.				

<table>
<tr><th colspan="5">Stage 4: Implementation</th></tr>
<tr><td colspan="5">Continue leadership training for all leaders. Include 'chimp management' training.</td></tr>
<tr><td colspan="5">Continue your rights-respecting journey.</td></tr>
<tr><td colspan="5">Consider utilising the GCI and accompanying training with middle leaders.</td></tr>
<tr><th>SLT</th><th>Middle leaders</th><th>All staff</th><th>Departments</th><th>Students</th></tr>
<tr><td>Restructure to address oversight of the five areas of the wheel of education and your GCI profiles.
Prioritise creating and updating welcoming usable spaces for staff to meet and collaborate.
Amend school day timings to facilitate proper staff interaction.</td><td>Appoint leaders to oversee and innovate on the five aspects of the wheel of education.
Trust leaders to innovate, initiate and experiment with new ways of measuring progress and leading change.</td><td>Continue training, shadowing and collaborating opportunities, as well as innovation opportunities, in the five areas of the wheel of education.
Ensure that staff are being used effectively and invest in non-teaching staff when/where necessary to enable all staff to play to their strengths.</td><td>Discuss and innovate cross-departmentally on how to develop more balance between the five areas of the wheel of education and how to measure them.</td><td>Make all targets learning goals that students set for themselves.
Make student voice central to your processes.
Equip students to take a leading role in your rights-respecting journey.</td></tr>
<tr><td colspan="5">Carry out another teachers' dozen survey. Share and act on the results.</td></tr>
<tr><td colspan="5">Carry out another student wellbeing survey. Share and act on the results.</td></tr>
</table>

References

Abolghasemi, H., Hosseini-Divkalayi, N. S. and Seighali, F. (2010) Blood Donor Incentives: A Step Forward or Backward, *Asian Journal of Transfusion Science*, 4(1): 9–13. Available at: https://www.ncbi.nlm.nih.gov/pmc/articles/PMC2847338.

Adams, R. (2019) Social Mobility in UK 'Virtually Stagnant' Since 2014, *The Guardian* (30 April). Available at: https://www.theguardian.com/society/2019/apr/30/social-mobility-in-uk-virtually-stagnant-since-2014.

Alexander, B. (2010) Addiction: The View from Rat Park. Available at: https://www.brucekalexander.com/articles-speeches/rat-park/148-addiction-the-view-from-rat-park.

Amortegui, J. (2016) The Surprising Reason You Should Stop Trying to Be So Productive, *Forbes* (8 August). Available at: https://www.forbes.com/sites/womensmedia/2016/08/08/the-surprising-reason-you-should-stop-trying-to-be-so-productive/#79cad5036e1a.

Aquinas, T. (1998) *Selected Writings*, ed. and tr. R. McInerny (London: Penguin).

Ariely, D. (2012) What Makes Us Feel Good About Our Work? [video], *TED.com* (October). Available at: https://www.ted.com/talks/dan_ariely_what_makes_us_feel_good_about_our_work.

Atwal, K. (2019) *The Thinking School: Developing a Dynamic Learning Community* (Woodbridge: John Catt Educational).

Augustine (2002) *Confessions*, tr. R. S. Pine-Coffin (London: Penguin).

Baard, P. P., Deci, E. L. and Ryan, R. M. (2004) Intrinsic Need Satisfaction: A Motivational Basis of Performance and Wellbeing in Two Work Settings, *Journal of Applied Social Psychology*, 34(10): 2045–2068.

Baraz, J. and Alexander, S. (2010) The Helper's High, *Greater Good Magazine* (1 February). Available at: https://greatergood.berkeley.edu/article/item/the_helpers_high.

Barber, M. and Mourshed, M. (2007) *How the World's Best Performing School Systems Came Out on Top* (London: McKinsey & Co.). Available at: https://www.mckinsey.com/industries/public-and-social-sector/our-insights/how-the-worlds-best-performing-school-systems-come-out-on-top.

BBC News (2019) Stafford Hospital Scandal: The Real Story Behind Channel 4's *The Cure* (19 December). Available at: https://www.bbc.co.uk/news/uk-england-stoke-staffordshire-50836324.

Belludi, N. (2008) Albert Mehrabian's 7-38-55 Rule of Personal Communication, *Right Attitudes* (4 October). Available at: https://www.rightattitudes.com/2008/10/04/7-38-55-rule-personal-communication.

Berenda, R. W. (1950) *The Influence of the Group on the Judgments of Children* (New York: King's Crown Press).

Bosely, F. (2017) What's the Ultimate Way to Defy Depression, Disease and Early Death? Exercise, *The Guardian* (3 October). Available at: https://www.theguardian.com/lifeandstyle/2017/oct/03/exercise-depression-disease-death-sit-less-move-more.

Bower, J. and Thomas, P. L. (2013) *De-testing and De-grading Schools: Authentic Alternatives to Accountability and Standardization* (New York: Peter Lang).

Bregman, R. (2020) The Real Lord of the Flies: What Happened When Six Boys Were Shipwrecked for 15 Months, *The Guardian* (9 May). Available at: https://www.theguardian.com/books/2020/may/09/the-real-lord-of-the-flies-what-happened-when-six-boys-were-shipwrecked-for-15-months.

Brown, S. (2014) *Speed: Facing Our Addiction to Fast and Faster – and Overcoming Our Fear of Slowing Down* (New York: Berkley Publishing).

Burkeman, O. (2016) Fetishing Busyness, *Oliver Burkeman Is Busy* [audio], *BBC Radio 4* (13 September). Available at: https://www.bbc.co.uk/sounds/play/b07v07pb.

Busby, E. (2019) Children Miss Out on Making Friends amid Shorter School Break Times, Study Finds, *The Independent* (10 May). Available at: https://www.independent.co.uk/news/education/education-news/school-breaks-lunchtime-friends-exercise-children-ucl-study-a8906756.html.

Butler, D. (2016) Tomorrow's World, *Nature*, 530: 399–401. Available at: https://www.nature.com/news/polopoly_fs/1.19431!/menu/main/topColumns/topLeftColumn/pdf/530398a.pdf?origin=ppub.

Cameron, W. B. (1963) *Informal Sociology: A Casual Introduction to Sociological Thinking* (New York: Random House).

Carnegie, D. (1948) *How to Stop Worrying and Start Living* (New York: Simon & Schuster).

Carter, K. (2019) Badly Behaved or Emotionally Strained? [video], *TED.com* (July). Available at: https://www.ted.com/talks/krissi_carter_badly_behaved_or_emotionally_strained.

Clear, J. (2018) How Vietnam War Veterans Broke Their Heroin Addictions. Available at: https://jamesclear.com/heroin-habits.

Collins, J. (2001) *Good to Great: Why Some Companies Make the Leap … and Others Don't* (London: Random House).

Collins, J. and Porras, J. (1994) *Built to Last: Successful Habits of Visionary Companies* (London: Random House).

Crabbe, T. (2015) *Busy: How to Thrive in a World of Too Much* (London: Piatkus).

Dahlitz, M. (2016) Basic Psychological Needs, *Science of Psychotherapy* (23 November). Available at: https://www.thescienceofpsychotherapy.com/basic-psychological-needs.

Department for Education (2019) *Relationships Education, Relationships and Sex Education (RSE) and Health Education* (25 July). Available at: https://www.gov.uk/government/publications/relationships-education-relationships-and-sex-education-rse-and-health-education.

di Lampedusa, G. (2007 [1958]) *The Leopard*, tr. A. Colquhoun (New York: Pantheon).

Doctor Oz (2019) Tiffany Haddish's Drama Teacher Taught Her How to Read [video] (26 August). Available at: https://www.youtube.com/watch?v=EevSKGxQn3I.

Duckworth, A. L. (2016) *Grit: The Power of Passion and Perseverance* (London: Vermillion).

Duckworth, A. L. and Seligman, M. E. P. (2005) Self-Discipline Outdoes IQ in Predicting Academic Performance of Adolescents, *Psychological Science*, 16(2): 939–944. Available at: https://www.academia.edu/5466301/Self-Discipline_Outdoes_IQ_in_Predicting_Academic_Performance_of_Adolescents.

Duncan (n.d.) Gallup's 12 Employee Engagement Questions + 1 It Forgot!, *Vetter*. Available at: https://www.getvetter.com/posts/174-gallup-s-12-employee-engagement-questions-1-it-forgot.

Dunford, J. (2016) We Should Measure What We Value, Not Value What We Can Measure, *TES* (12 December). Available at: https://www.tes.com/news/we-should-measure-what-we-value-not-value-what-we-can-measure.

Dweck, C. S. (1999) *Self-Theories: Their Role in Motivation, Personality and Development* (Philadelphia, PA: Psychology Press).

Dweck, C. S. (2006) *Mindset: The New Psychology of Success* (New York: Ballantine Books).

Dweck, C. S. (2010) The Effect of Praise on Mindsets [video]. Available at: https://www.youtube.com/watch?v=TTXrV0_3UjY&t=3s.

Dweck, C. S. (2012) *Mindset: How You Can Fulfil Your Potential* (New York: Constable & Robinson).

Dyer, F. L. and Martin, T. C. (1910) *Edison: His Life and Inventions*, vol. 2 (New York: Harper & Brothers).

Easwaran, E. (tr. and intro.) (2009) *The Dhammapada* (Tomales: Nilgiri Press).

Elkington, J. (1997) *Cannibals with Forks: The Triple Bottom Line of 21st Century Business* (Bloomington, MN: Capstone).

Frankl, V. E. (2004 [1946]) *Man's Search for Meaning* (London: Random House).

Frei, F. and Morriss, A. (2020) Begin with Trust, *Harvard Business Review* (May–June). Available at: https://hbr.org/2020/05/begin-with-trust.

Friedman, M. (1970) The Social Responsibility of Business Is to Increase Its Profits, *New York Times Magazine* (13 September). Available at: http://umich.edu/~thecore/doc/Friedman.pdf.

Fukuyama, F. (1996) *Trust: Social Virtues and the Creation of Prosperity* (New York: Simon & Schuster).

Gadsby, C. (2012) *Perfect Assessment for Learning* (Carmarthen: Independent Thinking Press).

Gandhi, M. K. (1964) *The Collected Works of Mahatma Gandhi*, vol. 12 (April 1913 – December 1914) (Delhi: Publications Division, Ministry of Information and Broadcasting, Government of India).

Gilbert, I. (2013) *Essential Motivation in the Classroom* (Abingdon and New York: Routledge).

Glucksberg, S. (1962) The Influence of Strength of Drive on Functional Fixedness and Perceptual Recognition, *Journal of Experimental Psychology*, 63(1): 36–41.

Goldbloom, A. (2016) The Jobs We'll Lose to Machines – and the Ones We Won't [video], *TED.com* (February). Available at: https://www.ted.com/talks/anthony_goldbloom_the_jobs_we_ll_lose_to_machines_and_the_ones_we_won_t.

Goleman, D. (2018) Emotional Intelligence at Work: Why IQ Isn't Everything [video]. Available at: https://www.youtube.com/watch?v=7ngIFlmRRPQ.

Government Office for Science (2008) *Five Ways to Mental Wellbeing* (22 October). Available at: https://www.gov.uk/government/publications/five-ways-to-mental-wellbeing.

Gyton, G. (2017) Just One in 10 Brits Feel Engaged at Work, Says Gallup, *People Management* (18 October). Available at: https://www.peoplemanagement.co.uk/news/articles/one-in-10-brits-engaged-work.

Handy, C. (2015) *The Second Curve: Thoughts on Reinventing Society* (London: Random House).

Hari, J. (2018a) Is Everything You Think You Know About Depression Wrong?, *The Guardian* (7 January). Available at: https://www.theguardian.com/society/2018/jan/07/is-everything-you-think-you-know-about-depression-wrong-johann-hari-lost-connections.

Hari, J. (2018b) *Lost Connections: Uncovering the Real Causes of Depression – and the Unexpected Solutions* (New York: Bloomsbury).

Harris, P. (2015) How Many Jobs Should You Expect to Hold in Your Lifetime?, *Workopolis* (8 October). Available at: https://careers.workopolis.com/advice/how-many-jobs-should-you-expect-to-hold-in-your-lifetime.

Hattie, J. (2013) Feedback in Schools, *Visible Learning*. Available at: https://visible-learning.org/2013/10/john-hattie-article-about-feedback-in-schools.

Haynes, T. (2018) Dopamine, Smartphones & You: A Battle for Your Time, *Science in the News* (1 May). Available at: http://sitn.hms.harvard.edu/flash/2018/dopamine-smartphones-battle-time.

Holmes Sr, O. W. (1858) The Autocrat of the Breakfast-Table, *Atlantic Monthly*, Vol. 2: 502.

Hotten, R. (2015) Volkswagen: The Scandal Explained, *BBC News* (10 December). Available at: https://www.bbc.co.uk/news/business-34324772.

Howkins, J. (2001) *The Creative Economy: How People Make Money from Ideas* (London: Penguin).

Hymer, B. (2016) How to Encourage Chessplayers (or Why Feedback Trumps Praise and Reward). Speech delivered at the 4th London Chess Conference, Kensington Olympia, 10 December. Programme materials available at: https://londonchessconference.com/wp-content/uploads/2017/02/Hymer-Praise.pdf.

Kelly, J. (2019) How to Future-Proof Your Career in a Fast-Changing, Unforgiving Global Job Market, *Forbes* (24 September). Available at: https://www.forbes.com/sites/jackkelly/2019/09/24/how-to-future-proof-your-career-in-a-fast-changing-unforgiving-global-job-market/#543f1fb13d83.

Kouzes, J. M. and Posner, B. Z. (2003) *The Leadership Challenge: How to Make Extraordinary Things Happen in Organizations* (San Francisco, CA: Jossey-Bass).

Longoria, M. (2020) What is the Situational Leadership Theory?, *Tough Nickel* (29 May). Available at: https://toughnickel.com/business/What-is-the-Situational-Leadership-Theory.

McGregor, D. (1985) *The Human Side of Enterprise* (New York: McGraw Hill).

McNair, D. (2010) Getting Results: Local CEO Tosses the Time Clock, *The Hook* (14 May). Available at: http://www.readthehook.com/67646/getting-results-local-ceo-tosses-time-clock.

Manson, M. (2016) *The Subtle Art of Not Giving A F*ck: A Counterintuitive Approach to Living a Good Life* (New York: HarperCollins).

Maslow, A. H. (1943) A Theory of Human Motivation, *Psychological Review*, 50(4): 370–396.

Maslow, A. H. (2013 [1943]) *A Theory of Human Motivation* (St Paul, MN: Wilder Publications).

Megginson, L. C. (1963) Lessons from Europe for American Business, *Southwestern Social Science Quarterly*, 44(1): 3–13.

Mervyn-Smith, J. and Ott, N. (2018) *Coaching Me Coaching You … Ahaa* (London: GC Index).

Milne, A. A. (1926) *Winnie-the-Pooh* (London: Methuen).

Morisy, A. (2004) *Journeying Out: A New Approach to Christian Mission* (London: Continuum).

MRI Network (2015) *Recruiter Sentiment Study: 2015 2nd Half*. Available at: https://www.mrinetwork.com/media/1036/2015_recruiter_sentiment_study_2nd_half.pdf.

Nishioka, R. (2017) Use the Gallup Q12 Questions to Manage Your Manager, *Business 2 Community* (5 October). Available at: https://www.business2community.com/human-resources/use-gallup-q12-questions-manage-manager-01926550.

O'Dwyer, M. (2019) London Drives Increase in Number of New UK Startups, *City AM* (14 January). Available at: https://www.cityam.com/london-drives-increase-number-new-uk-startups.

Open Business Council (2020) Working in the UK: The Top 5 Fastest-Growing Sectors (25 February). Available at: https://www.openbusinesscouncil.org/working-in-the-uk-the-top-5-fastest-growing-sectors.

Parungao, A. (2020) The Future of Remote Work After COVID-19: 3 Common Predictions, *Eko* (27 April). Available at: https://www.ekoapp.com/blog/the-future-of-remote-work-after-covid-19-3-common-predictions.

Peters, S. (2012) *The Chimp Paradox: The Mind Management Programme to Help You Achieve Success, Confidence and Happiness* (London: Random House).

Pink, D. (2008) *A Whole New Mind: Why Right-Brainers Will Rule the Future* (New York: Marshall Cavendish).

Pink, D. (2009) *Drive* (New York: Riverhead Books).

Pirsig, R. (1974) *Zen and the Art of Motorcycle Maintenance* (New York: William Morrow).

Plato (2007) *The Republic*, tr. H. D. P. Lee (London: Penguin).

Public Health England (2014) *The Link Between Pupil Health and Wellbeing and Attainment: A Briefing for Head Teachers, Governors and Staff in Education Settings* (November). Available at: https://assets.publishing.service.gov.uk/government/uploads/system/uploads/attachment_data/file/370686/HT_briefing_layoutvFINALvii.pdf.

Randolph, M. (2019) *That Will Never Work: The Birth of NETFLIX and the Amazing Life of an Idea* (London: Octopus Publishing).

Ressler, C. and Thompson, J. (2011) *Why Work Sucks and How to Fix It: The Results-Only Revolution* (New York: Portfolio).

Riley, K., Coates, M. and Martinez, S. P. (2018) *Place & Belonging in Schools: Opening Up Possibilities* (London: UCL Institute of Education). Available at: https://www.ucl.ac.uk/ioe/sites/ioe/files/place-and-belonging-unlocking-possibilities.pdf.

Robinson, K. (2015) *Creative Schools: Revolutionizing Education from the Ground Up* (London: Penguin).

Robinson, K., with Aronica, L. (2010) *The Element: How Finding Your Passion Changes Everything* (London: Penguin).

Robison, J. (2008) Turning Around Employee Turnover, *Gallup Business Journal* (8 May). Available at: https://news.gallup.com/businessjournal/106912/turning-around-your-turnover-problem.aspx.

Robson, D. (2009) The Sexist Myths That Won't Die, *BBC Future* (1 October). Available at: https://www.bbc.com/future/article/20190930-the-sexist-myths-about-gender-stereotypes-that-wont-die.

Rosling, H. (2019) *Factfulness: Ten Reasons We're Wrong About the World – and Why Things Are Better Than You Think* (London: Hodder & Stoughton).

Roy, G. (2015) 5 Writing Lessons from Tim Ferriss, *Medium.com* (27 January). Available at: https://medium.com/@eBooksIndiaMag/5-writing-lessons-from-tim-ferriss-2c11b39f6584.

Ruiz, D. M. (1997) *The Four Agreements: A Practical Guide to Personal Freedom* (San Rafael, CA: Amber-Allen Publishing).

Ruiz, D. M. and Ruiz, D. J. (2010) *The Fifth Agreement: A Practical Guide to Self-Mastery* (San Rafael, CA: Amber-Allen Publishing).

Ryan, R. M. and Deci, E. L. (2000) Self-Determination Theory and the Facilitation of Intrinsic Motivation, Social Development and Wellbeing, *American Psychologist*, 55(1): 68–78.

Schickel, R. (1968) *The Disney Version: The Life, Times, Art and Commerce of Walt Disney* (New York: Simon & Schuster).

Selva, J. (2020) Albert Ellis' ABC Model in the Cognitive Behavioral Therapy Spotlight, *Positive Psychology* (29 April). Available at: https://positivepsychology.com/albert-ellis-abc-model-rebt-cbt.

Sheetz, M. (2017) Technology Killing Off Corporate America: Average Life Span of Companies Under 20 Years, *CNBC* (24 August). Available at: https://www.cnbc.com/2017/08/24/technology-killing-off-corporations-average-lifespan-of-company-under-20-years.html.

Shuster, A. M. (1971) G.I. Heroin Addiction Epidemic in Vietnam, *New York Times* (16 May). Available at: https://www.nytimes.com/1971/05/16/archives/gi-heroin-addiction-epidemic-in-vietnam-gi-heroin-addiction-is.html.

Sinek, S. (2009a) *Start with Why: How Great Leaders Inspire Everyone to Take Action* (London: Penguin Random House).

Sinek, S. (2009b) Start with Why – How Great Leaders Inspire Action [video], *TEDx Talks* (28 September). Available at: https://www.youtube.com/watch?v=u4ZoJKF_VuA.

Sinek, S., Mead, D. and Docker, P. (2017) *Find Your Why: A Practical Guide for Discovering Purpose for You and Your Team* (New York: Penguin Random House).

Sloane, P. (2009) The Innovative Leader vs. the Command-and-Control Leader, *Innovation Management* (30 September). Available at: https://innovationmanagement.se/imtool-articles/the-innovative-leader-vs-the-command-and-control-leader.

Syed, M. (2011) *Bounce: The Myth of Talent and the Power of Practice* (London: Fourth Estate).

Syed, M. (2019) *Rebel Ideas: The Power of Diverse Thinking* (London: John Murray).

Taylor, C. (2019) These Are the Fastest Growing Jobs and Sectors in the UK, Researchers Say, *CNBC* (17 May). Available at: https://www.cnbc.com/2019/05/17/these-are-the-uks-fastest-growing-jobs-and-sectors-researchers-say.html.

Unicef (1989) *The United Nations Convention on the Rights of the Child* (20 November). Available at: https://downloads.unicef.org.uk/wp-content/uploads/2016/08/unicef-convention-rights-child-uncrc.pdf?_ga=2.86970783.641093437.1591280497-612875821.1591280497.

Unicef (2018) *Impact Report 2018: Creating Active & Engaged Citizens*. Available at: https://www.unicef.org.uk/rights-respecting-schools/wp-content/uploads/sites/4/2019/06/Summary-Impact-Report-2018_Final.pdf.

Ward, A. F. (2013) The Neuroscience of Everybody's Favorite Topic, *Scientific American* (16 July). Available at: https://www.scientificamerican.com/article/the-neuroscience-of-everybody-favorite-topic-themselves.

Weale, S. (2018) Teacher Crisis Hits London As Nearly Half Quit within Five Years, *The Guardian* (4 October). Available at: https://www.theguardian.com/education/2018/oct/04/teacher-crisis-hits-london-as-nearly-half-quit-within-five-years.

Weale, S. (2019) Fifth of Teachers Plan to Leave Profession within Two Years, *The Guardian* (16 April). Available at: https://www.theguardian.com/education/2019/apr/16/fifth-of-teachers-plan-to-leave-profession-within-two-years.

World Economic Forum (2016) *The Future of Jobs*. Available at: https://reports.weforum.org/future-of-jobs-2016/chapter-1-the-future-of-jobs-and-skills.

About the Author

Peter Radford is the founder of Beyond This, which provides staff training and student workshops focused on helping teachers and young people to live life better. As an experienced public speaker, teacher and trainer, Peter works with schools and businesses to help develop the strategies and momentum to meet the challenge of change and build a better future.

Peter has worked in education for over 25 years and has specific experience in effecting change at a whole-school level through addressing systems and mindsets that stifle progress. He has led two large secondary schools to achieve the Unicef Rights Respecting Schools Award, and now speaks to staff and students around the country inspiring change.

Please get in touch with Peter to arrange:

- Staff wellbeing INSETs.
- Leadership training.
- Student workshops – the READY programme:
  - R – Relationships
  - E – Emotional wellbeing
  - A – Aspiration and employability
  - D – Direction
  - Y – Your voice: politics and human rights

www.beyondthis.co.uk
peter@beyondthis.co.uk

BEYOND THIS
MOTIVATION • EDUCATION • TRAINING • DEVELOPMENT